Y0-BQN-054

Literary Seductions

What is it about their work that makes some writers so alluring? Profound, entertaining and hugely engaging, **Literary Seductions** examines the explosive collision of reading, writing and desire. It has already met with lavish praise:

'Wilson writes dazzlingly . . . A sexy firework of a book, seamed with enjoyable digressions.'
Independent

'Frances Wilson's book has all the sly delight necessary to pull off a literary seduction. Her prose is perfect, her humour funny and just . . . She does that daring thing of taking critical theory into the real world, showing how it might work amongst living, breathing people. The result is a truly woderful read – clever, crafty and almost impossible to resist.'
Kathryn Hughes, **Literary Review**

'Frances Wilson's wonderful, utterly riveting book is about people who lose themselves in the written word . . . **Literary Seductions** is a worthy and learned tome, but it is also a rollicking work of literary biography.'
Amanda Mitchison, **Daily Telegraph**

'One admires the elegance of Wilson's epigrams and the go-for-broke verve of her thesis. She herself writes extremely well – one does not even have to add that chilling "for an academic". And she has a deadly eye for the telling question.'
John Sutherland, **Independent on Sunday**

'One of the tenets of modern literary criticism is that the pleasure of reading is the same as the pleasure of sex: *la jouissance*. This beguiling book looks at why this should be so, and what happens when readers try to dive between the sheets. It's also packed with jokes: what more could you want? . . . Frances Wilson's book illuminates not only the fantasies driving all these impassioned lovers but also what goes on inside each of us when we abandon our self to a good read: bliss and terror all mixed up.'
Michèle Roberts, **Financial Times**

Literary Seductions

Compulsive Writers and Diverted Readers

FRANCES WILSON

faber and faber

First published in 1999
by Faber and Faber Limited
3 Queen Square London WC1N 3AU

Photoset by Parker Typesetting Service, Leicester
Printed in England by Clays Ltd, St Ives plc

A CIP record for this book
is available from the British Library

ISBN 0–571–19288–2

2 4 6 8 10 9 7 5 3 1

In memory of all books which lay
Their sure foundations in the heart of Man.

WILLIAM WORDSWORTH, *The Prelude*

I will a round unvarnish'd tale deliver
Of my whole course of love, what drugs,
    what charms,
What conjuration, and what mighty magic,
(For such proceeding am I charged withal)
I won his daughter.

WILLIAM SHAKESPEARE, *Othello*

Contents

Acknowledgements

One of the many pleasures in writing *Literary Seductions* has been the enthusiasm of other people for the project. I have had numerous conversations about seductive writers and diverted readers with strangers on trains and at parties, all of which have influenced this book, and to all of whom I am extremely grateful.

Of those who have fed me ideas, read and commented on the chapters, and recommended seductive reads and writers to me, I owe a debt of thanks to Barrie Bullen, Emma Clery, Nicola Humble, Christine Kenyon Jones, John Pilling, James Soderholm, and especially Ron Knowles, whose ideas gave me much food for thought. Tara Lamont and Frances Henderson lent me their homes to enable me to write in solitude, Anne Wilson sent me information more or less on demand at the early stages of my research and was invaluable as a babysitter and as a sounding-board at the final stages. Hugh Barnes encouraged the project from its earliest stage, and Andrew Wordsworth has been an endlessly supportive listener. Julian Loose has been an excellent editor, and is responsible for keeping my argument from too many diversions. The Head of the English Department at Reading University, Cedric Brown, kindly arranged for me to have a light teaching load so that I might finish *Literary Seductions* on time, and Diane Watts was patient with my computer problems. Had Christina Wieland not been there, this book would never have been written.

My deepest gratitude, however, goes to Amber Jacobs, for reading every line I wrote, discussing every idea I had, and lending me her library of Russian poetry.

Literary Diversions

She thank'd me,
And bade me, if I had a friend that lov'd her,
I should but teach him how to tell my story,
And that would woo her.

Othello

Someone has been led astray and seduced.

JEAN LAPLANCHE

'I love your verses with all my heart, dear Miss Barrett, – and this is no off-hand complimentary letter that I shall write . . . since the day last week when I first read your poems, I quite laugh to remember how I have been turning and turning again in my mind what I should be able to tell you of their effect upon me.' Robert Browning's first letter to Elizabeth Barrett describes a typical literary seduction: 'I do, as I say, love these books with all my heart,' he went on to write, '– and I love you too', as if the writer and the writing were indistinguishable.[1]

The story of the love affair that began with a good read between the still unknown poet of New Cross, an unfashionable location in South-East London, and the internationally celebrated poet of Wimpole Street, has been told so often that its strangeness as an encounter is overlooked. In the myth that has developed around the couple's epistolary courtship, secret marriage, and escape to Italy, attention has always focused on their clandestine meetings, on Elizabeth Barrett's mysterious illness and incarceration in her bedroom, and on the puzzling psychology of her father, Edward

Moulton Barrett, who forbade any of his nine children to marry. Yet the most striking aspect of the tale of Robert Browning and Elizabeth Barrett is not that she was ill or that her father was tyrannical, but that before he met Elizabeth Barrett the celibate Browning fell passionately in love with her *poems*.

In literary seductions it is writing that seduces and not the writer, and it was around Elizabeth Barrett's writing that Robert Browning's desire for her was structured; it was the effect of her writing on Browning that dictated the direction of his subsequent actions. But what the popular myth of the relationship between Elizabeth Barrett and Robert Browning also elides is the fact that the withdrawn Elizabeth Barrett, who never expected to see daylight again let alone romance, had, in her ballad 'Lady Geraldine's Courtship', overtly invited the seduction to take place.

For Robert Browning's astonishing introductory letter of 10 January 1845 was written in response to a poem of Elizabeth Barrett from her recent two-volume collection. 'Lady Geraldine's Courtship' contains a passage where a love-sick poet called Bertram reads Lady Geraldine – who 'only likes his verses' – some contemporary poetry, and Browning, who was still obscure outside the tightest literary circles, is praised alongside poets of established stature and reputation. Sitting with Geraldine on the hillside, Bertram recites from Spenser and Petrarch, or at times from

> . . . a modern volume, – Wordsworth's solemn-thoughted idyl,
> Howitt's ballad-verse, or Tennyson's enchanted reverie, –
> Or from Browning some 'Pomegranate,' which, if cut deep down the middle,
> Shows a heart within blood-tinctured, of a veined humanity.

If it were not flattery enough to be included in such a laudable line-up, Browning will have noticed that he was given more space than his celebrated peers, Wordsworth and Tennyson, and that his name was accompanied not by the usual adjectives of polite critical appreciation but instead by sensuous, carnal and erotic imagery. Elizabeth Barrett's fleshly metaphor was a reference to Browning's cryptically titled collection of plays and dramatic poems *Bells and Pomegranates*, and while she described the poet's heart as being itself like a pomegranate, it was his writing that she found lay blood-tinctured at the heart of him, and it was this that attracted her. As Anaïs Nin once wrote of her lover Henry Miller, what they had in common was that the core of each of them was a writer and not a human being.

Although Robert Browning said, when he had read 'Lady Geraldine's Courtship', that his own admiration 'went its natural way in silence', the effect of the poem on him led to his acting out of character, and he thus began to speak his mind on the alluring woman poet to their mutual friend John Kenyon. What 'if I were to *write* this, now?' Browning asked Kenyon of the feelings he was expressing towards Elizabeth Barrett. John Kenyon's reply was reassuring: she would be 'pleased' to hear how Browning felt, he said.[2]

Elizabeth Barrett was ecstatic. 'I thank you, dear Mr Browning, from the bottom of my heart,' she replied the next day, repeating in her letter the imagery of her seductive poem, and the measured presentation of her written response disguises the fact that Robert Browning's forthright letter did not come entirely as a surprise to her. Her poem's compliment to Browning's poems was calculated to inspire a reaction, for Elizabeth Barrett had been seduced by Robert Browing long before she read *Bells and Pomegranates* and issued her invitation to the poet. 'Lady Geraldine's Courtship' was the result of a literary seduction that had taken place ten years earlier, when she came across Browning's *Paracelsus* and exclaimed with great excitement that here was 'a poet in the holy sense', a poet of 'palpable power'. Given that passion on the page was the most Elizabeth Barrett could hope for in her limited circumstances, it is no wonder that she eventually threw down the gauntlet and challenged Browning to love her writing as she loved his.

The day on which they secretly married, in September 1846, was the first occasion on which Browning had seen Elizabeth Barrett outdoors. Prior to this, the couple had exchanged 573 letters which they took with them when they eloped to Italy after the wedding. Following their deaths, this extraordinary correspondence was left in the care of the Brownings' son, also called Robert, who published them in 1899. For Robert Wiedemann Barrett Browning his parents' collection constituted a step-by-step history of his own conception. Reading their love letters, he must have felt himself born of writing, the effect of his parents' poems. So it is most appropriate that two poets whose affair was organized around and experienced through ink on paper should affectionately call their offspring 'Pen'.

Literary Seductions tells this same story over and over again. In a literary seduction the reader first falls in love with writing in the form of a book, a poem, a single line or an isolated word and then falls for the writer himself. Rather than being captivated by a smile, a voice, or a gesture it is in the patterns of certain letters, the positions of particular vowels, the flow of the sounds or the story that the lover drowns. The passion between reader and writer is born from writing, conducted through writing, sustained by writing. In literary seductions words become flesh. The case of Elizabeth Barrett and Robert Browning is typical of the seductions explored here in that their mutual desire developed entirely through the medium of script, but by achieving the difficult transition from a love of one another's words to a broader love beyond the literary, Elizabeth Barrett and Robert Browning succeeded where other literary seductions fail. In pure literary seductions the lovers share a passion not for each other but for language and they find life on the page preferable to life beyond print. The lives of the writers and readers considered in the following chapters were lived through letters, in every sense of the word.

What does it mean to fall in love with the arrangement of signs on a page? Why were Elizabeth Barrett and Robert Browning so seduced by one another's writing that each was willing to sacrifice all he had? What was it about their relation to language that each left behind home and country on the strength of a good read, and bade goodbye to beloved family and friends in order to pursue its writer? Another way of exploring these questions might be to ask instead why it is that some writing is *not* seductive and why some writers – most writers – fail to inspire their readers into giving up life as they know it for the sake of a few lines of prose or poetry. Why do readers tend to be so *unmoved* by what they read? Why are literary seductions so rare?

Given that all writing strives to ensnare the reader, it is remarkable how few are ensnared. For as all writers know, their writing must be alluring and intoxicating or they have achieved nothing. Whether they are writing a poem, a postcard, or a novel, the writer's drive is to captivate the reader and make him forget for a moment the world beyond print. No writing is without what Roland Barthes calls the *love-me* element, and this desire to be desired is writing's appeal. By appeal I mean both the magnetic attraction of the words as well as their plea, and writing's appeal is for the reader's submission and devotion: come with me, absorb me, give yourself to me, it urges, and in this sense all writing attempts to seduce, and all seduction is an invitation to let go. Writing does not necessarily seduce because of its quality or its content. If a reader is receptive to the charms of writing, then even a shopping list harbours untold attractions, as Henry Miller explained in *The Books in my Life*. The writing of certain authors, he found, was so erotically charged that *everything* they wrote was exciting, and 'even the perusal of an author's expense account gives us a thrill'.[3]

Henry James, a generation younger than Robert Browning, was

intrigued by the discrepancy between the legend of Browning's seductive allure as a poet and the sheer ordinariness of his company. In his supernatural tale, 'The Private Life', James explored what he felt was Browning's unremarkable – 'bourgeois' – social presence and the rare appeal of his poetry. A party from London are on holiday in Switzerland and have with them the celebrated playwright Clare Vawdrey, 'the greatest . . . of our literary glories'.[4] Vawdrey, like Browning, proves himself an affable companion but no more: 'I never found him anything but loud and liberal and cheerful, and I never heard him utter a paradox or express a shade or play with an idea,'[5] the narrator complains. One evening, while Vawdrey is disappointing his dining companions downstairs, the narrator goes upstairs to Vawdrey's room and finds him there also, a ghostly shadow sitting at his desk in the dark, utterly absorbed in his brilliant work.

James's narrator then understands what has perplexed him during the vacation: there are two Vawdreys, the public man and the private writer, and they bear no relation to one another. 'The Private Life' dramatizes the difference defined by Gabriel Josipovici between the self one is and the self that writes,[6] and while James mourned that it was only possible to relate to the public man or, as he put it, that it is only 'the bourgeois whom we personally know',[7] Elizabeth Barrett found otherwise. Her relationship with Browning was with the silent, spectral figure furiously scribbling at the writing desk. It was the visible, public man who was a stranger to her. Browning, on his part, told Elizabeth Barrett that if she should say to him, ' "I am not *the* Miss B. – she is upstairs and you shall see her – I only wrote those letters, and am what you see, that is all now left you," ' he would not 'wonder at the event'.[8]

In 'The Private Life', Henry James realized what Elizabeth Barrett and Robert Browning had known all along: that physical presence is not necessary in order for seduction to take place, and James was so astonished by the idea of a writing with erotic potential on this scale that what should have been a tale of literary seduction became a ghost story, a tale of the incredible. Another version of this theme is explored in Antonio Skarmeta's novella, *Il Postino*. Here the postman, Mario Jiminez, delivers letters to the great Chilean poet Pablo Neruda, and when the tongue-tied Mario falls in love with the local barmaid, Beatriz, he turns to Neruda for metaphors with which to woo her and soon Beatriz is besotted. ' "With these metaphors, Don Pablo, he's got my daughter hot as a pistol," ' her mother exclaims. Beatriz's mother is well aware of the power of poetry and fears the loss of her daughter under such a spell. ' "We are in the thick of a very dangerous situation," ' she warns, when she finds Beatriz dreamily staring at the moon:

> 'All men who first touch with words go much further afterwards with their hands.'
> 'How could words be bad?' Beatriz said, hugging the pillow.
> 'There isn't a drug in the world worse than all that blah-blah-blah. It makes a village innkeeper feel like a Venetian princess. Later, when the moment of truth arrives, when life catches up with you, you'll realize that these words are no better than a bad check. I would much rather have a drunkard in the bar grab your ass than have someone tell you that your smile flies higher than a butterfly.'[9]

Mario's metaphors are not even his own, Beatriz's mother complains; he has 'stolen' them from Neruda and could therefore 'end up in jail', she tells her daughter, 'for telling you . . . *metaphors!*'[10] Like 'The Private Life', *Il Postino* plays with the idea that it is not the man who seduces but the writing. While they are Neruda's metaphors that divert her, Beatriz is unmoved by the poet himself. At the same time, Mario discovers that he is spoken by Neruda's language rather than speaking it: what he says has nothing to do with him and is no more than a tissue of quotations. Even words as intimate as 'I love you' have been said before.

Language is sensuous and to appreciate it, Mario Jiminez has learned from Neruda, '. . . you don't read the words – you swallow them. You have to savor words. You have to let them melt in your mouth.'[1] Words – their own or someone else's – were the means by which Mario Jiminez and Robert Browning each won the prized daughter; this was the only witchcraft used. What does it mean for the seduced party then to translate this taste and feel for letters, shapes, sounds, and stories to a love of the person who penned the lines? What is going on at the meeting point between the writer and the writing and the reader and the reading that effects such a powerful attraction? This is the question *Literary Seductions* sets out to explore.

It is also a subject that intrigued Thomas Hardy, and his story of a literary seduction, 'On the Western Circuit', is about a London lawyer who falls for a pretty but illiterate country girl at a summer fair. Not knowing that she can neither read nor write, he begins a flirtatious correspondence with her that she can only continue because her unhappily married mistress reads the lawyer's letters and composes the girl's replies. The lawyer is immediately enchanted by the letters he receives in the girl's name and soon proposes marriage to her. The mistress, for her part, has fallen in love with the lawyer through his missives but nonetheless agrees to attend the small wedding and to meet her correspondent in person. On his wedding day the lawyer discovers the true author of the love letters and he and his bride's mistress passionately embrace before they separate to spend their now ruined lives apart from one another. In this tale the writing overshadows the writer, coming before the love each has for his correspondent, but their translation of textual into sexual attraction is performed with shocking immediacy. These are no gentle readers: literary seductions are violent, extreme and irreversible.

The exchange of books for bodies in the literary seductions I explore here is never hard to achieve. The reader's love of the writing tends to become indistinguishable from his love of the writer – 'I love your verses,' as Browning put it, '. . . and I love you too' – so the reader himself is unclear whom or what it is he loves. Elizabeth Barrett responded positively to having her person thus identified with her poetry, but it wasn't long before Browning needed to separate his love for her verses from his love for her, much as he needed to see himself as separate from his own writing. This is why, although Robert Browning's pursuit of Elizabeth Barrett is the most famous example of a literary seduction in modern literature, he is not the subject of one of the following chapters. For Browning, unlike Elizabeth Barrett, is not the kind of writer who interests me here.

Seduction is a reaction: all seducers have been seduced themselves, and no writer will seduce who has not already found himself seduced by writing. The writers I discuss in *Literary Seductions* are those who have succumbed to the seductive allure of language; writing is their object of desire. They are driven to write and will risk – or forfeit – their lives for their vocation. These seduced writers are what I call compulsive: they feel *compelled* to write, addicted to the thrill of words and controlled by the power of written language. Sometimes this makes them prolific, and to varying degrees and in very different circumstances Anaïs Nin and Henry Miller, Laura Riding and Robert Graves, and Osip and Nadezha Mandelstam all wrote a great deal. But I am specifically interested in these writers for their remarkable *attitude* towards writing rather than because of the quantity of script they produced. No writer ever seduced a reader solely because of the amount that he or she wrote.

Once writing has begun, for the compulsive writer there is no going back. Compulsive writers know that writing involves a high degree of risk, and that the writer who is not prepared to sacrifice himself to his work is not writing. Thus Henry James, who spent his life writing and thinking about writing to the exclusion of all else, does not qualify as a compulsive writer. He was ruled by the fear that once he had let himself go in a book ('if only I could let myself go' is the constant refrain of his notebooks), he would drown in his own verbiage. Hence the rigorous plotting of his novels down to the last detail. His notebooks contain scores of these pre-planned structures, which function like framed grids in the event that his writing gets lured into temptation and goes off bounds. He refuses to be seduced by his own words and no one has, as far as I know, ever found *The Golden Bowl* a seductive read or had their head turned by a browse through James's works in a bookshop. James's readers feel the nervousness in his prose; his portentous style bespeaks his terrible awareness of the appeal of writing, which could suck him in like quicksand. In literary seductions there is a violent intimacy to the reading process, and in his obfuscating and anxious style James avoids this possibility, keeping his readers at arm's length. However superior they might be, writers like James, *who resist the full force of writing*, do not seduce.

Compulsive writers channel into writing emotions that would otherwise be expressed in sexual relationships, and for writers like this successful relationships are no more than an extension of writing. This was not, however, the case for Robert Browning, who became wary of the power of writing to displace physical passion in his courtship of Elizabeth Barrett. For instance, when Elizabeth, satisfied with their entirely epistolary encounters, continued to resist meeting him in person, Browning wrote to her in despair, 'Do see me when you can and *let me not be only writing myself.*'[12] The writers explored in *Literary Seductions* are striking precisely because they chose to 'write themselves' and preferred to experience themselves as writing. Aware that her and Browning's relationship was formed *through* 'writing themselves', Elizabeth Barrett was understandably cautious about meeting her lover in person.

If Elizabeth Barrett feared that her and Browning's attraction might extend no further than their verses, Robert Browning had resisted from the start the literary nature of his desire for Elizabeth Barrett. By responding as he did to 'Lady Geraldine's Courtship', he later explained to the poet, he was simply acting as any gentleman would do, only '*UNWILLINGLY*' so, '*on account of my purely personal obligation*, tho' of course taking that occasion to allude to the general and customary delight in your works'.[13] Why is Browning so defensive here? His first letter to Elizabeth Barrett doesn't read as if it were written under the pressure of duty: he was not bound by protocol, after all, to tell the poet that he loved her. What stands out in Robert Browning's initial letter is that, while it seems so *direct*, his frame of mind was entirely *diverted*. He may not have been a compulsive writer, but Browning was a great diverted reader and his reading of Elizabeth Barrett provided the most significant diversion of his life.

To be diverted is to be taken out of oneself, to go off the beaten track and down another path. To seduce also means to divert from one's path, and the implication is that the diversion directs one away from the truth and into the realm of deceit. Like seduction, diversion has risky connotations too and the pleasure yielded includes an element of danger: both reading and seduction lead one astray. Reading, as Robert Browning discovered, is an adventure without a known route or destination. In diversion, as in seduction, there is a pleasure involved in putting yourself in someone else's hands and letting go, and this is the pleasure of reading as well: it is a form of abandonment. Once you are diverted from the straight and narrow, there is no guarantee of return, and if you lose yourself in a book you might not find that same self again. There is nothing straightforward, therefore, about the stories in *Literary Seductions*: the next chapter charts the wayward journeys of an incestuous group of diverted readers who gave themselves up for a text, and of the three major couples I consider in *Literary Seductions*, all were diverted readers as well as being, at some point in their lives, writers who wrote with compulsive zeal.

All good reading involves diversion: 'If the reader is not at risk,' Harold Brodkey says, 'he is not reading.' Is the threat of this risk what lies behind the profoundly unsettling fear of being recommended a good book? We listen to the book's praise and block it out; the book is too much for us, we are not ready for it. We realize its risk and know that to read it will be dangerous, that to give ourselves to the book will be sacrificial. We would sooner not read, and stay as we are. Hence the great unreads of world literature, giant books that have moved and terrified nations and with which we would prefer to be only broadly conversant rather than intimately engaged. 'No one *likes* a good book if they have actually read it,' Brodkey rightly points out. This would be to underestimate the disturbing effect of being taken over by serious reading, where the reader finds himself not simply satisfied by the book but 'fanatically attached, restlessly attached, criminally attached, violently and criminally opposed, sickened, unable to bear it.'[14] When the diverted readers I explore said that certain writing had changed their lives, they meant it. For these couples, reading and writing were diverting in the most disorientating sense of the word, turning each seduction into powerful acts of possession, consumption, or containment.

But while the couples I look at in *Literary Seductions* take to an extreme the term 'lovers of literature', we have all of us been diverted and seduced by writing. The writers and readers here are only exceptional in having taken their literary seductions literally. For the commoner reader the process of seduction starts once we learn as children that written words unlock a secret world. Literary seductions begin not with the content of writing or its context, but at the level of the single black mark on a sheet of white paper. 'In reading,' Vladimir Nabokov says, 'one should notice and fondle details', and for the child these details are the basic elements of script itself. Before we learn to decode an alphabet we see its letters as patterns and shapes we respond to, much as a fetishist responds to the bit-parts of the body. There are certain letters that, for their curves or their straight lines, their enclosure or their left-facing profile, we love and wish we had in our own name, and there are certain letters we dislike for the same reasons. Vowels seduced Kafka and trapped him inside specific words where he circled in reverie, immune to the outside world: 'I can't understand it and I can't believe it,' he confided to his diary. 'I live only here and there in a small word in whose vowel ("thrust" above, for instance) I lose my useless head for a moment. The first and last letters are the beginning and end of my fishlike emotion.'[15]

Stories are seductive too, as are literary characters. Those of us who have lived in books since childhood have all read something without which we would not be the person we are now. We have all fallen in love with a fictional figure, a Heathcliff or Ayesha, Mr Darcy or Becky Sharp; perhaps this was our first love, never to be repeated, making all subsequent love affairs seem flat and disappointing. We have all felt that a book knew us better than we knew ourselves, that the book was, in fact, writing us. La Rochefoucauld had a dictum that we love as we do because we have learned from literature, and so perhaps it is our awareness of reading as a formative and seductive force that directs us to read the same books as the person we love. In the first throes of passion, readers instantly reach for the literary springs of their lovers' identities, which they explore through the reading that shaped them. If reading, as Schopenhauer said, involves nothing more than thinking with other people's brains, then by reading the books of our loved ones we are thinking our way into their very beings.

Reading, Barthes observes, is like those other solitary acts, praying and masturbation. Reading is both sacred and profane, also blocking out external events and folding readers into themselves. 'I went up sobbing to the very top of the house,' Proust wrote of the blissful abolition of the world performed by childhood reading, '. . . doubtless because it was the only place I was allowed to lock myself in for all those occupations of mine which required an inviolable solitude: reading, reverie, tears, and pleasure.' All readers notice how reading erodes time, that not only is it impossible to tell for how long we have been reading, but also it is an effort to recall who we are when we stop. We all indulge in the psychic dissolution of space when we read, the experience of being neither '*here* or *there*', as Michel de Certeau says of the reader straddled between the inside of the book and the outside of the other world, 'one or the other . . . simultaneously inside and outside, dissolving both by mixing them together'.[16]

The effect of childhood reading is more than merely impression-forming: we are forged from these pages, making it hard to separate the self one is from the reading self. 'I know that I have in my make-up layers of synthetic experience, and that the most powerful of my memories are only half-true,' Elizabeth Bowen writes of a childhood absorbed in books:

> Reduced to the minimum, to the what did happen, my life would be unrecognizable by me. Those layers of fictitious memory densify as they go deeper down. And this surely must be the case with everyone else who reads deeply, ravenously, unthinkingly, sensuously, as a child.[17]

How do those who did not read as children conceive of what they remember, Elizabeth Bowen asks; that is, if they are able to remember anything? For how can the senses carry imprints of the past without the help of stories to give these vague, inarticulate forms some structure? Freud felt the same: hysteria, he realized, listening to the disordered tales of his patients, was a loss of one's place in one's story, the letting-go of a narrative structure vital to one's sense of self. The task of the psychoanalyst is to enable the patient not to distinguish between fiction and reality but to recognize – and to read – the shape of the fiction she gives to experience. For Freud, psychoanalysis exposes how 'all tales lead back not to events but to other tales – to man as a structure of the fictions he tells about himself.'[18] *Literary Seductions* tells the tales of those for whom experience was structured by tales, and the pivotal event in each life was a moment of reading.

Samuel Richardson's *Clarissa*, the greatest tale of seduction in the English language, is also a tale of compulsive writing. This epistolary novel contains over one million words and the bulk of them are produced by Clarissa Harlowe and Robert Lovelace in their various correspondences. Clarissa is expected to marry Solmes, whom she loathes, and is pursued by the dashing Lovelace, whom her family think not good enough for her. Duped by Lovelace when she is locked up for refusing Solmes, Clarissa is taken to London and established by him in a brothel. Although she is clearly attracted to the man who has both saved and imprisoned her, Clarissa continues to hold on to her virginity. Lovelace eventually rapes her, after which he loses his power and Clarissa her mind. The letters she has written to her friend Anna Howe, through which her story unfolds, now stop and Clarissa's tale is continued by John Belford, who eventually rescues her and reports her drawn-out death.

Neither Clarissa nor Lovelace can put down their pens; throughout his pursuit of her Lovelace writes to Belford, and throughout her pursuit by Lovelace, her incarceration and starvation, Clarissa writes to Anna Howe as though her life depends on it, which in a sense it does. This continuous letter writing is the only means Clarissa has of affirming her identity and of rooting herself in time, her only way of remembering who she is when she is not writing. Kafka felt the same: 'But I will write in spite of everything,' he wrote in his diary, 'absolutely; it is my struggle for self-preservation.'[19] Flaubert also described Clarissa's precarious state, clinging on to her writing as to a cliff-face: 'My novel is the cliff on which I am hanging, and I know nothing of what is going on in the world,' he wrote to a friend.

So long as she pours out page after page, Clarissa knows that she is still alive, and she stops writing only when she gives up her life. Virginia Woolf likewise associated the end of writing with the end of living, and it is interesting, given her despair when not writing, that Woolf ever stopped at all: 'The only way I keep afloat is by working,' she wrote. 'Directly I stop working I feel that I am sinking down, down.'[20] Virginia Woolf felt suicidal each time she finished a book, and she affirmed her life through writing another one: 'I will signalise my return to life − that is to writing − by beginning a new book.'

Clarissa Harlowe is like other compulsive writers in that her drive to write was never affected by circumstance. The compulsive writer's task must continue at all costs and for many not even the absence of a reader would dissuade them from their tendency. Henry Miller's tireless writing wrecked his marriages and led to years of poverty; Anaïs Nin's writing created her marriages, but she wrote in her diary all day and every day, leaving little space for the sexual encounters she was writing about, and they were both well into middle age before anyone noticed their work. Robert Graves wrote through fighting in the trenches, shell-shock, the attempted suicide of Laura Riding and his own jump from a window; he exhausted everyone with his drive to write, while Laura Riding wore out friends and collaborators with her persistence, ignored the negative reactions she received from publishers and continued to write what no one wanted to read. Osip Mandelstam wrote through homelessness, starvation, and censorship, right up until his death in a concentration camp, while his wife poured out his memoirs in her old age before the ban on Mandelstam's name had yet been lifted. For all these couples writing was a necessity, like oxygen, and being unable to write was like being unable to breathe: its effects were suffocating, life-threatening. Writing also satisfied needs that their relations with one another failed to satisfy.

The writers in *Literary Seductions* wrote because nothing else mattered. But while the compulsive writer writes with a furious energy, what is most striking about him is the *ease* with which he works, and it is this curious lack of anxiety that is so enticing in the condition.[21] Writing comes to the compulsive writer almost too easily. He writes with Byronic speed and without the blocks and self-doubts that otherwise bedevil authors like Joseph Conrad and Henry James. Not one of the writers in *Literary Seductions* experienced for long the debilitating agony of confronting himself, day after day, before a blank page. None of the writers I explore was resistant to the seductive allure of his own writing, and none would be found repeating Joseph Conrad's hellish ritual:

> I sit down religiously every morning. I sit down for eight hours every day – and the sitting down is all. In the course of that working day of eight hours I write three sentences which I erase before leaving the table in despair . . . it takes all my resolution and power of self-control to refrain from butting my head against the wall. I want to howl and foam at the mouth but I daren't do it for fear of waking the baby and alarming my wife.[22]

Nor would they know what Flaubert meant when he wrote to George Sand, 'You don't know what it is to stay a whole day with your head in your hands trying to squeeze your unfortunate brain so as to find a word . . . Ah! I certainly know *the agonies of style*,'[23] or what Dostoevsky experienced: '*I worked and was tortured*. You know what it means to compose? No, thank God, you do not!'[24]

'What is one to do on a day when thoughts cease to flow and the proper words won't come?' Sigmund Freud asked in a letter to his friend Ferenczi. 'One cannot help trembling at this possibility.'[25] While he spent his life exploring drives and blocks, this vital question is pursued by Freud no further. 'Before the problem of the creative artist,' he wrote in his study of 'Dostoevsky and Parricide', 'analysis must, alas, lay down its arms,' and this is clearly – alas – what psychoanalysis did. In the vast body of work he produced

Freud said nothing at all, save a few isolated remarks, about the desire to write or the madness that ensues when that desire is thwarted. While exploring the ubiquitous presence of the unconscious in all its disguised appearances, psychoanalysis surrendered in the face of analysing either the demented capacity for endless writing experienced by some – 'I detest my own volubility,' Virginia Woolf despairs. 'Why be always spouting words?'[26] – or the profound dismay and paralysing horror of not being able to write experienced by others:

> Experience doesn't help, adds nothing, makes nothing easier
> . . . To want to write and to be incapable of doing so, like this
> morning, is for me a kind of tragedy. The ability is there but
> for some unknown reason it is unavailable.[27]

Only in *Moses and Monotheism* is there a hint that Freud had thought about writing's capacity to divert the writer: 'Unluckily an author's creative power does not always obey his will: the work proceeds as it can, and often presents itself to the author as something independent or even alien.'[28] The implication is that once it has begun, writing is as alien and threatening an experience as writing that cannot begin. Writing becomes like Frankenstein's monster, breaking free from its creator and taking control of him. Charlotte Brontë says something similar about the creation of Heathcliff in the editor's preface she composed for her sister Emily's *Wuthering Heights*:

> . . . the writer who possesses the creative gift owns something
> of which he is not always master – something that, at times,
> strangely wills and works for itself . . . Be the work grim or
> glorious, dread or divine, you have little choice left but
> quiescent adoption. As for you – the nominal artist – your
> share in it has been to work passively under dictates you
> neither delivered nor could question . . .'[29]

This would explain Péguy's feeling when he wrote: 'I never start a new book without dread. I live in the dread of writing,'[30] and Henry James's reaction to beginning his novels: both authors feared that the writing might take them over completely. As James confided to his notebook:

> The more I get into my drama itself the more magnificent, upon my word, I seem to see it and feel it; with such a tremendous lot of possibilities in it that I positively quake in dread of the muchness with which they threaten me.[31]

Like Freudian psychoanalysis, *Literary Seductions* also avoids examining the psychological dynamics of compulsive writing. A study of the pathologies of writing would be a rewarding venture – and one not yet undertaken – but it is the subject for another book. *Literary Seductions* is about compulsive writers themselves and not about compulsive writing as an activity or a disorder, and I restrict myself to describing rather than diagnosing the writing lives and relationships of those writers and readers for whom the literary is everything.

I do, however, think that compulsive writing is a perverse activity. I have no grounds for this assumption other than my sense of writing's strangeness and my sympathy with those who find it uncommonly so. The paralysing fear of translating one's self into letters on a page has always seemed to me understandable; likewise the horror of feeling that when writing begins it may never stop, or the sense that the writing might erase the writer and carry on chattering alone into infinity. The instinct to balk at the sacrifice of personal and domestic happiness that the writer must make if he sells his soul to writing would seem to be a rational enough response to the task ahead. It is the nearness of writer's block to our own mental states under pressure that makes films like *The Shining* and *Barton Fink*, both of which contain powerful images of the isolation of writing and of the self-destruction involved in being unable to write, so uncomfortably familiar and so disturbing. For all the horror of room 217, it is the typewriter in the middle of the huge, empty room at the heart of the huge, empty hotel that is the most terrifying image in *The Shining*. And the discovery by Wendy that her husband's finished manuscript, on which he has worked from dawn to dusk, contains no more than an endless repetition of 'All work and no play makes Jack a dull boy' is the film's most chilling moment.

Yet however close to insanity writer's block can push one, in comparison with the recklessness of compulsive writing, a writer's resistance to his craft shows, I believe, evidence of a healthy self-preservative mechanism. Hence my fascination with – even seduction by – the unguarded, unhesitant throwing of oneself into the abyss of prose or poetry practised by writers like Byron, Anaïs Nin and Henry Miller, Laura Riding and Robert Graves, Osip Mandelstam and George Yeats. Next to these compulsive writers' all-consuming drives to write, and compared with their single-minded pursuit of an ambition in which their lives are dominated by words, the horror of writing felt by Henry James and Joseph Conrad seems quite reasonable. Faced with the relentless aim towards a goal which only has to be reached again and then again, one can but sympathize with the despair of the writer either overwhelmed by the enormity of his task or enervated by its futility. 'I can't write any more,' Kafka wrote in his diary of the uselessness of committing one's life to prose. 'I've come up against the last boundary, before which I shall in all likelihood again sit down for years, and then in all likelihood begin another story all over again that will again remain unfinished. This fate pursues me.'[32] Kafka's diaries tell of his longing to write, but they also describe his dread of writing. And with reason – writing drained him of all else:

> It is easy to recognise a concentration in me of all my forces on writing. When it became clear in my organism that writing

was the most productive direction for my being to take, everything rushed in that direction and left empty all those abilities which were directed towards the joys of sex, eating, drinking, philosophical reflection, and above all music.[33]

The poet George Barker believed that 'the responsibility or onus of the poet is to assert and affirm the human privilege of perversity', and while Kafka recognized the perversity of allowing writing to take over from and destroy all his other pleasures, part of writing's perversity for George Barker is that 'a poet is a man who believes in silence so deeply that, if he speaks, it is simply because he dare not remain silent'.[34] The poet is perverse because he kills the thing he loves: there is a reckless desire in compulsive writers to say everything and to stop at nothing, to obliterate silence with endless words. 'I talk in writing,' Anaïs Nin wrote. 'I am truly mute without writing.' Poetry was the result, Laura Riding said in one of her introductions, of the poet's compulsion overtaking her inertia, poems are born of the tension between saying everything and saying nothing. Compulsive writers are bent on self-expulsion rather than self-containment, and I am fascinated by the contrast between the writer's desire to pour himself out and the silence and isolation of the medium in which he chooses to do so.

Perversion, like diversion, means a turn, and like seduction, the implication is that it is a turn from the truth, from the right direction. As with other perversions such as fetishism, voyeurism, and exhibitionism, compulsive writing becomes a ritual performance that diverts attention away from its own motives and desires. In psychoanalysis, a perverse activity is a survival technique disguising an underlying and repressed event. Rather than recall the painful memory, the pervert diverts it. The desire of the fetishist, for example, to be seduced by a shoe, suspender belt, or specific material, is perverse because the value afforded to the object is diverted from the mother's body where it originally belongs, and once detached it becomes an independent sexual item that, Freud says, then takes the place of the normal aim.

Compulsive writing is, I believe, perverse because, like all perversions, it heads off in a wayward direction, swerving from accepted understandings of what writing should be and do. Writing is traditionally understood to be an informative or entertaining medium, a cerebral pursuit undertaken with due care and attention on the part of the writer for the education or pleasure of the reader. For the compulsive writer, however, it is an activity disengaged from motivation or reward, aesthetic aim or narrative content. 'It's the writing, not the being read, that excites me,' Virginia Woolf wrote in her diary,[35] as if writing, like seduction, were a mission pursued entirely for its own sake.

Perversion, like writing, is a gender issue and *Literary Seductions* seeks to demonstrate the ways in which compulsive writing is experienced and treated very differently by men and women. Freud argued that women could not be perverse, and yet many activities that women undertake are treated as being so, not least compulsive writing. While compulsive writing in a man is regarded as evidence of a healthy libido and his drive to write is not questioned, we have a kind of revulsion towards women who write too much or too urgently, women like Caroline Lamb or Elizabeth Smart, whose lives as diverted readers I look at in the next chapter. Both of these readers were seduced by compulsive writers and then wrote charged accounts of their subsequent affairs. But the written versions of their relationships with Lord Byron and George Barker are seen as being anything but seductive. Caroline Lamb and Elizabeth Smart produced books that disturb – and in the case of Caroline Lamb, even repel – the reader. This is because *Glenarvon* and *By Grand Central Station I Sat Down and Wept* document an obsession not with writers but with writing, and each book's intoxication with words obscures the image of Byron or Barker it set out to create.

By writing about their seductions with such blind passion

Caroline Lamb and Elizabeth Smart make known the real nature of their love and the true object of their desire; it becomes apparent that they are the victims of metaphors rather than men, and herein lie their perversions. The writing of Caroline Lamb and Elizabeth Smart is regarded as an aberration of femininity, their writings and sexualities are understood as somehow contaminating one another, so that the one cannot be discussed without reference to the other. This is also the case with Mary Shelley, another seduced reader, whose disturbing novel *Frankenstein*, when it is remembered that she was the author, is continually assessed in terms of her failed motherhood; and with Anaïs Nin and Laura Riding, whose absorption in their own writing might seem less monstrous were that writing regarded as good.

While writing does no more than 'express' Henry Miller, Robert Graves, and Osip Mandelstam, it is seen as unsexing, oversexing, or generally perverting Anaïs Nin, Laura Riding and Nadezhda Mandelstam. While the most perverse aspect of each male writer is seen as his relationship not with writing but with his literary partner, each female writer is perverse not for her literary relationships but for the way in which she wrote, and this is why I pay more attention to the female half of each seduction.

Diversion is a gender issue too, and diverted reading is thought typical of the feminine disposition precisely because of its seductive tendencies. The majority of seduced readers I discuss in the following chapter are women; women are expected to be diverted by reading and to emerge from a novel with romantic notions and frustrated desires, unable to tell the difference between the world of the book and the real world. When women read they are thought more likely than men to abandon critical detachment; the woman reader will throw herself into texts with the recklessness of Laura Riding, who threw herself from a window for poetry, or of Sappho, who hurled herself from the rock of Leucas. For this reason Mary Wollstonecraft, the eighteenth-century feminist, warned women away from romantic fiction, fearing the detrimental effect such pleasure might have on feminist politics: women readers might give up wanting an education and settle for marriage to a dark-eyed stranger instead. Mary Wollstonecraft's assumption is that books are more dangerous for women to read than for men because women more readily lose themselves in literature, at the same time as they believe, like all seduced readers, that between these sheets their true selves can be found.

But however diverting they might find reading, the women I discuss in *Literary Seductions* all find themselves guiding their male partners' writing on its way. Anaïs Nin and Laura Riding were treated by Henry Miller and Robert Graves as muses, and while Nadezhda Mandelstam kept her husband and then his verse alive, the place of muse in their tale was reserved for Osip's greatest friend, the magnificent Anna Akhmatova. Akhmatova was also Russia's femme fatale, and it is as femmes fatales that Anaïs Nin and Laura Riding preferred to be seen: unsure of the seductive power of their writing, they cast themselves as dangerous temptresses as well, and confused sexual with textual desire all their working lives. All the couples I consider confused coupledom with triangles, and the literary seductions I describe each contain a third party without which the relationships would not have been possible. As Adam Phillips so seductively puts it, 'Two's company, but three's a couple.'[36]

First, though, I want to look at some of the twists and turns of the reading mind.

ONE

Seduced Readers:
Between the Sheets

'Reading a good book is not much different from a love affair.'

HAROLD BRODKEY

'Reading, reverie, tears, and pleasure'.

PROUST

Elizabeth Barrett had long dreamed of absconding with a poet. As a child growing up when the mania for Byron was at its height, she 'used to think seriously of dressing up like a boy and running away to be Lord Byron's page'.[1] Transgressions of this kind were seen as a natural reaction to the diverting pleasures of reading Byron. His racy poetry seduced readers as poetry never had done before; only when Byron had left the country, the Duchess of Devonshire said, could Regency husbands sleep in peace. No one had felt this about the effect of Pope's poetry, or Southey's, or William Wordsworth's, on the social and sexual behaviour of their readers. Following the publication of the first two cantos of *Childe Harold's Pilgrimage* in spring 1812, the twenty-four-year-old Byron was besieged by fans and fan-mail. Lady Caroline Lamb — whose husband never had any peace — was typical in responding to Byron's poem by sending him an anonymous letter, beginning 'Dear Childe Harold', and enclosing poems of her own. Warned by Samuel Rogers that the author of this melancholy tale bit his nails and had a club foot, Caroline Lamb determined that even if he were as ugly as Aesop she would meet him. Before the summer was out, she did dress up like a boy and run away to be Lord Byron's page.

Seduced readers desire not the writer — at least not initially so —

but something more. They want what the writer has: his desire for writing, which is why, once seduced, they so often become writers themselves. All the readers I look at in this chapter turned to writing in response to their seductive read. Caroline Lamb is one of the greatest, and most reviled, seduced readers of all time. Having read Byron, her life changed direction and she would never return. William Lamb's obituary of his wife argued that because Byron's attraction for Caroline had been literary her excessive behaviour should be forgiven: 'The world is very lenient to the mistresses of poets,' he wrote with a certain degree of anticipation, because 'their attachments . . . arise from imagination and not depravity.' And yet the reason that Caroline Lamb was unforgiven by her contemporaries was not her love for Byron, which was understood, nor her affair with him, for which she was envied, but precisely her *imaginative* attachment to the poet. Her seduction by Byron left her wanting to *be* him and not wanting to *have* him, and this degree of literary diversion was seen as depraved. Caroline Lamb wanted to appeal as Byron appealed and she was so diverted through reading him that she turned deviant.

What seemed particularly perverse to her critics is that Byron's presence was unnecessary to her obsession. Caroline Lamb quickly found that simulations of her lover would do instead of the real thing, and her response to him took the form of impersonating and reproducing the literary 'Byronic'. For example, she brilliantly forged Byron's handwriting in a letter to herself in order to gain a miniature of the poet from his publisher, John Murray. In so doing she not only possessed but *became* Byron's miniature, making herself indistinguishable from him on paper. In effect, she copied Byron in order to obtain a copy of Byron. She then wrote a mimicry of his epic *Don Juan* in her own verses, 'A New Canto', impersonating his style in such a way as to show that Byronism was reproducible and that no one was as good at being Byronic as herself. And she dressed as Don Juan for a masked ball, allowing his poetry not to disguise her but to express her.[2] When she built a bonfire to ceremonially burn his effigy and letters, she ensured that only copies of his letters were put on to the flames. As far as Caroline Lamb was concerned, the real thing and the reproduction were interchangeable and she had thus taken the typical literary seduction – in which the writer and his writing collapse – one stage further.

Caroline Lamb herself collapsed after Byron's rejection and her subsequent madness was such that she was removed by her family to their estates in Ireland. There she became paper-thin and hollow-eyed while back in London she was the object of society's derision for her abject pursuit of Byron, and Byron himself was soon courting Lady Oxford, a lock of whose hair he sent Caroline in exchange for her request for a lock of his. Byron's trick can be seen as his revenge on Lamb for her own cross-dressing and impersonations, but she was not to be beaten. Unable to let the image of Byron go, Caroline Lamb decided on her return home that she had to take control of the story of their relationship, which had fast become the property of public gossip. So, like many seduced readers, she turned her relationship with Byron into a story, and by including in her written version of their affair the cold letter of dismissal Byron sent her in Ireland from the home of Lady Oxford, she thus turned his private life into public property at the same time as impersonating his betrayal of her. *Glenarvon* was published in 1816, moments after Byron went into exile following the failure of his marriage. It was a best-seller not only because of its fortuitous timing – speculation about Byron was at its height and he was no longer there to represent himself – but also because it contained Lamb's own account of their scandalous liaison, and this everyone wanted to hear.

Her readers were disappointed. From beginning to end, *Glenarvon* is a narrative diversion. Rather than giving a straightforward rendition of her four-month affair with the literary lion of the day, the story takes an unexpected turn and heads off into unexplored country. *Glenarvon* tells the tale of Caroline Lamb and

Byron as the unconscious would tell it, in all its contradictions, evasions, and indirections. Like a dream, her novel has no sense of time or space, genders merge, and identities fade in and out of one another. Byron appears as two men: Lord Glenarvon, an Irish revolutionary, and Count Viviani, an Italian child murderer, while Caroline Lamb can be found divided between the three sentimental heroines but clearly identified most with the hero, who remains a dashing and romantic figure despite any attempt on the author's part to discredit Byron. *Glenarvon* was gleefully condemned as an artistic failure by those readers who expected her to write a conventional autobiography complete with facts and dates or to issue a public apology for her notorious behaviour, but Caroline Lamb's novel is remarkable for achieving without effort the representation of internal landscape that Freud would later map and that the modernist movement would aspire towards.

In its structure, self-exposure, and raw appeal, *Glenarvon* resembles Elizabeth Smart's *By Grand Central Station I Sat Down and Wept*, which is also the result of a literary seduction and abandonment. Elizabeth Smart came across George Barker in August 1937 when she was twenty-three and living in London. Browsing in 'Better Books' on the Charing Cross Road, she was so staggered by a collection of George Barker's poems that she spread the word that when she found the poet she would marry him. Smart's poetic novel about her relationship with Barker, published in 1945, was written during the first of her four pregnancies by him (he stayed with his wife), and she saw writing as a kind of pregnancy in itself, a fertilization and containment of words prior to the birth of the book. The sustained hyperbolic pitch of *By Grand Central Station* is an expression of both the agony and the ecstasy of the early stage of their relationship, and her opaque prose style reflects Elizabeth Smart's sense of writing as dangerous, something both enormously difficult to achieve and liable to take one over once it begins.[3]

The intensity of Elizabeth Smart's first reaction to George Barker's writing can be measured by her response to a later collection of his poems. 'Barker's new poems arrived,' she wrote, '. . . But when I opened the book my excitement made me too impotent to read. My head ached with too much greed. My eyes glazed with wanting too much at once.'[4] She said that she wanted to eat him up with eagerness; like Caroline Lamb, her desire was to consume the poet and make herself indistinguishable from him. Later in 1937, having left London for Mexico and still no nearer finding him, Smart wrote in her diary, 'George Barker grows into a long dangerous image . . . It is the complete juicy *sound* [of his poetry] that runs bubbles over, that intoxicates till I can hardly follow (and the recurring lines in 'Daedalus': "the moist palm of my hand handled fear like fear cramping my hand." OO the a-a-a!)'[5] 'It is clear,' her biographer comments, 'that Elizabeth was in love with the language of the man.'[6] Smart herself described the obsession in precisely these terms: 'You get into a state when you fall in love . . . The fact that I was madly in love with the English language and with poetry may have give vent to my feelings.'[7] In this sense, *By Grand Central Station* – half of which was written before she met him – is about the point at which Elizabeth Smart's relationship with writing became a relationship with George Barker.

Finding out from Lawrence Durrell that Barker had a job teaching English in a Japanese University, Elizabeth Smart wrote to him offering to buy one of his manuscripts (he was always in need of money, she was told). When Barker could stand academia no more he wrote to Elizabeth Smart and asked her to send him *two* tickets – this was the first she had heard of his wife – to get out of Japan before he went mad. In return he offered her the manuscripts of his private journals. Elizabeth Smart instantly began a campaign to raise the money and *By Grand Central Station* begins on the day when she first met the rescued Barker and his wife in Monterey in

July 1940. By the end of the month the poet and his reader were lovers. George Barker later said that he had fallen in love with her name before he met Elizabeth Smart.

Barker was described by his contemporaries as Byronic. His writing was compulsive in the same way as Byron's: their poetry had the same libidinal energy and quality of excess. Like Byron, he pushed life to the limit and was a great *bon viveur*; they shared a disdain for the professional poet (Byron refused to be paid for his work), and for both men, women took second place to writing: Barker was 'married to poetry.'[8] Elizabeth Smart was, like Caroline Lamb, an obsessional character – 'I am the obsessional type,' she once said. 'Which type are you? If you are the butterfly type you will never forgive my intensity'[9] – and, like Lamb's, her writing is pensive and introspective where her lover's is rapid and Rabelaisian. For both readers, the desire for her poet's *writing* – as a noun and a verb – made her representation of him as a man impossible to achieve. George Barker is eclipsed behind the metaphors in the abstract portrait Smart drew of him in *By Grand Central Station*, while Byron had the unsettling experience of watching himself, at the hands of Caroline Lamb, fade out altogether, to reappear in *Glenarvon* as the first prototype of the Byronic hero.

The official image of Byron is the one produced by his most seduced reader. The 'Byron' who is broadly recognized today – the type of the music-hall villain twiddling his moustaches – is closer to Caroline Lamb's construction of her demon lover than it is to any objective historical account of the poet's character, and her creation of Clarence de Ruthvyn, Lord Glenarvon, was to have enormous repercussions. Later in 1816 Byron's doctor, John Polidori, was looking for a name for the vampire in the story he was basing on Byron. What could be more appropriate than to call his anti-hero 'Ruthven', after Caroline Lamb's portrayal of the poet? Polidori's readers would instantly make the connection between the two dastardly milords. The character of Polidori's villain in *The Vampyre* was a continuation of the ambiguous figure drawn up in *Glenarvon*, and later his seductive, aristocratic vampire became the model for the tragic hero in Bram Stoker's *fin de siècle* novel, *Dracula*. It is quite a thought that the image of horror that has haunted twentieth-century cinema was born of one woman's literary seduction in the early 1800s.

But if Caroline Lamb turned Byron into a literary figure, she was only continuing the process he had begun himself. Byron was a self-conscious product of bibliogenesis and his popularity with readers was to do with what was perceived as his fictional status: he was like the Gothic heroes of Ann Radcliffe's novels, he was Milton's Satan, or those alluring seducers of the eighteenth-century novel, Valmont and Lovelace. Moreover, Byron's fans had collapsed the isolated and brooding heroes of his poems into the worldly figure of the poet himself, and Byron, while protesting his difference from his poetry, was content to accommodate these fantasies. He had to fight, however, to dissociate himself from the mythology that Caroline Lamb was fast constructing around him, and while he claimed that his portrait in *Glenarvon* could not be good because he didn't sit long enough, readers as sophisticated as Goethe took Caroline Lamb's novel to be historical fact.

Yet Caroline Lamb wanted less to write *about* Byron than to *write* and thus to be like Byron. For Byron boasted that his early narrative poems were mere indulgent diversions, rushed off in a matter of evenings between various parties, and this indifference to his literary charm was part of his appeal. So when she put it about that she had written *Glenarvon* in a month, sitting up all night while dressed as a boy, Caroline Lamb was doing no more than impersonate Byron's own literary energy:

I wrote it unknown to all (save a governess, Miss Welsh), in
the middle of the night. It was necessary to have it copied out.
I had heard of a famous copier, an old Mr Woodhead. I sent to

beg he would come to see Lady Caroline Lamb at Melbourne
House. I placed Miss Welsh, elegantly dressed, at my harp,
and myself at a writing table, dressed in the page's clothes,
looking a boy of fourteen . . . He would not believe that this
schoolboy could write such a thing.[10]

Caroline Lamb determined to ensure her literary appeal by turning
herself into a page, literally. Byron had, after all, been little more
than this when she fell for his poetry four years before.

When Lady Oxford left him to go abroad, Byron complained that
he felt 'Carolinish' about his loss. So who was reproducing whom?
Caroline Lamb had, it seems, seduced Byron into an identification
with her, and identification is the backbone of seduction. The
seducer compels the seduced party to feel as they do, to mimic their
responses and repeat their desires. Thus it was that in 1824, the year
of Byron's death, Caroline Lamb seduced a reader of her own, or
rather, her seduction by Byron seduced a reader also seduced by
Byron. And this was entirely to do with both parties' identification
with the Romantic poet. Like Lamb (and like most of the foppish,
literary young men of the generation), the young novelist Edward
Bulwer Lytton modelled himself on Byron, and Caroline Lamb's
feelings for him were inspired by his imitation of her previous lover.
'You are, like me,' she wrote to Bulwer Lytton of his verses, 'too
fond of Lord Byron.' With Caroline Lamb at his side playing the
cruel muse, Edward Bulwer Lytton – who would soon be as prolific
a writer as his hero – would sit dressed as Byron to read his poetry.

The relationship between the older woman (Lamb was thirty-
nine – the same age as Elizabeth Barrett when Robert Browning
first wrote to her) and the younger man (he was twenty-one)
outraged its observers much as Lamb's and Byron's relationship had
done, and Lamb was once more decried as a malevolent seducer, not
least when this time – in true Byronic fashion – she threw her lover
over for another model. For his own part, Bulwer Lytton's feelings

towards Caroline Lamb were fuelled by her affair with Byron, which had, and not least because of *Glenarvon*, become legendary. Although only just buried, Byron was now mythical, and for Edward Bulwer Lytton to be touching the hand that Byron had touched was like going back in time. For him, Caroline Lamb was a page in history.

This curious diversion in the lives of both Lamb and Bulwer Lytton recalls Henry James's 1888 tale, *The Aspern Papers*, which was inspired by James's shock on hearing that Claire Clairmont, a lover of Byron's and the sister-in-law of Shelley, had only recently died, having lived the length of the nineteenth century. A sea-captain, James heard, had tried to extract Shelley's letters from the old woman, and out of this kernel James devised his plot in which a publisher is so obsessed with Jeffrey Aspern, a Romantic poet, that in his attempt to get hold of the poet's manuscripts he seduces the ancient niece of Aspern's still-living muse, Juliana. *The Aspern Papers* is a tale of bibliomania and in this sense a love story. The publisher is to some extent in love with the past, with Aspern, and with Aspern's writing, but it is the *materiality* of writing he craves, the tangibility of the papers with which he is in love. Regardless of what is written on them, he wants the papers themselves, and the tale's irony is that the publisher has no idea of nor interest in their content. For all he knows, the Aspern papers are little more than a laundry list, but this would not disappoint him: it is the scratch of pen on paper he is after and for which he would sacrifice himself. Caroline Lamb and Edward Bulwer Lytton, Juliana and the publisher – both couples who straddle the Romantics and Victorians – live with ghosts, and the women in each relationship serve as mediums to the earlier age. As in 'The Private Life', each reader, like Elizabeth Barrett and Robert Browning, is involved in a relationship with the spectral writer working in the dark upstairs, rather than with the public figure enjoying his dinner down below.

The year after Caroline Lamb died, Edward Bulwer Lytton

received a letter from another woman infamous for her lovers and the exposure of her writing. Harriette Wilson's *Memoirs* had been published in 1825 and the society courtesan had agreed only in exchange for a payment to exclude from her book the names of men with whom she had slept, hence the fabled retort of 'publish and be damned' from the Duke of Wellington when she threatened to reveal his identity. Her memoirs make a riotously good read – Harriette Wilson was a born entertainer. Because her occupation required her to feign seduction in order to disguise the financial imperative that was driving her, the status of her supposed seduction by the writing of Edward Bulwer Lytton – with whose 'talents' she pronounced herself 'in love' – is questionable. But then seduction is by its nature artificial, making it impossible to distinguish between the real and the contrived. Harriette Wilson makes it plain in her opening letter to Bulwer Lytton that she is well aware of the seductions of reading, particularly in the post-Byronic age. The diversions of reading crush authenticity, she believes: 'I am very ignorant and can't spell, but there is this advantage in not reading, *you are all of you copies and I am the thing itself*.'[11] Harriette Wilson had read *Glenarvon* and followed the story of Caroline Lamb with interest. If Lamb had become a copy of the writing by which she was seduced, Wilson would copy Lamb's affair with the writer rather than her seduction by the writing. Harriette Wilson seems, in this sense, to have been more seduced by Caroline Lamb than by Edward Bulwer Lytton.

Her letter to Bulwer Lytton is a flirtatious attempt to marry his literary talents with her sexual ones, to match one ravishment with another:

Sir –
Though I have disliked reading all my life unless it be
Shakespear's [sic] plays, yet I got to the end of *Pelham*. It was not
a book to my taste either, for I thought the writer was a cold

hearted man, and his light chit-chat was pedantic, smelling of the *Lamp* – not so good as my own. But then it was a sensible book, the fancies brilliant, the thought deep, the language very expressive. In short I got to the end of it

. . . Now for *Devereux*, I have nearly finished the first vol. and am so charmed with it, that I have laid it aside to tell you how proud I should be if you felt disposed to honour me with your acquaintance. I merely *suggest* this to you because life is too short and too miserable for us to afford prudently to risk the loss of a possible pleasure for want of asking for it, and it is just *possible* that we might derive pleasure from being acquainted.

. . . I am only in love with your *last* work as far as I have read it, and have pleasure in expressing to the author my perfect glowing admiration of every line up to page 266.[12]

Bulwer Lytton resisted (or feigned resistance to) Harriette Wilson's considerable charms and refused to read the proofs she sent him of her novel, *Clara Gazul*. But he cannot have been altogether displeased by the encounter nor by the fact that he was in the position to turn down a literary seduction. His 1826 novel, *Falkland* is, after all, a fantasy of himself as the arch-seducer of the age, and only Byron had previously been appealed to in such a way by readers who offered themselves to him on the strength of an unfinished read.

When Claire Clairmont wrote to Byron in spring 1816, under the guise of wanting his encouragement to become an actress, he too could have ignored her letter, but instead allowed himself to be distracted because she had caught him at a low point in his life. His marriage was over and he was anticipating exile. Claire also wrote excellent letters, and it is easy to imagine how Byron might have been weakened by her lively prose. Claire Clairmont had written to the most famous figure in England because her step-sister, Mary Wollstonecraft Godwin, was courting Percy Bysshe Shelley, and

Claire wanted to ravish a poet of her own. By the time Byron left the country, Claire was already pregnant with their child – although neither of them then knew it – and she pursued Byron to Lake Geneva, where she appeared with Shelley and Mary, who had respectively run away from his wife and her father. Byron only agreed to the rendezvous with this girl who, he complained, 'pranced' half way across Europe to get into his bed because he was intrigued to meet Shelley, whose poem *Queen Mab* had impressed him.

Byron's and Claire Clairmont's encounter was over before the end of that dark and thunderous summer of 1816, although they continued to communicate about the welfare of Allegra, their daughter, who was born in September. Having initially wanted to send the child to his sister, Byron then insisted that Claire bring Allegra to Italy to live with him and she reluctantly agreed, on the condition that Allegra would be brought up by her father and no one else. Byron broke his word: he placed the five-year-old in a convent, where she soon died of typhoid, being unvisited by her father during her illness. Claire Clairmont was heart-broken.

Claire was a child in 1801 when her mother married the radical philosopher, William Godwin. The 'widow' Mrs Mary Jane Clairmont reputedly introduced herself to her neighbour from the balcony of her house: 'Is it possible that I behold the immortal Godwin?' she proclaimed. Mrs Clairmont was not bookish and was therefore thought a surprising choice of second wife for someone of Godwin's intellectual calibre and fame. Like her daughter, she was seen as lacking blood, brains, and breeding, and yet they were a contented couple and Godwin, a widower bringing up a daughter of his own as well as raising the daughter of his deceased wife and her previous lover, badly needed a partner. In 1797 Godwin had married Mary Wollstonecraft who, like Caroline Lamb and Harriette Wilson, was known for her 'loose' sexuality and the shocking content of her writing. As author of the feminist polemic,

A Vindication of the Rights of Women, Mary Wollstonecraft was determined to defy the stultifying givens of social convention, and having fallen in love with the married artist, Henry Fuseli, she suggested that she move in with him and his wife. She proposed a *ménage à trois* to her next lover as well, an American called Gilbert Imlay, who fathered her daughter, Fanny. In despair when Imlay abandoned her, Mary Wollstonecraft threw herself off Putney Bridge into the Thames and was fished out by boatmen. This was her second suicide attempt. Her daughter Fanny would successfully kill herself when she was twenty-two, swallowing laudanum when life in the Godwin household became too much for her.

William Godwin, a bachelor in his mid-thirties, had first met Mary Wollstonecraft in 1791, before her trials with Gilbert Imlay began. She was thirty-six and he forty when Godwin became acquainted with her again at a dinner party in January 1795. He was then at the height of his fame, the recent success of the *Enquiry concerning Political Justice* being followed the next year by that of his novel, *Caleb Williams*. After what was an inauspicious meeting with Mary Wollstonecraft, Godwin read her newly published *Letters Written During a Short Residence in Sweden, Norway, and Denmark*, and wrote: 'If ever there was ever a book calculated to make a man fall in love with its author, this appears to me to be the book.'[13] Diverted and distracted, Godwin was drawn to call on the author but found she was not at home. He also discovered that he was not the only reader to feel this way about Mary Wollstonecraft's literary 'genius', which, he said, 'commands all our attention' and 'dissolves us in tenderness'. Her *Letters* generated a number of other letters and she was pursued by readers across Europe. However, it was Godwin who interested Mary Wollstonecraft and in April she returned his call. By July 1795, their affair was consummated.

Godwin was bewildered by the emotional complexities of this, his first real love affair. 'I had rather at this moment talk to you on paper than in any other mode,' he wrote to Mary after they first slept together, and while Mary Wollstonecraft was more experienced and less sexually inhibited in relationships, her previous encounters had made her equally cautious, and she also expressed herself in writing rather than in person until their emotions had become more established. Her feelings for Godwin, while strong and loving, had none of the passion that she had felt for Fuseli or Imlay, and she married him because he was, as her biographer Claire Tomalin writes, 'clever and famous and sought after; she was fond of him, wanted a companion and bedmate, a father for Fanny', and because she became pregnant and 'he was willing'.[14] The couple who had each argued against the institution of marriage decided that to marry would be in the best interests of the baby – as well as of the mother, who had one illegitimate child already – and the knot was tied quickly and discreetly on 29 March 1797 at their local church of St Pancras in North London.

The short period of marital life they shared was happy, and Mary become 'a worshipper of domestic life', Godwin recalled. When Mary Wollstonecraft Godwin died that September, after giving birth to their daughter, William Godwin was too grief-stricken to record the event in his diary. '20 minutes before 8' is all he wrote, and his wife was buried at the church where they had recently married. Godwin was not ready to attend her funeral there five days later.

Within two weeks of Mary Wollstonecraft's death, William Godwin had begun to write about her. She was the most remarkable woman of her own or of any age, he believed, and by taking up his pen he wanted to record her extraordinary life as well as to give his relationship with her some kind of narrative structure, before the disintegrating effects of mourning erased her memory in him. Besides, Godwin had always preferred to 'talk to you on paper', as he had previously put it to Mary, and in a sense this is what he was doing in writing his way through the misery of his loss: he was talking to her, for her, and with her. His *Memoirs of the Author of A Vindication of the Rights of Women* (Godwin identified his wife by her most famous book rather than by her name), published four months after Mary Wollstonecraft was buried, is like Caroline Lamb's *Glenarvon* in that it describes a relationship that began with a good read and ended with an outpouring of writing and grief. Godwin inadvertently did for Mary Wollstonecraft what Caroline Lamb would do for Byron, and so it is fitting that these two great mythologizers soon began a correspondence of their own. Godwin's portrait of Wollstonecraft established her popular reputation and reception for years to come. But where Caroline Lamb radically embellished her lover, creating a manic fantasy of Byron, Godwin stuck earnestly and straightforwardly to the truth, which was seen by the reading public as equally sensational. He revealed her love affairs, her times as a kept mistress, her suicide attempts and her pregnancies alongside Mary Wollstonecraft's rational philosophical beliefs. So much for his placing reason above passion, Godwin's readers thought, as they mocked the two philosophers.

At the same time as the *Memoirs* were published, Godwin brought out a four-volume edition of Wollstonecraft's posthumous works, which included her love letters to Gilbert Imlay. Astonishingly, he failed to see what the public reaction to this exposure of his wife's private life would be, and with these two books he in moments managed to bury Mary Wollstonecraft's reputation so deeply that the feminist movement she had represented was unable to mention her name for several generations to come. Their heroine had become an embarrassment to the cause of women's liberation.

The young Mary Godwin was not expected to survive. As it was, she grew up haunted by her mother's life and her part in her mother's death, themes that recur in the novel she would write when she was not yet nineteen. When Mary Godwin was five, her father's marriage meant that the small household in which she had grown up expanded. As well as containing herself and Fanny Imlay, who adopted the name Godwin, the house in The Polygon now included Mary Jane Clairmont's daughter, Jane Clairmont, who adopted the name Claire, her brother Charles Clairmont, and soon young William, the son of Godwin and Mary Jane. The extended Godwin family were continuously penniless and Godwin's years of fame were so far behind him that when, in early 1812, Percy Bysshe Shelley heard that his hero was still alive, he wrote to Godwin instantly: 'The name of Godwin has been used to excite in me feelings of reverence and admiration, I have been accustomed to consider him a luminary too dazzling for the darkness which surrounds him . . .' This first letter, William St Clair points out, resembles a fictional letter Godwin included in his novel *Fleetwood*, and later Shelley wrote to Godwin, 'I had pictured to my fancy that I should first meet you in a spot like that in which Fleetwood met Ruffigny,' Ruffigny being the teacher of Fleetwood's wisdom. The nineteen-year-old Shelley, recently sent down from Oxford for atheism, and now – through Godwin's and Wollstonecraft's example – married to Harriet Westbrook, was 'evidently already viewing his own relationship with Godwin in pre-set literary terms'.[15] The stage was set for his meeting with Godwin's daughter, who also structured her life according to her parents' writing and her writing according to her parents' life.

In May 1814, the sixteen-year-old Mary Godwin returned from an extended stay in Scotland to find that Shelley had become a regular visitor to the noisy house in Skinner Street, and that he was involved in a tangled financial relationship with the perpetually broke Godwin. The philosophy of both men approved the situation in which any money Shelley had he should give to his mentor. In late June of the same year, Mary Godwin took her father's disciple to her mother's grave and declared her love to him, which he reciprocated. 'Nothing that I have ever read in tale or history could present a more striking image of a sudden, violent, irresistible, uncontrollable passion,' Thomas Love Peacock wrote in his *Memoir* of Shelley, perhaps not realizing that it was tales and history that presented to the couple the image of passion that they were determined to repeat. Much of Mary's and Shelley's courtship had taken place at the St Pancras cemetery, where the couple used to come with Claire to sit on Mary Wollstonecraft's gravestone and read her letters and books.

When Shelley announced to Godwin his plan to leave Harriet (who was pregnant with his child) and live abroad with Mary, he thought he was acting in a Godwinian manner that would impress the philosopher. Godwin, who had written eloquently of his deceased wife's freedom to live with the man of her choice, was, however, appalled by Shelley's desire to live with the woman of his choice and although he adamantly refused to give the poet his approval of the match, he continued to take large sums of money from him. In the early hours of 28 July Shelley, Mary and Claire left London and got the next boat from Dover to Calais. Just as Godwin had been unable to record any more than the time of Mary Wollstonecraft's death in his journal, the elopement of his daughter, his step-daughter, and his young friend was reported as simply 'five in the morning'.

Running away together, the couple continued to believe that they were doing what Mary's parents would have done. They agreed that in the freedom of their lifestyle they were more Godwinian now than Godwin; that they embodied the New Philosophy of the 1790s that William Godwin had clearly forgotten. Taking Claire with them as a third party made their situation even more enlightened; Mary Wollstonecraft had, after all, always suggested living in threesomes and Godwin was also an advocate of unpossessive love. But Claire was not the only extra presence on the journey: Mary had packed her parents' love letters and she showed them to the delighted Shelley when they arrived in France. Running away with your own love letters, as Robert Browning and Elizabeth Barrett had done, is one thing; absconding with the amorous correspondence of your parents is quite another, bespeaking as it does a voyeuristic desire to observe your own literary primal scene. But in the context of Shelley's and Mary's relationship this extraordinary act makes sense.

Godwin was wrong to accuse Shelley of seducing Mary. It was he, Godwin, who had seduced Shelley. Harriet Shelley, describing her husband (who wanted her to join them in France) as now 'dead' and replaced by a 'vampire', was more clear-sighted about what had been going on, and she put Shelley's behaviour down to his reading Godwin's *Political Justice*. 'The very great evil that book has done is not to be told,' she wrote to a friend. But what she called Godwin's 'false doctrines' could not alone be held accountable. Mary Godwin was also responsible for the seduction, Harriet said, as it was she who 'heated his imagination by talking of her mother, going to her grave with him every day.'[16] It was not the talk so much as the mother's writing that had heated Shelley's imagination, and Harriet – knowing where Shelley's passions lay – was well aware of this. Mary Wollstonecraft had herself seduced Shelley through the person of her daughter, the product of her philosophy. As for Mary Godwin, she was repeating the story of her mother's life in what she saw as her own visionary and impulsive passion for a man who was the child of her father's intellect. This was a literary seduction by proxy: Mary Godwin and Percy Bysshe Shelley had found in one another a living incarnation of the writing of her parents.

Mary's and Shelley's desire to forge their own relationship out of the story of Godwin and Wollstonecraft becomes one of the most unsettling themes in *Frankenstein*, whose concern with the power of stories and the longing for a meaningful narrative in which to place oneself recurs in the other literary seductions in this book. Not only is *Frankenstein* full of poignant and apparently pointless anecdotes that divert from the main story, but it is constructed from stories enclosed inside one another like a Russian doll, and each narrator seduces his listener as he tells the tale of someone else. The epistolary novel is framed with Walton writing to his sister Margaret from his ship, and relating the tale that Victor Frankenstein, whom he has rescued, tells him; and Frankenstein's story encloses his monster's narrative. Within the monster's story of his life is the story of the De Laceys and of Safie, on whom we gather the monster has been spying. As he listens to their tales, the monster's identity, sympathies, ideas, and desires develop around them. Through their narratives, and through discovering *Paradise Lost*, Goethe and Plutarch, he learns to experience himself as a sympathetic human being.

Everyone in *Frankenstein* is in need of a story to hear and a story to tell; each character needs a listener to whom he or she can speak and each tale is about someone they can neither make contact with nor separate from. The narrators in the novel find their *own* story through the tale of another. More than anything, *Frankenstein* bespeaks the need to *have a story to tell about the self* and reveals the horror of finding, when your story is begun, that it is not even yours to tell, that it belongs to someone else instead. Hence Walton's tale is about not himself but Frankenstein, and Frankenstein's is about the monster, and so forth. Mary Shelley, like Freud, suggests that there is no such thing as the free, autonomous self, that we are all inhabited by another voice and another person, by a tale other than our own. This is the nightmare of being a child: we carry around with us the history of our parents that we are destined to repeat. In *Frankenstein*, the creator and created, like mother and child, haunt and inhabit one another, becoming indistinguishable. Not only was this the story of Mary Shelley's relationship with Mary Wollstonecraft, but it also describes Mary's and Shelley's affair with her parents' story.

As they journeyed across Europe in the summer of 1814, with Mary feeling increasingly wretched from the first stages of pregnancy, Shelley read aloud from Mary Wollstonecraft's *Letters from Sweden*, the book that had seduced Godwin back in 1795.

Inspired by the idea, Mary used it as a model when she later wrote up their own journey as the *History of a Six Weeks Tour*. When the trio returned to England and set up home together in London, they worked their way through the oeuvre of both Mary's parents and scoured the pages of Godwin and Wollstonecraft for enlightenment and guidance as to how to lead their future lives. Still unforgiven by Godwin, Shelley, Mary and Claire left the country again in the summer of 1816. This time Claire was pregnant with Byron's child, and they met up with the exiled poet on the shores of Lake Geneva, where one rainy night John Polidori, Byron's doctor, began composing his vampire tale and Mary Shelley had the waking dream that resulted in *Frankenstein*.

Later that year Harriet Shelley's pregnant body was found in the Serpentine in London. Six years later, Shelley drowned whilst sailing in Italy, leaving behind his wife and one surviving child. Mary Shelley continued to write but she was never again seduced by the literature of either parents or poets. Writing, in Mary Shelley's experience, had the power to generate life and death, which gives her own literary fate an irony. It was soon forgotten that her first novel was written by her, or indeed that it was *written* at all: in modern myth, *Frankenstein* is thought to be self-generated, or at least generated by cinema. Mary Shelley's writing had such power that, like the monster she described, it killed off its creator and broke free in a strange diversion of its own. But that is another story.

TWO

Literary Possession:
Anaïs Nin and Henry Miller

I write a love letter, to write, and not because I love.

FLAUBERT

I cannot write myself out.

ANAÏS NIN

Writing, for Anaïs Nin, was not compulsive so much as patho-logical: she was a scribomaniac, and this much she was to have in common with Henry Miller. Anaïs Nin was also a consummate seductress and the mutual pleasures of the word and the flesh were to dictate and shape her entire life. When she was twenty-nine, her introduction to Henry Miller inspired her to write more than at any other period, filling six journals in a year. He also inspired her seductions and she was to have a complementary six lovers over the next two years. These affairs she wrote about intensively before editing them out of the published journals for fear of shocking her husband.

In April 1932, the month after her thirteen-year-long relation-ship with Henry Miller began, Anaïs was so anxious that the obsessional self-absorption of her journal writing was blocking her ability to write fiction, that she took the advice of Eduardo, her love-sick cousin, and consulted his psychoanalyst, René Allendy. 'I realize I *am* too personal,' she said, '– that all of my writing springs from my self. As soon as I write objectively, as soon as I talk in the third person, my work freezes.'[1] Anaïs was reluctant about being analysed, believing that her journal was her therapy, and so Eduardo shrewdly tempted her to see Allendy by arguing that a therapist would be a father-figure. Given Anaïs's very real attraction to fathers (which would soon become apparent) and Eduardo's attraction to Anaïs, this was a somewhat self-sabotaging move. Particularly as Eduardo's motivation for getting Anaïs to see Rene Allendy was that the analyst might persuade her to sleep with her cousin on the grounds that Eduardo's psychological health depended on it. René Allendy talked with Anaïs about Eduardo's passion for her and then noted with concern how his patient's only reality seemed to be in her journal writing; how, as Anaïs put it, 'What is left out of the journal is also left out of my mind.'[2] Anaïs's obsessive writing had the effect of making 'the rest of life, and people around me seem unreal and irritating, and useless.'[3] Allendy also observed how during therapy sessions she would be restless and distracted in her eagerness to rush home to put the experience down on paper.

Anaïs Nin's zeal to *record* the interchange between analyst and analysand rather than *respond* in it was no doubt exacerbated by the fact that at this stage in the treatment she had become bored with the traditional therapeutic method and had decided instead to show Allendy her breasts. After this the sessions ceased being concerned with discussing Anaïs's writing, which Allendy saw as a neurosis, or with analysing what he called her 'completely artificial' appearance and her need to be seductive, both of which he said disguised the fact that inside this polished exterior she was really 'a hidden wreck'. The therapeutic hour now became the scene of another seduction that Anaïs could then write about. Owing to Allendy's impotence, the couple were restricted to heavy petting sessions in his consulting room, but Anaïs soon persuaded him to ask her to a hotel, where he snapped out a whip and induced her to indulge in a frantic bout of flagellation, which she found amusing because it still failed to arouse him. Anaïs then sent her husband and her sister-in-law (with whom she was also conducting a flirtation) to consult Allendy, in the expectation that they would all talk about how desirable she was.

Shortly after the Allendy episode, Anaïs, her husband, Hugo, and Henry Miller began reading Otto Rank together, and Anaïs was diverted by Rank's *Art and Artist*. This was a book she would like to have written herself. She felt that Rank's view that 'the artist [is] created not *because* of the neurosis but in spite of it'[4] made him the right man to help her; far more suitable than what she saw as the pathetic Allendy, with his whips, his hotchpotch of theories, and his mad books on *The Symbolism of Numbers* and the 'Emerald Table of Hermes Trismegistes'. Otto Rank had been Freud's most brilliant disciple until he disgraced himself in 1924 by defecting from Freudian orthodoxy with his book on *The Trauma of Birth*. He was duly expelled from Freud's circle in Vienna and he came to Paris, where he pursued his own independent line of psychoanalytic thought, which had a broader sociological base than he found in Freudianism. Anaïs Nin saw herself as the embodiment of his theories about the human urge to creativity and the visionary role of the artist.

So in late 1933, Rank became the next analyst whose professional and sexual services Anaïs Nin employed in the hope of separating herself from her prose. Rank read with great admiration and interest the journal extracts she gave him and then attempted to ban her from writing altogether during the term of her therapy with him. But having dutifully marooned herself in a hotel room without writing materials, Anaïs soon found herself crawling up the walls in a state of cold turkey, and resorted to asking hotel staff for scraps of paper and a pencil so that she could rush down her thoughts. This afforded her great relief. Eighteen months later Rank, still hopelessly in love with her, was to write a preface to Anaïs's childhood journal in the false expectation that her writing would soon be published.[5] Anaïs was delighted by this change in their relationship. From being walking evidence of Rank's philosophy, and from falling, Narcissus-like, for the image of herself she found reflected in his work – 'I'm falling in love with your books,' she warned him. 'Are you jealous?'[6] – she had ended up luring Rank into *her* world of writing. From being seduced by the language of psychoanalysis ('his work was his seduction'), Anaïs succeeded in turning the tables and seducing the analyst with her own work. Rank now met her on her terms: 'The very man who killed off the diary as neurosis has now given me back the urge to continue it.'[7] They were now writing twin diaries, exchanging them each week. Meanwhile, she had also sent Hugo to Rank for analysis, presumably for the same reason as she sent him to Allendy.

The patient had even become the therapist. In 1935 Otto Rank enthusiastically arranged for Anaïs to join him in New York, where he was setting up a new psychoanalytic practice. Yet more terrifying than the thought of being analysed by a completely untrained Anaïs Nin is the fact that, unbeknown to Rank, she had smuggled Henry Miller into New York with her and she referred some of her patients to him. Henry was as qualified to approach the unconscious mind as he was to perform a lobotomy; his comment on his four clients a day and on Rank's technique was that he didn't 'give a fuck' because he was 'totally indifferent' to psychoanalysis.[8] It was better, however, than doing nothing while his lover carried on with her lover, and he worked out his own particular brand of Milleresque relief for his patients' neuroses: get them reading. He would recommend to them 'a little of the juice of St Augustine and a little Emerson', and if that didn't cure them then they weren't worth curing. Otto Rank died suddenly in 1939, a few months after he married his secretary. Anaïs and he were no longer in contact, but she did write a preface to the seductive *Art and Artist*, in which she praised Rank's wisdom, courage, and originality.

From the beginning writing and seduction were interchangeable terms for Anaïs Nin because she began to write as an act of seduction. 'Every act related to my writing was connected in me

with an act of charm, seduction of my father,' she reflected in her old
age, when she was still writing and seducing as if her life depended
upon it, which in a sense it did. Eduardo's observation that Anaïs
needed a father was perceptive, and she was to find Henry Miller
attractive because he could be, she believed, 'a father, a guide'.
When the foppish and decadent Joaquín Nin abandoned his family
in 1914, he left his older and plainer wife, Rosa Culmell, to sail
from Spain to New York to make a new life for herself and her three
young children. It was then that the eleven-year-old Anaïs began
her journal in order to assuage her hurt and grief. The story goes
(and everything in Anaïs Nin's life is a story, thinly attached to
external fact) that the monumental journal – all 35,000 pages of it –
started out as her letter to her father, a last-ditch attempt to lure him
back to her. But, however apocryphal the tale, the act of writing
quickly developed attractions of its own for Anaïs and she was soon
less concerned with winning her father back than with supplement-
ing his loss: 'When I have written a thing I no longer fear the loss of
it,'[9] she discovered. Writing was the perfect panacea and in order to
prolong its pleasure Anaïs set herself an impossible task: 'I will
never be able to stop writing my Journal until I find peace,' which,
she added in qualification, she would 'never find'.[10]

There is a psychoanalytic dictum that it is in the nature of desire
to thwart its own fulfilment because desire, as opposed to love, has
no object and is an autoerotic act: the pleasure of desiring is in the
pursuit and not in the goal. Anaïs Nin's writing functioned like the
law of desire in that it became less about seducing her father than
about the pleasure of writing *per se*; it was less an instrument of
communication with an end in sight than a sensual act of its own,
an experience in and for itself. 'So, Sir Diary,' she wrote as a child, 'I
name you my prince of princes and my only king on earth. I am
madly in love with you . . .'

Her journal writing didn't stop after June 1933 when Anaïs had
succeeded in a genuine seduction of her father, or rather they had

performed a mutual seduction. This experience (which was encouraged by Otto Rank) had, so far as Anaïs was concerned, set the record straight and enabled her to avenge Joaquín's betrayal. She left him longing for her, believing her (if we are to believe her) to be, at last, '*the* woman of my life', while she returned home to her husband and four lovers. The tale of the frenzied holiday affair between father and daughter that took place in the sleepy French village of Valescure, near St Raphaël, is edited out of the first publication of the journals and told in typically portentous and novelettish prose in *Incest*, the second of the recently published unexpurgated volumes (in an account which is indistinguishable from the novelette she did endlessly write, rewrite, and revise about the encounter, eventually called 'Winter of Artifice'). In her breathless rendition of the seduction, it would seem that the taste of revenge was sweetest for Anaïs when Joaquín said that he felt jealous of her diary and referred to it as his 'rival', which indeed it had once been, only now it replaced him altogether. Joaquín begged his daughter not to write about their affair in the same way as he might beg her not to laugh with another partner about his performance, but as far as Anaïs was concerned there would be little point in having had intercourse with her father if she couldn't tell her journal. Anaïs Nin's writing had taken the place of the men, whom it was intended to beguile; having her writing – 'Sir Diary' – rid her of the need for other committed relationships.

What Anaïs Nin and Henry Miller were to share was this erotic love of the written word – their own, each other's, and that of other people. If people were seductive because of the words they wrote, then Anaïs wanted to go one stage further and ensure her appeal by aspiring, like Henry Miller, to 'realize myself in words'.[11] When she began her journal she decided not to write *about* herself but to *write herself*, and she dealt with the pain of her father's rejection by opting to *become* her writing. As a precocious thirteen-year-old she told Joaquin: 'I am nothing but dust . . . I want to spread myself on a lot of paper, turn into lots of sentences, lots of words so that I won't be walked on.'[12] Anaïs felt that by being absorbed in inky signs she could reinvent herself, and her journals are a monumental endeavour to trade flesh and blood for a life as blotches and specks on a page. She was to identify this same quality in Henry Miller: 'The same thing which makes Henry indestructible is what makes me indestructible: It is that at the *core* of us is a writer, not a human being.'[13] The joys of writing had utterly seduced her.

II

Anaïs Nin's journals are her attempt to tell herself the story of her life because 'that life would be more bearable if I looked at it as an adventure and a tale'.[14] She had no need, however, to invent a mysterious family romance about her parentage or to exaggerate the drama of her childhood, as Henry's wife, June Mansfield, would do. Anaïs's father was the impoverished and ambitious son of minor Spanish nobility and her mother was the clear-sighted and determined daughter of a wealthy Danish merchant and his French-Cuban wife. Rosa Culmell was in love with the stunningly handsome Joaquín Nin, who was eight years her junior, and while her family were anxious about their courtship, Rosa insisted on the marriage. Joaquín, meanwhile, was more attracted to the help Rosa's money could offer him in his drive to be a world-famous concert pianist. Their wedding present from Rosa's doubtful father was a passage to Paris, a grand piano, and a steady income until Joaquín made enough money to support them both. Rosa's own promising career as a soprano never came to anything: she devoted herself to supporting her husband and to raising their children. Joaquín, in turn, beat and abused them all. Anaïs's birth in Paris on 21 February 1903 immediately disappointed her father, who had wanted a boy rather than, as he said, an 'ugly little girl', and Anaïs was to remember this slight all her life, delighting, in years to come, in any compliments he might pay her. Joaquín's sadistic behaviour and his dictatorial compulsion for order and cleanliness dominated her childhood. He would frequently spank and fondle Anaïs as well as torment and humiliate her by his obsession with photography – the camera lens would appear around the door without warning when she and her two younger brothers were in various states of undress.

In *Secret Life*, his autobiographical account of an addiction to sex that he believed was procured from childhood molestation, Michael Ryan makes an observation that is applicable to Anaïs Nin and to the pattern of her behaviour following Joaquín's abuse: 'I believe the most insidious part of sexual abuse is in the creation of desire in the molested child, the way it forms a shape for desire that can never again be fulfilled, only substituted for and repeated, unless – if he's lucky and can find help – he ceases to identify with the molester.' Anaïs Nin wanted to become a Donna Juanna to compete with her father's reputation as a Don Juan, and just as her desire to seduce was never fulfilled, nor was her thirst for writing. Her writing also became a craving for satisfaction, for 'the essential thing', which could never be completed. Her sexuality and her writing became indistinguishable, as she told Edmund Wilson: 'My writing is *me* and my life and writing are one whole, integrated and indivisible unit.'[15]

When he deserted them, Joaquín left Anaïs with an image of her father as a man who had to be pleased, a man who was loved by adoring audiences and whom she must love also, a perfectionist for whom she must attain perfection. She was later to say that the reason she wrote was 'to give to the world one perfect life', and it is clear that this image of perfection was, like her perfectly decorated stage-set houses, her perfectly turned-out appearance, and her cataloguing of every flattering remark she ever received, a gift to her father, should he return to her. When Joaquín did see her Paris house, Anaïs records him as saying – and allow here for the Nin-speak in which everyone addresses her in the same humourless manner: 'You know, Anaïs, I have been in many homes – and I have never seen any like yours. None gave me the same feeling. You understand a home.'[16] The habit Anaïs was later to acquire of indexing what she did every day would seem to be as much to do with pleasing the retentive and fastidious Joaquín as it was with keeping abreast of her own lies. It is also clear that her desire to support men and not to compete with them was born of her fear of displacing her self-important father, and it took her years of analysis (with a woman analyst this time, Dr Martha Jaeger) to realize how profoundly she resented this role. It is easier to forgive Anaïs Nin's gargantuan self-adulation and egotism in the light of her miserable childhood. It is also possible to see the reasons why she chose to weave herself into her writing as a way of ensuring that she would no longer be the victim of betrayal and abandonment. From now on she would be the only person doing any abandoning, and she turned it into an art.

Psychoanalysis has it that women cannot be perverse because perversion is tied to the traumatic experiences of masculine sexuality alone. Perversion and fetishism result from the boy's shocked reaction to the woman's 'castrated' body, and the pervert's drive is to disavow the mother's 'lack' by focusing instead on what disguises it or comes before it, like shoes, stockings, or underwear. So the fetishist is in a state of limbo between knowing and not knowing, seeing and not seeing, and his sexual life becomes an endless re-enactment of this cross-eyed moment. As the bearer of this lack and the source of this shocking knowledge, the woman can choose to reveal or to disguise her castration, either representing herself as a comfort to men (in the guise of a fetish) or as a threat: you, too, could be castrated.

Yet, for all her purring and soothing, for all her desire to reassure her male readers that she means them no harm, there *is* something perverse about Anaïs Nin's compulsive writing, just as there is something perverse in the pleasure readers get from her tireless prose. Her journal took on for her the importance of a sexual fetish, taking over and dictating her entire life. Writing it was as necessary to her as eating and sleeping. 'What distinguishes a perversion is its quality of desperation and fixity,' Louise Kaplan writes in *Female Perversions*. 'A perversion is performed by a person who has no other choices, a person who would otherwise be overwhelmed by anxieties or depression or psychosis.'[17] Perversions, like diaries, are both secret and revealed: Anaïs Nin revealed her writing to her lovers with theatrical relish. The dramatic performance of the perverse act serves to redirect attention from its underlying motives, disguising the repressed desires that lie at its source. Perversion is therefore a psychological strategy for survival: 'The enactment, or performance, is designed to help the person to survive, moreover to survive with a sense of triumph over the traumas of his or her childhood.'[18] The pervert is unconsciously driven to perform his perversion and 'when deterred from doing so he feels desperately anxious, panicky, agitated, crazy, even violent'.[19] Precisely how Anaïs Nin felt, in fact, when during her analysis with Otto Rank she was locked in her hotel room without a pen.

But Anaïs Nin experienced none of the *shame* that accompanies the perverse performance. There is a marked absence of embarrassment in her writing, an absence that is supplemented by her readers, and her skill as an artist is revealed in this dynamic. She is the most embarrassing woman writer of the twentieth century and the degree to which her readers blush on her behalf is testament not only to the strange force of her prose but also to the degree of shameful *pleasure* her writing incites. It is useful here to distinguish between types of pleasure: in Anaïs Nin can be found none of the pleasure of the well-crafted classic text, what Roland Barthes describes as those pleasures which can be 'spoken about', such as irony, intelligence, and delicacy, the check-list of textual pleasures that lead to literary criticism. Pleasure such as this generates satisfaction and self-confirmation: the reader nods approval at the text. He enjoys a harmonious encounter between the rounded text and the rounded self, each confirming the other. Anaïs Nin's writing conforms instead to Barthes' other definition of textual pleasure: the perverse, seductive *jouissance*, which translates as 'bliss' but whose meaning is closer to 'orgasm'. Anaïs Nin's reader may not *like* her writing, may not think it good or even interesting, but he or she finds that these critically evaluative terms and reactions are curiously irrelevant. The reader becomes perverse: just as the perverse child *knows* that the mother does not have a penis but *believes* all the same that she does have one, so the reader knows that Anaïs Nin is a minor writer of limited ability whilst also knowing that she is utterly absorbing and unputdownable. Her readers credit her with the tremendous power they fear she does not have.

During her otherwise inauspicious education in New York, Anaïs Nin had some writing published in the school paper, and this led to her insistence that she leave school early to pursue what she believed looked to be a promising career as an author. This was the only writing that Anaïs Nin would see in print for years to come and so it is as well that she found a wealthy husband to support her and her family, who were continually without money and dependent on her help. Rosa was confident of her daughter's capacity to secure a good match: Anaïs was head-turningly striking, tallish and fragile (indeed, 'underweight', as she would remind people), with a childlike heart-shaped face, high cheek-bones, large eyes (which she emphasised with copious quantities of kohl), an aquiline, slightly turned-up nose (which she would have surgically corrected, twice), and wide, thin lips (which she would have surgically enlarged when she was in her sixties). In 1921 she met the well-heeled and handsome Hugh Parker Guiler – 'Hugo' – at a dance held at his family home in the salubrious district of Forest Hills, Queens, and they spoke together of their mutual love of writing poetry, reading literature and keeping journals. Like Anaïs's, Hugo's childhood had been restless, leaving Boston for Puerto Rico and then settling to an education in Scotland, where he remained until his father moved him to Queens in 1914, the same year that the eleven-year-old Anaïs docked in New York, able to speak only Spanish and French. Hugo studied Economics and English at Columbia and chose a career in banking that would give him the financial security he needed in order to become an artist. Anaïs and Hugo married, against his family's wishes, when Anaïs was twenty and Hugo twenty-five. Hugo's father never forgave him for marrying a Catholic and cut his son out of his will.

Whatever was to become of their marriage, Hugo never regretted his decision and in many ways the couple met one another's needs ideally, as the early days of their relationship show. Greatly in love, the young newlyweds were anxious to retire to their bedroom in the evenings as soon after supper as possible. They would then close the door on the rest of the household (they were living with Anaïs's mother and her lodgers) and write in a common diary. Two shy virgins, it took them over a year to consummate their marriage.

Following his early retirement from banking, Hugo did indeed become a relatively successful artist and avant-garde film-maker, working under the name of 'Ian Hugo'. But by then Anaïs was bigamously married to the much younger (although he didn't then know it) Rupert Pole, a forester-turned-school-teacher with film-star good looks, whom she supposedly met in a lift. Because Anaïs lived secretly with Rupert for half the year in Los Angeles, she missed out on enjoying her other husband's fifteen minutes of fame in New York. But this was no bad thing: she was jealous and resentful of Hugo's acclaim. Not only was Anaïs the artist in the marriage but she had seen all the men in her life attain a recognition which she had long wanted for herself, and the rejection of her work was a rejection of her offer of seduction and of her very existence. She told Dorothy Norman, 'When I am not printed I feel as if my very being were entombed, my existence denied. This is not merely an egotistic pain. It is for me an act of love that is rejected.'[20] While she was struggling to get her own writing published, Anaïs felt that it was owing to her continued love and support that Hugo and Henry Miller, amongst other of her 'children', had achieved their publicity and reputation.

This was certainly true in many ways, but it remains to be asked *why* Anaïs Nin spent so much time promoting the work of the men with whom she surrounded herself, as opposed to selling her own talents with more vigour, and why her personal sacrifice was so painfully *self-conscious,* as if she were only *playing the part* of a devoted mother, starving so that her son can eat? When she first met Henry Miller, for example, Anaïs had written a pioneering and brave 'Unprofessional Study' of D.H. Lawrence, a writer not taken seriously by literary circles in the 1930s and someone whom Henry hadn't at all appreciated until he read Anaïs's book. Henry then became so inspired by Lawrence that he decided to write his own book about him, which Anaïs duly put in her briefcase and carried over to England to show to Rebecca West, in the hope that she might help Henry to get it published. Rebecca West found it bizarre that someone of Anaïs's talents (she thought Anaïs Nin had 'genius') should waste her time promoting someone operating on Henry Miller's level. Her verdict was that Henry's book was 'completely silly'; not only could she do nothing for him but she recommended that Anaïs should also give him a wide berth and concentrate on her own skills.

During the period of her analysis with Martha Jaeger, it was suggested to Anaïs that she felt intense guilt about competing with men through her writing, and that it was this same guilt that made her want to please her father sexually rather than intellectually. Anaïs was powerfully resistant to Jaeger's observations, as indeed she had been to Allendy when he had made the same point: 'Have you not wished to surpass men in their own work? To humiliate them by your success?' To Allendy she replied, 'Indeed not. I constantly help men in their work, make sacrifices for them. I encourage, admire, applaud them.'[21] But to Jaeger she was more insistent: 'I did not want to rival man. I did not want to *be* a man. I did not want to steal man's creation, his thunder . . .'[22] Jaeger's analysis of Anaïs Nin's ambiguous behaviour obviously hit a nerve, and her portrait of her patient as a woman terrified of threatening men with her intellectual skills while deeply resentful of the nurturing role she allotted to herself, recalls the contemporary study of an 'intellectual woman' by Joan Riviere, published in *The International Journal of Psychoanalysis* in 1929.

Riviere's 'Womanliness as a Masquerade' describes the case of a woman who seemingly had everything: a happy marriage, a well run and organized home, a good sex life, and an impressive job, which involved both 'speaking and writing'. She found, however, that after giving public performances, which required her to present herself with authority and dignity, she would suffer from attacks of anxiety and she became

> obsessed by a need for reassurance. This need for reassurance led her compulsively on any such occasion to seek some attention or complimentary notice from a man or men at the close of the proceedings in which she had taken part or been the principal figure; and it soon became evident that the men who were chosen for the purpose were always unmistakably father-figures.[23]

The patient wanted to be reassured professionally but also sexually, and afterwards she would find herself putting on a 'performance' of femininity and flirting with the same men she had tried so hard to impress with her 'performance' of rigour and objectivity; she would sell herself short, having just commanded intellectual admiration and respect.

Joan Riviere's analysis of the woman's behaviour was that she was caught up in Oedipal rivalry with both of her parents. She identified with her father, who was an intellectual, but she also competed with him. Feeling uncomfortable in the 'masculine' position in which she found herself, she never lost the fear that her display of intellectual ability would be a threat to her father, and so her flirtatious behaviour was an attempt to 'ward off her anxiety' about his anger by offering herself to him sexually. As she wanted to be the object of her father's desire, her mother naturally became her rival and the patient would try to surpass her in terms of housewifely skills. She became a *superwoman*, running her home like a company whilst maintaining a high-profile job. She was also fiercely jealous of other women and found that she needed to be the centre of attention.

So what was this woman's sexual identity? What came more 'naturally' to Riviere's patient: the woman at home, pleasing her husband, or the mannish role at work, which was then displaced by the display of overt 'womanliness'? Who was she when she wasn't putting on a performance of either masculinity or femininity? Womanliness, Riviere concludes in a sharp observation, *is a performance* to disguise masculinity, and women learn how to 'look' like women and 'act' like women, as an actress learns her part. Womanliness can be 'worn' as clothes are worn; it can be put on like a 'mask' (women often say they are 'putting on their face') when she needs to disguise her 'possession of masculinity and to avert the reprisals expected if she is found to possess it – much as a thief will turn out his pockets and ask to be searched to prove that he hasn't stolen the goods'. Women therefore *play the part of being women*, knowing full well that femininity is a kind of *pretence*, but a pretence that is so unconscious as to have become 'natural'. In fact, the more 'artificial', the more waxed and painted and trimmed a woman is, the more of a 'natural woman' she is seen to be: unwaxed and unpainted women are often treated as 'unnatural', as violations of the norm and as 'man-haters'. So what is the difference between *being* a 'genuine' woman and the *pose* of being a 'genuine woman'? 'The reader may now ask how I define womanliness or where I draw the line between genuine womanliness and the masquerade,' Riviere writes. 'My suggestion is not, however, that there is any such difference; whether radical or superficial, they are the same thing.' The 'genuine' woman is therefore the same as the 'masquerading' woman: they are as authentic or inauthentic as each other: womanliness *is* a masquerade.

'Womanliness as a Masquerade' goes a long way to explaining the otherwise inexplicable behaviour of Anaïs Nin, who identified strongly with the male world of achievement and success (both professional and sexual) and also sought approval from her father whilst working to displace him. She made writing and seduction interchangeable so that she could counter any 'masculine' display of intellectual energy, as she wrote like a Fury, with the 'feminine' characteristics of flattery and servility. In her essay 'On Writing', Anaïs Nin noted how the woman writer has a worrying 'tendency to imitate man and adopt his goals'.[24] And so after allowing her diary, which she said was for her eyes only ('It is surprising how well one writes if one thinks no one will read you'[25]), to be read – and only men were invited to read it, the approbation of other women being irrelevant to her – Anaïs would let her writing be admired (in fact, nothing else was acceptable), but it was her *desirability as a woman* that needed reinstating. She would invariably go to bed with her reader and fake an orgasm.

In this endless display of her pleasure she is utterly perverse: Anaïs Nin would pretend to be seduced as if a genuine seduction were terrifying to her, as if she could not let herself go for a moment. Pretending to be seduced 'cuts all seduction short', Jean Baudrillard says: it terminates the very event she was driven to create.[26] Because Anaïs Nin even posed to herself as sexually satisfied in her journals (this is in many ways their point), it comes as a shock to find extracts in which it is revealed that the sex that has been so transporting has left her unfulfilled. As Joan Riviere said of her masquerading patient's sex life: 'The gratification it brought was in the nature of a reassurance and restitution of something lost, and not ultimately pure enjoyment. The man's love gave her back her self-esteem.'

Along with Riviere's patient, Anaïs erased the importance of women from her life whilst powerfully identifying with a feminine ideal. She told Allendy that, receiving no love from her father, she had experienced herself *as* her mother in the most corporal way: 'I suffered within Mother's own body the injuries she suffered.'[27] Rosa Culmell, meanwhile, lived with her daughter for thirty years, until she got so fed up with Henry Miller's being in the 'guest room' that she moved out, but she is never mentioned in Anaïs's journals. Just as her mother was erased, so was Anaïs unable to treat her own body (as opposed to her mother's) as carnal, describing it instead as if it were either entirely abstract or simply a line of poetry. All women she felt to be potential rivals and Anaïs was not able to form female friendships until she was in late middle age. And as with Riviere's patient who, because she identified with her father, found that she also identified with her husband's feelings for a woman with whom he had an affair, so too would Anaïs *identify* with Henry Miller's desire for his wife, June – 'By the end of the evening I was like a man, terribly in love with her face and body'[28] – rather than experience an autonomous desire of her own.

Anaïs Nin's journals are in the odd position of giving you all there is to know of someone and leaving you knowing nothing. She believed that she told 'everything and let the mask of delicacy, sweetness, and softness drop from my face and from my body',[29] and yet she also felt that if she let the mask drop there would be no one underneath; she was terrified that if she stopped writing about herself she would vanish. Yet it is this very suggestion of emptiness in her writing that seduces. 'The great stars or seductresses never dazzle because of their talent or intelligence, but because of their absence,' Baudrillard writes. 'They are dazzling in their nullity, and in their coldness.'[30] Like Garbo's face, it is the surfaces of Anaïs Nin's journals that fascinate, and the suggestion that they contain all there is to see. There is precisely nothing – no space, no volume, nothing – behind their appearance. Writing therefore became as much a masquerade as Anaïs Nin's womanliness.

Her journals impersonate a depth that is never achieved. As with orgasm, they create an emptiness in the place of fulfillment: the pleasure they leave behind is the bliss of loss rather than the satisfaction of completion. Anaïs Nin made out that her published diaries were the product of automatic writing. She said that they were 'dealing always with the immediate present, the warm, the near, being written at white heat [the diaries] developed a love of the living moment, of the immediate emotional reaction to experience'. They were, in fact, pruned, censored, rewritten and embellished constantly and for years, making the final version a veritable palimpsest of truth and lies. It is now impossible to tell whether a certain passage in the journals was written on the day in question or thirty years later, and given that we don't know whether the event happened at all in the first place, the dividing line between fact and fiction in her writing is rendered meaningless. Her writing is therefore criticized for being as deceptive and duplicitous as her femininity. Anaïs Nin aimed at making her writing feminine and alluring: her style is as slim, ethereal, flirtatious and flattering as she tried herself to be. She was always anxious to present her wisdom as the 'intuition' and 'instinct' of the Eternal Feminine as opposed to the thought-out conclusions of a serious thinker.

Anaïs Nin's critics have long puzzled over the tricky collapse of reality and fantasy (or of 'truth' and 'lies') in her life and writings, and while some have tended to *excuse* it in the name of 'art', others see it as a flaw in her work, and treat her lies as discrediting her status as a serious writer. 'When . . . or where, or even why, was it decided that literature had to be founded on "truth"?' Anaïs Nin's most recent biographer, Deirdre Bair, asked in despair, when she was endlessly told that Anaïs Nin didn't deserve to have a biography because she 'lied'. Henry Miller is seen, on the other hand, as a valuable writer because he was so 'honest', and you find this description of Miller as an honest-John who 'tells it as it is' in most of the work done on him, although Henry Miller also embellishes and fantasizes with maniacal enthusiasm. However, to see Anaïs Nin's fictionalizing of herself in her journals, and her fictionalizing of the journals themselves in her editing, as dramatizing a problem at the heart of feminine identity rather than as simply representing a collection of facts that are 'true' and fictions that are not, suddenly makes her writing more interesting than it is usually given credit for. To see her womanliness (both in her person and her writing) as a masquerade, and her masquerade *as* womanliness, sorts the issue out for her critics: fantasy and reality need no longer be treated as separate terms.

Anaïs Nin's fiction is also preoccupied with the woman as a masquerade, and many of her stories, such as 'Stella', are organized around a highly desirable woman's uncomfortable sense that her shadowy self-image is not the same as, but inseparable from, the powerful image she projects on to the world: 'Stella sat in a small, dark room and watched her own figure acting on the screen. Stella watched her "double" moving in the light and she did not recognize her. She almost hated her . . . The image was not she . . . It was a work of artifice . . .'[31] The masquerade both covers and exposes a non-identity, and it is this sense of not having a 'whole' self that Anaïs Nin describes thoughout her journals: 'I feel that an initial shock has shattered my wholeness, that I am like a shattered mirror. Each piece has gone off and developed a life of its own.' The refrain of her journals is her desire for and fear of 'wholeness', and she oscillates, in a matter of days, from statements like, 'I hate lies, double lives, continuous insincerity, shifting, transition, deceits. I want wholeness, wholeness with Henry!' to, 'Oh, God, there are moments when my sincerity and my wholeness kill me – I cannot *act* anymore!'[32] All her life Anaïs either represented herself as in pieces or as others saw her. For all her celebrated subjectivity, Anaïs Nin's journals give us principally objective descriptions of herself. She is always her own audience, standing outside her body looking in:

> I want to copy here things Hugh has written about me in his journal which please me. While travelling through Italy: 'And that is another reason for me to worship Anaïs – above all the other women I have ever seen or known she is exquisitely feminine. Such beauty, reflected from within, is hers; her lovely, liquid sad eyes, her soft, delicately moulded mouth, her fine nose and chin, her downy skin, so white that it actually illumines, her fine, wispy hair bound high over her head, her goddesslike grace . . . Travelling with her is like a continuous Fourth of July parade, so much does everyone stare at her.'[33]

Accounts of herself such as this (and there are a great many) suggest that Anaïs Nin rested uncomfortably in her womanliness, wanting urgently to *prove* she was a woman, in case there was any doubt of it. Even after she aborted Henry's baby (or it may have been Hugo's) Anaïs's main anxiety was that she should look like a woman in the clinic, as if her refusal of motherhood had unsexed her:

> I had sat up on the operating table to look at the child. The doctor and nurses were amazed by my aliveness and curiosity. They expected tears. I still had my eyelash makeup on . . . Sleep. Morning toilette. Perfume. Powder. The face all well . . . Everybody was amazed by my appearance. The morning after the birth: pure complexion, luminous skin, shining eyes.[34]

There is something excessive about her display of femininity, as if she were a transvestite, and something excessive about her need to display her womanliness to *herself* in her journals. All her eyelashes and perfume and powder seem rather overdone and this is what René Allendy pointed out when he commented on Anaïs's 'completely artificial' appearance, on the way in which she wore her make-up like a mask. This is the impression that her writing gives as well. Her ideal reader was, after all, her father, and her *raison d'être* was to seek his approval by being *the* ideal woman, the image of Woman herself.

III

Hugo Guiler may have won his acclaim before his wife won hers, but he is known less now for his contribution to the arts than for his snow-blind uxoriousness, and for being a gull and a cuckold on an epic scale. In order to protect their marriage, Anaïs edited his existence, and thus the source of all her money and comfort, out of the diaries when they at last began to be published in 1966. She also censored all mention of the sexual relationships she enjoyed with the scores of male 'friends' she wrote about. It is only with the recent appearance of the 'unexpurgated' diaries, *Henry and June*, *Incest*, and *Fire,* all of which are lovingly, dotingly even, edited and prefaced by Rupert Pole, that Hugo first appears in print, and he stands in a line-up with a dazzling entourage of rivals, from Antonin Artaud to George Barker.

It is only now therefore that the truly strange nature of the journal and the densely complicated relationship between Anaïs and Hugo can be fully appreciated. Never able to break her ties with him, even after thirty years of inexhaustible lies and exhausting travel between her west-coast home and her east-coast home, Anaïs and Hugo remained married until she died, in Los Angeles in 1977, with Rupert at her side, and Hugo was to stay doggedly ignorant of all she confided to her journals. Rupert Pole's fate has been the opposite, and as Executor of The Anaïs Nin Trust he knows more about the full content of the journals than anyone else. Following Hugo's death in 1985, the task of re-editing and republishing the 2150 diaries in their full splendour (they had originally been miraculously condensed into seven volumes, with the help of Anaïs Nin's editor, Gunther Stuhlmann) was immediately begun by Anaïs Nin's other husband, who is as helplessly seduced by her writing as she was herself. Deirdre Bair describes how the now septuagenarian Rupert sits down each day at the kitchen table on which he and Anaïs had once eaten their toast, and reads through page after page of her original journals, sifting out the compliments she recorded so that he can be sure to include them in the next 'unexpurgated' edition.

It is fascinating to speculate on why and how Hugo Guiler bought all of his wife's lies, for the degree to which he was willing to believe her tales and excuses suggests not only how greatly he feared losing Anaïs but also the extent to which he inadvertently colluded in her double life and encouraged her disengagement from crude facts. Anaïs delighted in her ability to manipulate Hugo, to convince him that black was white and that anything he saw or surmised relating to her infidelities could be readily explained away, either as the product of his fevered imagination or, even more oddly, as the product of hers. On one occasion, when Hugo returned home unexpectedly early from a business trip and saw Henry Miller run naked out of the marital bedroom, Anaïs's defence was that Hugo could not have seen what he thought he saw because it hadn't happened. And Hugo went along with it: 'Pure Hugo, he needed to believe. He wanted consolation, support, protection, security . . . he was tired and worried about money matters. I gave him enormous tenderness . . . He went to work almost gay.' [35] In a perfect example of his peculiar complicity in Anaïs's affairs, this episode ended with Hugo agreeing to telephone in future before arriving home early and, in case this wasn't enough warning for her, he assured Anaïs that he would toot the car horn as he drove through the gate. This way he wouldn't again impinge on his wife's privacy, whilst protecting himself from potential hurt.

During this same period, Anaïs deliberately left her diary open in a room in which Hugo was alone, and he was able to read a full account of her sexual adventures which was so freshly written that the ink was still wet. Now *this*, she diligently explained to the agonized Hugo, was in fact a *fictional* diary of a possessed woman, but she also had a *real* diary which he could see, telling of her true and faithful life with him. Delighted by her own cleverness, Anaïs then rushed out to buy the second journal and wrote in it at top speed an 'innocent' version of her life up to the current date.[36] For the thirty-five-year span between meeting Henry Miller and the publication of the first volume of her diaries, when she was made able to support her two husbands, Anaïs gave Hugo's money away as gifts for her lovers, while explaining to him that her allowance was going on housekeeping necessities and wardrobe requirements, of which Hugo obviously saw no evidence. Reverse the roles and Anaïs's complicated plots remind one of the spate of female paranoia films that came out during the war years, such as *Gaslight* and *Dangerous Voyage*, in which a scheming husband convinces his wife of her own madness by insisting that her version of reality is in fact a delusion, the spawn of her twisted and paranoid imaginings.

Aided by her tales, Hugo managed to rationalize to himself his wife's continual overnight absences, comforted by the saccharine love notes that Anaïs would pin to his pillow in the certain knowledge that he would be reassured that she was with her friend, Natasha (an aristocratic Russian exile who used to paint Anaïs: it would be fascinating to know more about her, but Princess Natasha Troubetskoi, like Rosa Culmell, is another woman literally written out of Anaïs's life). And yet, in his own diary, Hugo described his anguished suspicions and fear of betrayal in such a way that it is possible to conclude that he spent his whole married life in a perverse state of suspense between knowing everything and registering nothing (thus in much the same position as Anaïs Nin's readers): 'This morning I asked Anaïs to tell me everything about her experiences. Another paradox. It hurts me to hear about them. I suffer. But I . . . would rather hear them even if I suffer, than not to hear.' Again, 'I love A. more than my life and suffer that she may have other experiences not only with men but now with women. The thought of anyone having a physical relationship with her just stabs me.'[37] The pathetic irony of these passages is enough to move a stone.

Anaïs Nin has seduced her critics (or rather, 'commentators' in this case) in much the same way as she seduced Hugo. No other writer is treated as Anaïs Nin is treated; no one would dream of writing about Virginia Woolf or Dorothy Richardson with such abjection. For like Hugo, Anaïs Nin's critics are also concerned to flatter her, to leave her remarks unchallenged, and to let the sanctity of her world go undisturbed. By overlooking bad writing, weak metaphors, repetition and monotony – aspects of a text to which a good critic should be alert – Anaïs Nin scholars believe they are saving her feelings, knowing that she could never take criticism. That is, if we assume that these untextured aspects of Anaïs Nin's writing *are* being overlooked by her readers as opposed to being precisely what is looked for and enjoyed: bliss resides in the textual abrasions, Barthes argues in *The Pleasure of the Text*. Textual ecstasy is a complicated experience that bears no relation to learned and cultured critical responses. *Jouissance* includes feelings such as shock, emptiness, disturbance, and loss.

Anaïs Nin's writing creates a kind of trap so that she is only ever taken on her own terms, be it in her marriage or in her literary reception. Even Philip Kaufman's film of *Henry and June* was the kind of film that Anaïs would have made herself, in which every flattering description she recorded is treated as biographical evidence of what she was 'really like' rather than presented as her attempt to write herself into the person she would like to be. Kaufman's 'Anaïs Nin' is not only without neuroses but she never once picks up a pen, and so the film forgets that this story is *her* story and is the story of her seduction by writing. It would be like filming the life of George Best and missing out the football, or *Alice's Adventures in Wonderland* without showing that it was all Alice's dream.

The female critics of Anaïs Nin tend not only to accept her terms but also to adopt her prose style, and they write about her in the same precious way in which she wrote about herself, as if using any other kind of language would be offensive, like going to France and not speaking French. This is because the text of bliss, as opposed to that of contentment, is outside criticism, *'unless it is reached through another text of bliss*: you cannot speak "on" such a text, you can only speak "in" it, *in its fashion* . . .'[38] So just as Anaïs wanted to turn into her writing, so too do her readers: reading Anaïs Nin is so seductive that you *become* her, helplessly imitating her style and becoming just as embarrassing. Noel Riley Fitch writes her entire *Erotic Life of Anaïs Nin* in the present tense, referring to her subject as 'She' in a manner otherwise only found in H. Rider Haggard. The whole book is swathed in mists and swirls; Riley Fitch writes like this of the influence Anaïs Nin has had on 'the Age of Aquarius' (which is even the title of an Anaïs Nin newsletter): 'Six books of criticism. Two dozen university dissertations. A French perfume. A legend.'[39] Elisabeth Barillé's 'biography' of Anaïs Nin, *Naked under the Mask*, is a fictional fantasy also involving a lot of enigmatic references to 'She' and 'Her', but they are interrupted by earnest soliloquies on Anaïs's aura, given by Hugo, Rosa, June, and other participants in Anaïs Nin's beautiful life. Barillé's writing becomes increasingly heavy and weird, documenting, for example, Anaïs Nin's abortion as if it were a biblical event:

The carnal chain is broken. Anatomy abolished. Her destiny
is to be creative.
From this death, she brought forth a story, 'Birth'.
From this death, she brought forth words.
The journal: a long pregnancy.
Writing: giving birth to words, nourishing fantasies.[40]

These examples are what Philip K. Jason calls 'the School of
Beauties criticism', in which he includes the critics who gush about
how much Anaïs 'means' to her readers, and other 'attempts' to give
a 'creative, responsive criticism that result . . . only in earnest
bursts of cheerleading'.[41] Nancy Scholar perceptively identifies part
of Anaïs Nin's literary seduction as lying in her use of sincerity, and
she argues, as Philip Jason puts it, that

> Nin's art of sincerity traps the reader into an uncritical
> response. Thankful for Nin's supposed directness and trust,
> the reader is predisposed to approve. Flattered by being given
> access to what was undertaken in private, the reader is seduced
> with privilege. By claiming that the *Diary* is not art but life,
> Nin forestalls objections on artistic grounds.[42]

The literary agent William Burford is therefore a classic
seduced reader. He rejected her journals for publication but
claims, in his essay on her, that while there are weaknesses in Anaïs
Nin's prose, 'all these marks of the second-rate writer are made
oblivious by the sincerity of her effort'.[43] Would anyone dare to
make a remark like this about Ernest Hemingway or Norman
Mailer? Yet oddly, this was the kind of reception Anaïs Nin
seemed to want. She was *only* interested in seducing readers and
didn't at all like the idea of participating in an intellectual debate.
Having fought all her writing life for the respectable literary
status that she started to edge towards in the 1960s, she then
colluded in ensuring that she was never subject to the academic

discussion a professional writer would expect for herself, and she did this by ruling over her literary reputation with an iron rod. She took it upon herself to edit an 'Anaïs Nin Newsletter' and she dismissed defectors who dared to 'criticize' her. These critics were readers who at least took her writing seriously enough to think it worthy of evaluation.

IV

'1931 – the year Henry Miller and his wife, June, came to visit me in Louveciennes – was really the beginning of the interesting part of my life', Anaïs Nin reflected.[44] By the time she met Henry Miller, in December, she had been furiously writing for almost twenty years and had just finished her study of D.H. Lawrence, in whom she 'found herself' and for whom she felt her 'first really passionate love for a writer'.[45] In Lawrence, Nin found a seductive expression of her own 'entanglements' of 'reality and unreality, fantasy and life'. In Henry Miller she met someone who would also 'twist, distort, deform, beg, borrow, steal, cheat, lie, hoodwink, do anything and everything' in order to write, as his friend Michael Fraenkel said. And when he was writing, Miller was likewise in the 'grip of a mania over which he has no control whatsoever'. And Henry Miller, too, was becoming interested in D.H. Lawrence.

Hugo and Anaïs had moved to Paris in early 1925 where Hugo was still working at the bank and Anaïs had been indulging in the idle flirtations that had tortured Hugo enough to make him confide in his diary. They were living with her mother and brother, Joaquin, in a house in the unfashionable suburb of Louveciennes, which was a short train journey away from central Paris, and this cheaper lifestyle was to enable them all to live within Hugo's income. Now that she had written her first book, Anaïs looked forward to meeting another writer, and she had read with excitement Henry Miller's appreciation in the *New Review* of Luis

Buñuel and Salvador Dalí's surrealist film, *L'Age d'Or*. But more significantly, Richard Osborn, the lawyer who introduced Anaïs to Henry Miller, had shown him an article she had written on Lawrence and had shown her extracts from Henry's work-in-progress. These extracts would soon become part of his extraordinarily original 'fuck everything' book, *Tropic of Cancer*, for which Anaïs would later write a preface, after she had paid for it to be published by Obelisk Press, having borrowed the money to do so from Otto Rank. Henry Miller's struggle to become a writer was often aided by the financial support of the lovers of Anaïs and of his wife, June.

Tropic of Cancer, which is known chiefly as the sex odyssey of its protagonist, 'Henry Miller', was published in France in 1934, and so was available to the French years before it won court battles over publication in the States. Although France was subject to the same censorship laws as America, the book slipped through the net because it was written in English and so couldn't violate the French sensibility (unless they could read English, of course). Henry Miller had a charmingly stolid faith in his own talents and he publicized his book – which he believed to be a work of genius – with gay abandon, sending copies to the doyens of the literary world and then sending on to each of them the compliments he had received from the others. And *Tropic of Cancer* did receive compliments: it was praised by T. S. Eliot, Ezra Pound, George Orwell, Samuel Beckett, Herbert Read, Aldous Huxley, William Carlos Williams, and Cyril Connolly (all of whom received their copies from the author). It is a rich and wonderfully gross book, an assemblage of sensual and sexual impressions, tastes, and encounters, and Miller rambles around on any one page from the 'tasteful' – 'Indigo sky swept clear of fleecy clouds, gaunt trees infinitely extended . . . I am reminded of another Paris, the Paris of Maugham, of Gauguin, Paris of George Moore' – to the tasteless: 'The trouble with Irène is that she has a valise instead of a cunt. She wants fat letters to shove in her valise . . . Llona, now, she had a cunt. I know because she sent us some hairs from down below.'[46] *Tropic of Cancer* is written in continual free association. 'Henry Miller' blahs on about sex and then food and then friends and back to sex again, reminding us that this is how the mind works: thoughts of high and low, of Gauguin's modernity and of whores, are balanced together in the same moment, somewhere between the conscious and the unconscious self.

The 'Henry Miller' of his books is styled as an anarchistic (or at least a messier) version of Miller himself. Henry Miller looked like a bank manager: he was shortish, slightly built, balding and myopic, dressing with neat formality. In his reckless alter ego, the middle-aged author had done with his own pedantic desire for precision and order (Miller was like a Dutch houseboy, Norman Mailer thought); gone was his need for meticulous tidiness. This other Henry Miller is fashioned as fantastically chaotic and iconoclastic, a fuck-you hedonist with none of the charm and appeal of the original. Miller may have been unlike his literary persona but he was keen to stress that he *was* like his finished writing. The distinction is important: 'For me the book is the man and my book is the man I am, the confused man, the negligent man, the reckless man, the lusty, obscene, boisterous, thoughtful, scrupulous, lying, diabolically truthful man that I am.'[47]

Anaïs Nin thought that she was like her writing too, and so given that she and Henry Miller had already read one another, they didn't really need to meet in person. This initial attraction to the other's work was to develop throughout, indeed to define, their long relationship. What did they find in each other's writing? How could their *writing* have been more mutually seductive than their initial introduction in the flesh? And how did their *writing* continue to fuel a thirteen-year affair which was otherwise sexually flagging? They each bought into the raw sexual stereotype of one another's style: Anaïs saw Henry's writing as charged by testosterone while he wrote about her journal as being a pure example of the feminine. They were always to describe one another's prose as representing the epitome of heterosexual male and female sexualities, and their books and their bodies were treated as interchangeable.

Readers and critics also treat their respective writing as inseparable from their sexualities. Henry's compulsive writing, for example, is seen as evidence of his sexual health while Anaïs Nin's compulsion to write raises questions about the stability of her feminine sexuality. What is of interest here is less the pathologization of Anaïs Nin than the consistent representation of Henry Miller as a 'regular guy'. For compulsive writing *is* a perverse activity, but perversions are treated as a regular aspect of masculine sexuality. So writing himself in and out of relationships, using writing as a continual displacement, is seen in the case of Henry Miller as an endearingly blokeish affectation, like fetishizing stiletto shoes or spending too much time in the pub, while Anaïs Nin's writing is perverse not because she preferred it to living but precisely because it is a transgression into a masculine terrain. So in deciding to turn *herself* into a male fetish object (her masquerade), Anaïs Nin would seem to be disguising her own fetish for writing, her perverse desire to write. Her excessive femininity is therefore a mask over what is an unsightly masculine trait.

But Henry Miller's was an entirely different kind of prose from Anaïs Nin's. Compared to her pretty, introspective, passive-aggressive observations, Miller is like the shock of graffiti on a museum wall. But for all his bawdy iconoclasm and his scandalous reputation, his writing is not perverse. He wrote colourfully, noisily, with jubilant energy and in a language that was closer to the 'gutter' speech of his native Brooklyn than to the literary English employed by Anaïs. But beneath all this linguistic excess and disturbance lies that same rage for order noted by Norman Mailer. In Miller is the 'maniacal exactitude of language, [the] descriptive madness' that Barthes finds in straightforward, common-or-garden textual pleasure as opposed to the fragmentation found in textual bliss (fetishists are lovers of fragments: lace, leather, lipstick in some cases; semi-colons, capital letters, question marks in others) and typified by Anaïs Nin.

Another difference between their two styles is that Anaïs Nin was always trying to slide herself into a language she saw as a giant structure that had been there long before her. She wrote as if language were something outside and separate from her that she wanted to become a part of, *to turn herself into*. This is quite possibly because English was her third language, and she had initially written her journal in French, of which her father thought she possessed a weak grasp and which therefore needed improvement. When she learned English as a young adolescent she immediately developed a 'passion for the . . . language – a passionate curiosity, a passionate interest which usually only a foreigner will experience. Because I didn't take English for granted, *I felt like an explorer, discovering it had an infinite variety of words.*'[48] While Anaïs was outside looking in, Henry – whose family was German – saw the English language as already a *part* of his body, something inside him from birth, and he wrote as if he were belching and farting out words. Henry enjoyed words with a gusto and confidently controlled them, bending them to his purpose, while Anaïs believed that words were speaking *her* rather than the other way round; that writing controlled *her* and knew more about her than she did. While she was in awe of the seduction of words, Henry just fucked them.

The effect of Henry Miller's writing, as George Orwell describes it in 'Inside the Whale', is that you are *being read* rather than doing the reading. It is easy to see why the narcissistic Anaïs Nin would find this appealing: 'read [Miller] for five pages, ten pages, and you feel the peculiar relief that comes not so much from understanding as from *being understood*. "He knows all about me," you feel; "he wrote this specially for me." '[49] This is how Anaïs would feel when she came to read Otto Rank's *Art and Artist* and fell in love. Compare their two styles. First look at Anaïs Nin on the impact of Henry's writing, which she saw as a tantalizing balance between 'delicacy and violence'. It is savagely seducing and invading her, inseparable from *his* body and forcing itself into *hers*:

> His life – the underworld, Carco, violence, ruthlessness, monstrosity, gold digging, debauch. I read his notes avidly and with horror. For a year, in semisolitude, my imagination has had time to grow beyond measure. At night, in a fever, Henry's words press in on me. His violent, aggressive manhood pursues me. I taste that violence with my mouth, with my womb. Crushed against the earth with the man over me, possessed until I want to cry out. [50]
>
> Then at certain moments I remember one of his words and I suddenly feel the sensual woman flaring up, as if violently caressed. I say the word to myself, with joy. It is at such a moment that my true body lives. [51]

His words impress themselves on her person and galvanize her. Reading him puts her in raptures of physical pleasure, which she invites us to watch (turning her readers into voyeurs, making us the perverse subjects).

This is Henry Miller on the pleasures of reading on the lavatory, a subject he devoted an entire chapter to in his remarkably unique (and shamefully underrated) hymn to the joys of reading, *The Books in my Life*. Writing and the body are joined in perfect harmony, books are read, digested and expelled. Notice the precision of his descriptions, the 'maniacal exactitude' of his language, which belies Miller's hectic and lawless literary persona:

> O the wonderful recesses of the toilet! To them I owe my knowledge of Boccaccio, of Rabelais, or Petronius, of *The Golden Ass*. All of my good reading, you might say, was done

in the toilet. At the worst, *Ulysses*, or a detective story. There are passages in *Ulysses* which can only be read in the toilet – if one wants to extract the full flavour of their content.[52]

I am a man who pisses largely and frequently, which they say is a sign of great mental activity . . . Here [in a urinal], on a balmy night in spring, through what concatenation of events I do not know or care, I rediscovered my old friend Robinson Crusoe . . .

What impressed me, in the urinal by the Luxembourg, was how little it mattered what the book contained; it was the moment of reading it that counted, the moment that contained the book, the moment that definitely and for all time placed the book in the living ambiance of a room with its sunbeams, its atmosphere of convalescence, its homely chairs, its rag carpet, its odour of cooking and washing, its mother image bulking large and totemlike, its windows giving out on the street and throwing into the retina the jumbled issues of idle, sprawling figures, of gnarled trees, trolley wires, cats on the roof . . . The story of Robinson Crusoe owes its appeal – for me, at least – to the moment in which I discovered it. [53]

Both Anaïs Nin and Henry Miller saw writing and reading as something solid, corporal, and erotic; a form of living and not just a reflection of it. 'Lawrence's language made a physical impression,' Anaïs wrote in her study of him; he would give writing 'the *bulginess of sculpture*, the feeling of material fullness', much like Henry Miller, who also 'projected his physical response into the thing he observed'.[54] 'Books are as much a part of life as trees, stars or dung,' Henry Miller held,[55] always ready to demystify the literary world that Anaïs was busy mystifying.

Although they approached the pleasures of language from different angles, they both succeeded in 'making the text *an object of pleasure*', as Barthes puts it, comparable to other, more obvious, pleasures.[56] So for Henry, the pleasure of reading competes with the pleasure of going to the lavatory or the pleasure of a meal: 'What is better than reading Vergil [sic] or memorizing Goethe?' he asked. 'Why, eating outdoors under an awning for eight francs at Issy-les-Moulineaux.'[57] The memory of reading is as much to do with the memory of the sensuality of the book, its 'feel', as with its content. The pleasure of reading is also to do with place, with circumstance, with the weather. Henry Miller turns reading from the solipsistic and solitary act of the intellectual or escapist into a 'vital experience' marking the events in one's life:

> With childhood reading there is a factor of significance which we are prone to forget – the physical ambiance of the occasion. How distinctly, in after years, one remembers the feel of a favorite book, the typography, the binding, the illustrations, and so on. How easily one can localise the time and place of a first reading. Some books are associated with illness, some with bad weather, some with punishment, some with reward. In the remembrance of these events the inner and outer worlds fuse. These readings are distinctly 'events' in one's life.[58]

It was the *activity* of reading and writing that they enjoyed so much and you get this impression when you read Anaïs Nin or Henry Miller. Neither of them is writing *about* anything so much as writing because they have no choice, and because writing is as necessary as 'breathing' to them (an image Anaïs used on several occasions, once rather pretentiously stating in her journal that she had just 'breathed some notes'). It is ironic therefore that they were both censored so much for their subject matter, Anaïs censoring her own work and Henry being censored by the state for his; because what they wrote *about* was just an excuse for writing. Similarly, Henry Miller recalled 'how little it mattered' what *Robinson Crusoe* 'contained; it was the moment of reading it that counted'. They each wrote about sex because sex had *become* a kind of writing, as

Anaïs's comments after consummating her relationship with Henry were to show, when she expected him to turn into his vocabulary in bed. Henry was writing because he liked to feel words like 'fuck' and 'cunt' quiver on the page. In fact, sex had become a kind of contentless *list* for them both, and Henry Miller, like Anaïs Nin, loved lists, often turning entire paragraphs and pages into lists of things such as rivers, diseases, and people who lent him good books; even listing, in *The Books in my Life*, all the books he could 'ever recall reading', a 'thankless task', which 'gave me extreme pleasure and satisfaction'.[59]

Now turn to Henry Miller's description of Van Norden, in *Tropic of Cancer*. He is one of a long list of featureless, garrulous figures who populate the book and his life is a long list of identical fucks, not too different from the sexual encounters of the narrator, 'Henry Miller': 'Mornings – he means by mornings anywhere between one and five p.m. – mornings, as I say, he gives himself up to reveries. Mostly it is about the past he dreams. About his "cunts". He endeavours to recall how they felt, what they said to him at certain moments, where he laid them, and so on.'[60] The women he refers to are *meant* to be a hollow list – that is the point. There is nothing much (or at all) to *say* about all these encounters but that is no reason not to write them down; as far as empty experiences go these were good ones, and they provided him with lots to *write*, only not much to write *about*. For Anaïs Nin, sex and bodies have no solid form and so she describes sex as something fragmented. Like a true fetishist, she experiences her own body as bits and pieces, and she lists its parts. Her descriptions of sex with Henry Miller read like a join-the-dots picture:

> Henry, kiss my eyelashes, put your fingers on my eyelids. Bite my ear. Push back my hair. I have learned to unbutton you so swiftly. All, in my mouth, sucking. Your fingers. The hotness. The frenzy. Our cries of satisfaction . . . Driving in a

spiral. The core touched. The womb sucks, back and forth, open, closed. Lips flicking, snake tongues flicking. Ah – the rupture – a blood cell burst with joy. Dissolution.[61]

Given that women are not just the sum of their genitals, as Henry Miller describes them, and that wombs don't suck and women don't have 'cores', as Anaïs Nin would have it, it seems that for both of them the imaginative possibilities of sex on the page were much more satisfying than the scary reality of having sex with a whole other person.

V

Henry Miller and Anaïs Nin each wrote far too much, going well beyond what they were incited or invited to say, going well beyond what was interesting to read or what was even good writing. Imagine their excitement therefore when they read, in the radical journal, *transition*, Jolas's manifesto, 'The Revolution of the Word', in which he decreed that 'The writer expresses. He does not communicate.' At last, a vision of a different kind of writing, a writing that need not be *about* anything beyond itself, which can just be an endless celebration of Writing itself. 'You write in order to find out what you're writing about,' Henry Miller once said. 'The object is not to know where you're going.'[62] When Henry Miller's biographer, Robert Ferguson, concludes that 'As a writer, it is clearer now that Miller was only occasionally an artist,'[63] it is interesting to recall Roland Barthes' distinction between the 'writer' and the 'author'. For Barthes, it is not the *writer* who 'expresses' rather than 'communicates', it is the *author*. The 'writer' is someone who writes *something*, just as the painter paints something, while the 'author' just *writes*, and Henry Miller and Anaïs Nin are in this sense 'authors'. The 'author' aims not to take us through his writing into a different reality, as if the writing were a window onto another world, but instead to draw our attention to the *writing itself*, as an action with no other end in mind: 'The author performs a function, the writer an activity.'[64]

Barthes also distinguishes between what he calls 'readerly' and 'writerly' texts, the readerly texts being the reader-friendly ones that you don't notice you're reading, and these include classics like *Middlemarch*, while the 'writerly' texts are the unreadable ones, like *Ulysses*, where your eye staggers and stalls on the surface of the page, unable to see 'through' the self-conscious texture of the writing to any green pastures that might lie beneath. Barthes suggests that 'writerly' texts – and Anaïs Nin and Henry Miller fall into this category, being the great unreads of twentieth century literary mythology – are the seductive ones. 'Readerly' texts cannot seduce because of the sheer effortlessness of reading: they practically read themselves. 'Writerly' texts seduce because we are invited to "join in" and be aware of the interrelationship of the writing and reading, and which accordingly offers us the joys of cooperation, co-authorship (and even, at its intensest moments, of copulation) . . .'[65] The best seductions are, after all, the hardest won.

In the case of Henry Miller, he no longer even has to be *read* in order to either seduce or repel (as with Anaïs Nin, readers respond to Miller with either desire or disgust: there is no middle ground). Many people feel that they don't *need* to read him because they already know what he's about. He can be found in Italo Calvino's classifications of 'Books You Needn't Read', 'Books Read Even Before You Open Them Since They Belong To The Category Of Books Read Before Being Written', and 'Books That Everybody's Read So It's As If You Had Read Them, Too'.[66] *The Books in my Life*, which contains Henry Miller's discussion of the phenomenon of the unread book that prophesies his own fate, anticipates this passage of Calvino's at the beginning of 'If on a winter's night a traveller'. Miller can be found in his third category:

. . . many of the books one lives with in one's mind are books one has never read. Sometimes these take on amazing importance. There are at least three categories of this order. The first comprises those books which one has every intention of reading some day but in all probability never will; the second comprises those books which one feels he ought to have read, and which, some at least, he undoubtedly will read before he dies; *the third comprises the books one hears about, talks about, reads about, but which one is almost certain never to read because nothing, seemingly, can break down the wall of prejudice erected against them.*[67]

Erica Jong wrote a book on Henry Miller after he introduced himself to her in a fan letter about her novel, *Fear of Flying* (a case of literary seduction, but this is as far as it went). In *The Devil at Large* she laments the status of *Tropic of Cancer* as an unread modern classic, and tells an interesting anecdote to show how unread it is: 'Even as careful a reader as John Updike recently wrote to me . . . "Strangely, I don't think I read either of the Cancers through . . . Just a peek inside and the perusal of a paragraph was, well, inflammatory." '[68] Presumably John Updike meant that he read neither of the 'Tropics' through rather than the 'Cancers', but this proves the point about Henry Miller's being someone who is rarely read carefully or *deeply*, although this isn't by any means the only way of reading a book.

Apart from student followers who highlight and underline his iconoclastic wisdom, Henry Miller is mainly read horizontally rather than vertically: he is someone who is *skim-read* – which is exactly how you read a list. Not that skim reading isn't enormously pleasurable and a valuable kind of reading in itself: who has ever read every word of a book, and who says that this is how a book *should* be read or even *can* be read? For Barthes skimming and skipping over a text is the most pleasurable kind of reading: 'It is the very rhythm of what is read and what is not read that creates the pleasure of the great narratives,' he argues.[69] So the eye caresses the page as it would the surface of a picture: feeling its textures, admiring its shape, and enjoying its contours.

It is not clear why we continue to associate reading with steadily and continuously perusing the words on a page from left to right and from top to bottom. This is, after all, only the Western way of scanning a page; Hebrew and Arabic scripts are read from right to left and Chinese and Japanese writing is read in columns. A hundred years ago the French ophthalmologist Émile Javal showed how, when we read, our eyes do not in fact move systematically from left to right but rather leap about the page rapidly. The activity of 'reading' only takes place in the pauses between leaps (or what Barthes might see as in the gaps of tantalizing flesh peeping between clothing – pure bliss). Barthes reminds us that

> [w]e do not read everything with the same intensity of
> reading; a rhythm is established, casual, unconcerned with
> the *integrity* of the text; our very avidity for knowledge impels
> us to skim or to skip certain passages (anticipated as 'boring')
> in order to get more quickly to the warmer parts of the
> anecdote . . . we boldly skip (no one is watching)
> descriptions, explanations, analyses, conversations; doing so,
> we resemble a spectator in a nightclub who climbs onto the
> stage and speeds up the dancer's striptease, tearing off her
> clothing, *but in the same order* . . .[70]

There is a certain kind of reading that is continually interrupted and that takes place in these interruptions: 'Has it never happened, as you were reading a book, that you kept stopping as you read, not because you weren't interested, but because you were: because of a flow of ideas, stimuli, associations? In a word, haven't you ever happened *to read while looking up from your book?*'[71] While this reader is 'insolent' in his interruptions, like an inquisitive child, he is also seduced and his seduction is apparent in his continual return to the text. This is how Anaïs Nin and Henry Miller are read – by readers gazing into the distance with an open book before them. For all their efforts to focus on themselves alone, Nin and Miller detract attention away from themselves and on to other things, other ideas, other books. Like true seducers, they lead one astray.

Anaïs Nin's journals have rarely, I am sure, been read chronologically from cover to cover (unless the reader is either obsessive or masochistic); she will always be a writer who is dipped into and skimmed over for the 'dirty bits', if only because the bulk of what she writes is so boring. This is not an evaluative remark or a criticism: there is real pleasure to be found in a boring book, just as there is in a slow and clichéd film, in pornography (deadly dull, even at its best), or in a languorous Sunday afternoon spent watching the cricket. Just as there is a profound pleasure for Barthes in being with a lover whilst thinking of something else, so one of the pleasures of Anaïs Nin's writing is the way in which it settles into the background, like wallpaper or lounge music. Barthes says that the best textual pleasure is in writing that makes itself heard indirectly, and this is precisely what Nin's journal achieves, not least because its bulk and length give the impression of its going on all the time, like a radio that hasn't been turned off.

The rich pleasures of 'boredom' have been overlooked in the theory of reading and should be recognized as an important theoretical category. It is often the most boring part of a book that gives the *most* pleasure, such as the description of the contents of a sock drawer or the laborious realistic accuracy an author gives to an account of a sunset or a street scene. Boredom hits the spot like orgasmic bliss: 'it is bliss seen from the shores of pleasure'.[72] After all, we each yearn to be bored one day. For the *fin-de-siècle* decadents, boredom was a cult, and a cult that was cultivated by Anaïs Nin in her opium-den houses and her stylized opulence and ennui. Just because boredom has gone out of fashion, like Abba or Camp coffee, it doesn't mean we wouldn't still choose to have it.

Reading Henry Miller is often as boring as being stuck with a braggart at a party, but George Orwell points to the minute attention to detail in *Tropic of Cancer* as one of the pleasures of this kind of grotesque realism: 'Why is it that these monstrous trivialities are so engrossing?'[73] Henry Miller's strength as a writer lies in his depiction of 'vulgar reality' (Anaïs Nin's phrase), with all his scrawny cats and overcooked cabbage – 'What is not in the open street is false, derived, that is to say, *literature*' – he expounded. It is only Henry Miller's women who appear either chopped in half and seen from underneath or mythologized beyond recognition; the rest of his writing is as down-to-earth and packed with comic detail as a Breugel painting. There is a peculiar enjoyment, Barthes rightly perceives, in this kind of theatre of mediocrity, in the representation of daily life in a text and in the inclusion of petty details: 'schedules, habits, meals, lodging, clothing . . .' We are disappointed if we don't know what time breakfast was and whether the toast was burned; we feel as if we have been cheated of vital information. One of the pleasures of Sex 'n' Shopping novels lies in the host of material details available for the reader to consume: a meal is described down to the last delicious mouthful; a wardrobe of clothes is given the rigorous attention of an inventory as the choice of what to wear is made (last year's blue velvet mini-skirt, favourite grey lycra body, borrowed black leather trousers, too-tight red chenille crop-top . . .); bank balances are regularly surveyed; and every pound of weight lost or gained by the heroine is documented. And all this indulgence at the expense of good writing, plot development and subtle characterization.

In his essay on Henry Miller, Orwell describes the effect of *Tropic of Cancer* on the literature of the 1930s: 'The callous coarseness with which the characters in *Tropic of Cancer* talk is very rare in fiction, but it is extremely common in real life . . . English is treated as a spoken language, but spoken *without fear* . . . The thing has become so unusual as to seem almost anomalous, but it is the book of a man who is happy.'[74] Two of Henry Miller's biographers have picked up on his *joie de vivre*, calling their studies after Miller's own descriptions of himself: *Always Merry and Bright*, and *The Happiest Man Alive*. But his infectious celebration of life was in part a celebration of literature, of the 'magic' we are 'dealing' with in books, in which 'signs and symbols' come to life: '*They were alive and they spoke to me!*' was Henry Miller's jubilant cry when he started to read.[75] What excited him were the imaginative possibilities of reading and writing, the way in which discovering Dostoevesky could transform the moment, making the mundane seem mythical: 'Such a day it may be when you first encounter Dostoevski [sic]. You remember the smell of the tablecloth on which the book rests; you look at the clock and it is only five minutes from eternity; you count the objects on the mantelpiece because the sound of numbers is a totally new sound in your mouth . . . It was exactly five minutes past seven, at the corner of Broadway and Kosciusko Street, when Dostoevski first flashed across my horizon.'[76]

Reading is a carnal experience, but Henry Miller's reading body is not the same as the 'classical body', the hairless, organless, self-enclosed, and noble statue-on-a-plinth of whom we all think when we hear the word 'body' used in this context. Henry Miller's is a *grotesque* body, open at both ends, and his aesthetic is carnivalesque, as the Russian critic Mikhail Bakhtin would describe it: 'Before me is always the image of the body, our triune god of penis and testicles,' Henry Miller wrote.[77] For Bakhtin, the medieval carnival's celebration of low-life culture, with its cacophony of different voices and speech types, its inversion of power-relations, its noise and laughter, and its representation of the body as something that 'copulates, defecates, overeats' and of 'man's speech' as 'filled with genitals, bellies, defecations, urine, disease, noses, mouths and dismembered parts'[78] is life affirming, filled as it is with images of regeneration and renewal. Bakhtin's study of the carnivalesque, *Rabelais and his World*, is now classic, but in Henry Miller we also find a writing that 'celebrates the anarchic, body-based and grotesque elements of popular culture, and seeks to mobilise them against the humourless seriousness of official culture',[79] the culture that expects a writer to use a literary language that no one speaks, which never mentions the body either as an organ or as a pleasure zone. Henry Miller loved overturning this culture of vapid gravity: '*Laughter!* counseled Rabelais. For all your ills *laughter!*'[80] and it is worth recalling that Henry Miller is *funny*, that he makes you belly-laugh. His irreverent and anecdotal style also makes good lavatory reading, and laughing and urinating are the great levellers. For Henry Miller, even the sound of 'the name Swift' – another carnivalesque writer – 'was like a clear, hard pissing against the tin-plate lid of the world'.[81]

It is Henry Miller's challenge to the haughty arrogance of 'high culture' and good taste with their repression of all things physically and socially 'low' that Anaïs Nin picked up on in her preface to the first edition of *Tropic of Cancer*: 'In a world grown paralysed with introspection and constipated by delicate mental meals this *brutal exposure of the substantial body* comes as a vitalizing current of blood. The violence and obscenity are left unadulterated . . . And it is flesh and blood that is here given us. Drink, laughter, passion, curiosity . . .'[82] This may well be right, but what is extraordinary here is that it is *Anaïs Nin* writing this; Anaïs Nin, who precisely describes herself as the idealized, sculptured, and odourless body that Henry Miller was 'gobbing' at.

Anaïs was so horrified by bodies that she took as a compliment June Mansfield's insulting remark that she was cold to the point of being 'odourless': ' "You are so dead that your body has no smell – no odor" [sic] . . . About my odor – yes – I know you noticed that – I suppose that's part of my frailty, lightness of texture, the fact that, not being fat, I don't perspire . . .' In his autobiography, *Palimpsest*,

Gore Vidal, who knew Anaïs when she was in her forties, contradicts this one of her particular self-deceptions. Anaïs Nin even returned to June's remark again later, *apropos* of nothing, in one of her anecdotes:

> The *pendant* to June's remark about my odorlessness: Emilia goes to clean the bathroom after I have taken a bath and says, 'It is so wonderful to go into the bathroom after the *señora* has been there; it smells good – fragrant – and before, the other two ladies I worked for – after their baths, I hated to go in, it was so smelly.'[83]

What disturbed Anaïs Nin even more than physical secretions was the association of her body with flesh, and she describes with horror, in 'Winter of Artifice', the father's remark that his daughter is

> 'an Amazon . . . a force.' She looked at herself in the mirror with surprise. Certainly not the *body* of an Amazon. What was it her father saw? She was underweight, so light on her feet that a caricaturist had once pictured her as having floated up to the ceiling like a balloon and everybody trying to catch her with brooms and ladders.[84]

And at one point in her early diaries she remarks that when she is returning from a holiday with Hugo and weighs herself on the station scales, the dial does not move an inch. 'That is the only thing you have failed to make an impression on these last few weeks,' the inexhaustible Hugo says.

VI

Henry Miller was like her, Anaïs thought when she met him: someone else whom 'life makes drunk'. Anaïs Nin had little engagement with 'life' beyond her journal, and so to prove the strained similarity between herself and Henry she showed him her writing. While he might not have found her also drunk with the ribald carnival of life, he found her disorderly with writing and he was clearly like her in this. In an early letter, he raged: 'God, it is maddening to think that even one day must pass without writing. I shall never, never catch up. It is why, no doubt, I write with such vehemence, such distortion. It is despair . . .'[85] In the first year of their acquaintance, Henry wrote Anaïs over 900 pages of letters, even though for the bulk of that time he was in the same city or even the same bed as her. Why say what can be written instead? Even when he had shared a house with Lawrence Durrell, Henry often chose to write rather than to speak to him.

Before arriving penniless in Paris, Henry Miller had been scraping a living together in New York where he lived in a hand-to-mouth fashion with his second wife and life-long muse, June Mansfield, an ex-taxi dancer (a woman you paid to dance with in dance halls). He was raised as the son of a tailor in a family of anti-semitic German immigrants in Edwardian Brooklyn, and he spent his childhood saturating himself with reading. While Anaïs Nin grafted herself out of her childhood writing, Henry Miller was forged out of his childhood reading, and his major experiences were in books: 'It was in the days before I undertook to write, I must confess, that reading was at once the most voluptuous and the most pernicious of pastimes.'[86] His compulsive writing was born of compulsive reading, and with hindsight he claimed to have read (and note the Milleresque list)

Sir Walter Scott, Dickens, Dumas, Victor Hugo, and American writers too, especially the poets, practically all of them, up to a certain period. Include Ambrose Bierce, Lafcadio Hearn, Frank Norris, Dreiser, Anderson, Ben Hecht, many, many others . . . while in my teens, I believe, I read Petronius, Rabelais, Pierre Louys, Rémy de Gourmont, Jules

Laforge, Maeterlink, Pierre Loti, to mention a few. Nearly all of them very important to me. As were the Greek tragedies, the Restoration dramatists, and the 19th century dramatists of most European countries.[87]

Allowing for a certain amount of self-mythologizing, it is not unlikely that the word-hungry child consumed this many books; the printed page was, after all, where life was happening. At the back of *The Books in my Life*, written in 1950, he originally listed 5000 titles that had thus far been important to him. Henry was so locked up inside a literary universe that he 'used to think,' he wrote, 'that all the tragic events in life were written down in books and that what went on outside was just diluted crap'.[88] Henry Miller is an important writer precisely because he read everything from the Bible to Frank Harris and yet was directly influenced by so little (apart, he said, from Whitman, Rabelais and Hamsun); his startling originality came seemingly out of nowhere, and his first attempts at writing were appropriately automatic. Sentences suddenly appeared in his head during an afternoon walk after he had been studying the dictionary, and he hurried back to write them down.

In *Tropic of Cancer*, Henry Miller describes himself as shedding all this accumulated literature and accepting that there is nothing left to write:

I no longer think about it, I *am*. Everything that was literature has fallen from me. There are no more books to be written, thank God.

This then? This is not a book. This is libel, slander, defamation of character. This is not a book, in the ordinary sense of the word. No, this is a prolonged insult, a gob of spit in the face of Art, a kick in the pants to God, Man, Destiny, Time, Love, Beauty . . . what you will.' [89]

It is easy to see why the writer of *Sexus, Plexus* and *Nexus* would have left City College after one semester because 'Nothing on earth . . . could induce me to tackle anew Spenser's *Faery Queene*.[sic]'[90] Anaïs Nin, who solidly read through the stock of her local library from A-Z, also felt – 'almost indignantly' – that 'One reads books and expects life to be just as full of interest and intensity. And of course it isn't so.' She accused Henry of giving her the impression that he *was* a book and she was therefore disappointed by the reality of his company when Hugo went away and she lived with Miller alone for a few days, expecting that she would be *reading* him rather than just 'being' with him; hoping that 'all our talks [would] be feverish, portentous. I expected you always drunk, and always delirious'.[91]

When Henry met June he was married to Beatrice Wickens, a dark-haired concert pianist who had given him music lessons. Beatrice didn't live up to the literary promise of her name, and Henry found her all too easy to forget once he had set eyes on June in the dance hall where she worked. June approached him because she had overheard him say something about Strindberg, and she had to let him know: 'Henriette is me, myself!' and that she was also Knut Hamsun's Victoria.[92] This was music to Henry Miller's ears, and while he felt lingering guilt about leaving Beatrice and their young daughter, Barbara, it was never enough to encourage him to get a nine-to-five job so that he could pay them some maintenance. In *Sexus*, Henry boldly represents Beatrice as forgiving and compliant, thoroughly accommodating and supportive of her ex-husband's life of sexual abandon, realizing its worth and her own foolish prudery. Back on planet earth, the abandoned Beatrice remained chiefly significant to Henry as the unlikely person who introduced him to Knut Hamsun's *Hunger* – at last, a book he wished he'd written himself, like Rank's *Art and Artist* was to be for Anaïs Nin – and just at the point when he was first trying to write and needed a literary role model. He frequently cited the importance of *Hunger* on the generation of *Tropic of Cancer*. The incongruity of associating the prosaic Beatrice with one of his most seductive reads was part of his strange literary destiny, Henry believed.

June Mansfield – 'America on foot, winged and sexed', as Henry was to mythologize her – was a tiny five-foot-two; not at all the statuesque figure that Henry and Anaïs would present her as being. Anaïs even claimed, in *Henry and June*, that June's feet were too big to fit into a pair of her sandals, which is unlikely, given that Anaïs took a size nine shoe. June is seen as physically excessive: her real body is lost to Henry and Anaïs and what replaces it is *over-represented*: her body is allowed the consciousness of which she herself is deprived. In her book, *In the Freud Archives*, Janet Malcolm repeats a story that Jeffrey Masson told her about the power of his transference relationship with his analyst. Masson said that throughout the analysis he had seen his analyst as taller than himself – as 'an immense man' – and it was only when the analysis was over and the transference spell had broken that he realized to his shock that his analyst was in fact a small man, a head shorter than Masson. June seems to have had this effect on Henry and Anaïs, who continually depict her as striding into rooms like a colossus. In *Tropic of Capricorn*, Henry describes first seeing June: 'What a walk. Tall, stately, full bodied, self- possessed.' In the film of *Henry and June*, the miscasting of the six-foot tall Uma Thurman to play June is because in Anaïs Nin's journals June is simply presented as an Amazon, and there would be no way of knowing that she wasn't this huge.

June's attractions are never described as being either mortal or healthy. Instead she is 'destructively' beautiful, she has, as Lionel Abel describes her, an 'almost frightening beauty': she is 'like Garbo' with her luminously clear skin and long, slender neck.[93] June is always seen as being like someone other than herself; for Fred Perles, Miller's flatmate in Paris, who loathed June and her effect on Henry, she was 'one of those dark *femme fatale* types one comes across in certain French novels'.[94] She is one of the deadly beauties who inhabit the art of *fin de siècle* decadence. Anaïs Nin would always describe June as 'death', as though her beauty promised castration itself, and Anaïs wrote, after meeting June, tonight 'I saw for the first time the most beautiful woman on earth', as if June were an alien and had been beamed down to Anaïs's garden. In the face of all the literary production going on around her, June is seen as unproductive, barren and sterile: hardly a woman at all. In this sense she is not so much the classic devouring femme fatale – the excessive woman – but the more archaic phallic mother. June is the woman whose lack is entirely disavowed, the woman of primal fantasies who is endowed with both penis and vagina and is therefore more man than Henry Miller and more woman than Anaïs Nin. Both male and female, she is powerfully self-sufficient and self-contained, without need of other people to satisfy her desires, whilst needed and desired by both sexes.

Part of June's fascination for Henry and Anaïs was that she lied inconsistently and at random, inventing a variety of the usual exotic tales that Freud describes in his essay, 'Family Romances', as being a common and healthy part of a child's fantasy life. June's stories were of the orphaned only-daughter-of-aristocratic-and-Romany-parents and the running-away-to-join-the-circus variety, and her fantasies fed Henry's imagination as well as her own, lingering on after the more mundane truth about her family became known. Perhaps it was because June invented herself so freely that Henry felt he had carte blanche to do the same: it is as if she relinquished all rights to a truthful representation and became a free-floating idea to do with as you will.

Anaïs's obsession with June was organized around June's masquerading; beneath her theatrical appearance – 'She is an actress every moment' – there was no one: 'There is no June Mansfield. She knows it.'[95] June was the sum of her performance of womanliness, and it was this very lack of 'core' (as Anaïs called it) that made her so desirable. Anaïs's writing is seductive for the same reason. Being the construction of other people's fantasies added to June's appeal: 'June has no ideas, no fantasies of her own. They are given to her by others, who are inspired by her being.'[96] In *Tropic of Capricorn*, Henry Miller eulogizes June's mystery. She 'changed like a chameleon. Nobody could say what she was really like because with each one she was an entirely different person.' Anaïs described June's fictions as luring her in like the sirens' song, and, in her journal account, June ceases to be the subject of her stories and becomes the fictional object – of Proust, of Miller, of Anaïs Nin herself:

> June is a storyteller. She is constantly telling stories about her life that are inconsequential. I tried at first to connect them into a whole, but then I surrendered to her chaos. I didn't know at the time that, like Albertine's stories, to Proust, each one was a secret key to some happening in her life which it is impossible to clarify. A lot of these stories are in Henry's novel. She does not hesitate to repeat herself. She is drugged with her own romances. I stand humbly before this fantastic child and give up my mind.[97]

The life on a page that Anaïs yearned for was June's idea of hell, and Henry's obsession with writing about June (which Anaïs was to share) was something that his wife found hard to forgive. She saw Miller as a reckless self-publicist who was turning her into literature in order to spice up his own image. Ironically, it is Anaïs who recorded in her diary June's complaints against her husband, at the same time as Anaïs herself was both sleeping with Henry and competing with him as to who could best describe June. So even here June's voice is silenced, turned instead into Anaïs's bosom-heaving prose: 'It is Henry who has made me complex, who has devitalized me, killed me,' Nin has June say. 'He has introduced literature, a fictitious personage . . .'[98] Of course, June's point was that fictionalizing oneself (or masquerading) and being fictiona-

lized by another are two entirely different things, and once Henry
got hold of her as a symbol of the guts and gait of modern America,
her freedom to fashion her own identity was over. The Millers'
relationship was to become a battle of interpretation over who June
really was (this same discussion about June would initiate Henry
and Anaïs's relationship) and Henry was to continue warring it out
in his books long after June had disappeared off the scene.

In *Tropic of Capricorn*, his major 'June' novel, Henry describes how,

> [p]assing beneath the dance hall, thinking again of this book,
> I realized suddenly that our life had come to an end: I realized
> that the book I was planning was nothing more than a tomb
> in which to bury her – and the me which had belonged to her.
> That was some time ago and ever since I have been trying to
> write it. Why is it so difficult? Why? Because the idea of an
> 'end' is intolerable to me.

What does Miller mean here? The end with the real June Mansfield
was achieved with relative ease, and so one can only conclude that
the idea of an *end to writing* is intolerable to Miller; especially the
idea of an end to writing about June. When Anaïs Nin's diaries
began to be published, it was the heavily edited version of herself
that caused June more offence than Henry's cultish depiction of her
as a sex-monster (or goddess, depending on whether you are Henry
or June). In her immaculate editing of the journals, Anaïs removed
all evidence of her part in the break-up of the Millers' marriage and
she consequently made June look ridiculous, stomping around
histrionically whilst telling Anaïs how desirable she found her.

VII

Her real name was June Smerth, or it could have been Juliet Edith
Smerth; her parents were Austrian, and she was born some time in
January 1902, a year before Anaïs Nin, although she made herself a

year younger on her marriage certificate. When the Smerth family arrived in New York, in 1907, they became American citizens and changed their name to Smith. June later decided, for her own reasons, to change her name to Mansfield. Henry referred to her as the June-Smerth-Smith-Mansfield-Miller woman, as if it were her fate to have an unfixed identity. After their first encounter at Wilson's dance hall they left together and Henry besieged June with letters until she agreed to meet him again. They married in 1924, six months after Henry's divorce from Beatrice was finalized, and with June's encouragement, Henry set out to become a successful writer.

Henry and June modelled themselves on their favourite literary characters: June was Fanny in Dostoevsky's *Crime and Punishment*, although Henry saw her more as Proust's Albertine, while Henry was Dostoevsky and Proust themselves, busy creating June. Henry was convinced that the lesson of all his years of reading was not to 'translate literature into life but to alchemise life into literature',[99] and June would be the subject of his writing just as he found her present in all that he read. After meeting the Millers, Anaïs Nin found to her dismay that 'the more I read Dostoevsky the more I wonder about June and Henry and whether they are imitations. I recognize the same phrases, the same heightened language, almost the same actions. Are they literary ghosts? Do they have souls of their own?'[100] Jealous of Henry and June's mutual literary seductions, Anaïs celebrated the 'rare hybrid of man and book'[101] that Henry Miller was on his own and she wrote in her journal with heightened lyricism and intense excitement of his absorption in literature. With June out of the way, he could invite Anaïs instead into his world of reading: 'He walks inside of Proust's symphonies, of Gide's insinuations, of Cocteau's opium enigmas, of Valéry's silences; he walks into suggestivity, into spaces; into the illuminations of Rimbaud. And I walk with him.'[102]

Life wasn't this glamorous back in Brooklyn, before Anaïs was to romanticize the Millers. Always desperate for money, when they were first married Henry and June resorted to bizarre means of getting it. Henry started selling mezzotints (prints made from copper plates) of his writing, and having no success as a salesman he passed the job on to June, who could sell coals to Newcastle. This entailed changing his pen name to June E. Mansfield in order that June could pass Henry's macho writing off as her own. So June added another identity on to her already full cast of characters, and Henry passed himself off as a name that he must have felt he had about as much right to as June did herself. What Robert Ferguson says about this period in their lives and the effect that June's adoption of Henry's personality as a writer had on their already troubled relationship is worth quoting in full:

> . . . in essence what now happened was that June
> requisitioned Henry's talent . . . acquiring for herself a new
> and wholly false identity as a writer. Even her friends and
> acquaintances were not party to the deception. This was a
> psychologically pregnant development in their relationship
> in which it appeared that June, a character who had found her
> author in Henry, now moved to appropriate his place in the
> drama too. Henry, while appearing to relinquish the role, was
> able to observe this development and use it to add depth and
> mystery to the act of creating her in which he was
> continuously involved. [103]

June's customers tended to be love-sick admirers and her sales technique drew on her skills as a professional flirt. She had no qualms about selling the mezzotints to abject swains, knowing that they bought them in the hope that they might have a chance of winning her affection – if only her invalid mother back at home wasn't so demanding (June would say she was a struggling single woman). Oddly, given the threat that it posed to their marriage, Henry's habit of writing under June's name was to stick and, after the mezzotint affair, 'June E. Mansfield' had a serious of smutty stories published in a magazine for which the Millers earned $50 per issue.

Then an episode occurred that was to be June's one experience of a literary seduction almost of her own and Henry's first experience of a literary seduction by proxy, and the strange tangle of disguised identities involved in the tragedy shows how unpredictable and various literary seductions can be, how confused the relation between writer and writing can become. When June showed Roland Freedman, a successful joke writer for the *New Yorker* cartoons, some of Henry's mezzotints, he was so impressed by the quality of what he thought was June's spunky writing that he offered to support her in her struggle as an up and coming author and to pay for a trip to Europe if she managed to finish a book. So while Freedman wooed June with a constant flow of love letters, Henry would pass on to her freshly typed sections of the rabidly anti-Semitic and big-cocked *Moloch,* which she would then take for Freedman to read. Freedman would pay June for the pleasure of her company, for the privilege of being able to read her work (with which he was in love) and for being allowed, in turn, to write to her. Henry and June would blow his money with their customary carelessness, roaring with laughter at Freedman's hopelessly futile crush on June and at his stunning credulity; at his belief (which *is* pretty incredible) that the exquisite, low-voiced June could have written lines like, 'Keep your libraries. Keep your penal institutions. Keep your insane asylums. Give me beer', [104] sentiments that can only be paralleled by Flann O'Brien's, 'A PINT OF PLAIN IS YOUR ONLY MAN'. Some years after this, and no closer to captivating June, Roland Freedman killed himself. But by then Henry and June had enjoyed a six-month trip to Europe at his expense.

When Henry arrived in Paris alone in 1930, he was thirty-nine and had been writing for twelve years to no avail. He had one unpublished novel, *Moloch*, and one unfinished novel, *Crazy Cock* (or *Lovely Lesbians*), about a nightmare triangular relationship between two lesbians and a husband, based on June's affair with her friend Mara Andrews (or Jean Kronski, as June would call her), which had driven Henry to despair with jealousy and humiliation. Mara is recreated in *The Rosy Crucifixion* as Stasia, the lesbian who becomes infatuated with Mona (one of June's incarnations in Henry's writing). Although *Crazy Cock* was deeply offensive to June — or maybe because it was — she encouraged Henry to take some more of the Roland Freedman seduction money to buy a passage to Europe in order to finish the book. She was to join him in Paris on four separate occasions before giving up the ghost, walking out on the marriage and going back to New York, where Henry was next to hear of her in 1947, when she was cold, starving, and living in poverty. She had been abandoned by her second husband and had spent some time in a psychiatric hospital.

Henry had hated New York and so he threw himself into low-life Paris, with its whores, its cheap wine, and its café culture. Paris in the depression years of the 1930s was a thriving centre for wandering bohemians and artists; the current vogue was Surrealism, and 'Proust, Gide and Valéry were the pillars that supported the superstructure of literary life'.[105] Nothing could have suited Henry Miller more and he stayed until Bastille Day, 1939, when the war brought an end to this twilight life and he went to Greece. His tremendous capacity for making the right friends and for cadging free meals and beds enabled him to survive for a year. He organized himself so that he was seeing fourteen friends in rotation, and each one conveniently at a meal time. Anaïs Nin brought an end to all this: she supplied him with excellent meals, her own bed, her husband's income, and her typewriter to boot.

Weighing up the pros and cons of having an affair with Henry Miller two months after they met, Anaïs decided that the main argument against was, ' "I just don't want to be pissed on." ' She wrote this in inverted commas in her journal because this was Henry's language and not hers, but the very fact that she was using his vocabulary shows that he had got to her. Hugo was terrified of the power of Henry's writing on his wife's imagination and so tried to win Anaïs back in the only way left to him, and Anaïs fondly noted how he now 'sits down to write also, to woo me with writing'.[106] What eventually persuaded Anaïs to sleep with Henry in early March 1932, only six days after she had told him, in purple ink on silver paper, that 'The woman will sit eternally in the tall black armchair. I will be the one woman you will never have . . . We will not live, we will only write and talk to swell the sails,'[107] is no doubt the quantity and quality of letters that he wrote to her from Dijon. Hugo had arranged for Henry to leave Paris in January to teach in a lycée, a job that Henry had loathed and stuck for only a few weeks. If this was an attempt to keep Anaïs away from Henry's appeal, Hugo's plan badly misfired. Nothing could have been more seductive than the armloads of letters about Proust, Nietzsche, Dostoesky, and Goethe; about June; about each other's writing; about everything, which kept Anaïs occupied while Henry was gone. She even pinned them to her study wall.

June had left Paris in late January after one of her doomed attempts to save her marriage, and she was only to return once more, in the October of that year, when she discovered the affair between Anaïs and her husband and asked for a divorce. In January, when they had just met, she and Anaïs had become embroiled in a complicated flirtatious game that involved lots of champagne and caviar, an endless exchange of mutual compliments, a long kiss in a taxi and a walk where June had held Anaïs's hand over her naked breast. Anaïs was not bisexual and she had no idea what two women could think of doing together sexually until, inspired by her nights with Henry, she went to see a sex show with Hugo and discovered what and where the clitoris was. It is clear from her journal accounts of this intense period in all of their lives that Anaïs was deeply threatened by the reality of June, as she was by any woman who might command more attention than herself. What captivated, or 'possessed', her was Henry's *idea* of June – particularly his masochistic accounts of the way she taunted him with her relationship with Jean – and Anaïs delighted in the extent to which June inspired her writing. While she was obviously pleased with her analysis of June in the journal ('I understood June') and with the portentous prose in which she couched her understanding ('For June is destruction'), there is nothing new in Anaïs's descriptions of June Mansfield. Rather than finding a fresh and liberating way to write about feminine sexuality, for which Anaïs Nin has often been celebrated (principally by Henry Miller), she does no more than give a traditional masculine depiction of a femme fatale, and so much so that Henry was to borrow Anaïs's analysis of June's character for his own work. Anaïs gives us a tiny-voiced enchantress, hopelessly in need of a good man, and notice how she dreams of the petite June only '*as if* she were very small':

> June. At night I dreamed of her, as if she were very small, very frail, and I loved her. I loved a smallness which had appeared to me in her talk: the disproportionate pride, a hurt pride. She lacks the core of sureness, she craves admiration insatiably. She lives on reflections of herself in others' eyes. She does not dare to be herself. There is no June Mansfield. She knows it. The more she is loved the more she knows it.[108]

Later, when Henry and Anaïs became lovers, Anaïs would look with jealousy at the photograph of June that stared down at them from the mantelpiece in the bedroom. She must have seemed very real then.

VIII

So Anaïs and Henry began their 'literary fuck fest', as Henry aptly called it, after she had read his books, *Moloch* and *Crazy Cock*, and he had read her journals, and she had read to him her account of the effect that reading his notes had had on her. While Henry was teaching in Dijon, Anaïs was in Switzerland, and by the time the couple's affair began back in Paris they were in a frenzy of writing and reading. As far as Anaïs was concerned Henry's reading her journal had made them inextricably intertwined, they were like man and wife anyway and so what more need they do to consummate their relationship? 'Last night Henry and I got married . . . I let him read most of my journal (even half of what relates to June's kisses etc.)'[109] One is reminded of Anaïs's honeymoon activity with Hugo after the bedroom door was closed, and of the diary she shared with Otto Rank to cement their love. Henry told Anaïs that she could only write with this amount of intensity because she 'hadn't lived' what she 'was writing about'. In other words, because, as she lucidly put it in an earlier diary, 'I am so preoccupied with telling all I am going through that I don't have time to realize what I am doing.'[110] Henry was determined to give her an experience that she could live through before writing about it, which must have been challenging for someone who gave her journals ominous and anticipatory names, such as 'Possessed' and 'Fire', before she had begun filling them, as if her metaphors would dictate the direction of her experiences.

Their first sexual encounter is typically described by Anaïs as if she did not have a body, and her evasive, idealized description is about as far removed from Henry's carnivalesque celebration of orifices as it is possible to be: 'His room, I do not see. When he takes me in his arms, my body melts. The tenderness of his hands, the unexpected penetration, to the core of me but without violence. What strange, gentle power.'[111] Anaïs was surprised that Henry didn't make love in his prose style, or indeed in D.H. Lawrence's prose style, which she also described as being both 'tender and violent'.[112] She had expected that his 'words' would 'press in' on her rather than his person, and the seduction of his writing is seen as far more sexually invigorating than this pale physical replacement – note Anaïs's previously described sensation of 'the sensual woman flaring up' in her when she 'remembered' one of Henry's 'words'. Anaïs's description of their sex is like her account of her feelings when Henry read her journal, where she also melted into him: 'I almost wept because of that absolute *breaking up of myself*, this absolute dissolution of myself into him.' She then described how, after sex, his writing fell away from him, leaving her with no idea of either who he was or what she was in love with, if they were no longer in love with each other's writing alone: 'His mountain of words, of notes, of quotations are sundered. I am surprised. I did not know this man. We were not in love with each other's writing. But what are we in love with now?'[113]

Even here, in her struggle to experience something purely physical and without the mediation of writing, she is herself *quoting*, and it is, comically, Henry Miller's comments about himself in *Tropic of Cancer* to which she resorts, to his claim that 'everything that was literature has fallen away from me'. It is as if in her panic at this sudden literary nakedness she is trying to reclothe Henry Miller in his own notes and quotations; to make him more like June, who was nothing but notes and quotations. But where this literary 'sundering' gave Henry a sense of relief and freedom – 'I *am*' – it caused Anaïs Nin great confusion: 'I do not know this man.' Literature quickly enveloped Henry again, however, and Anaïs's confusion was soon cleared up when he wrote to her two days later to say that he was 'drunk with desire', not to see or speak to her, but to 'write [to] you. listen; [sic] I'll call you in the morning: tonight I'll write or bust'.[114] Soon they were able to introduce their writing to the bedroom: 'Afterwards he was

languid, and I was gay. We even talked about our craft: "I like,"
said the retentive Henry, "to have my desk in order before I begin,
only notes around me, a great many notes." [115] The incessant
descriptions of their sex life that follow gradually start to
incorporate Henry's sexual vocabulary and Anaïs occasionally
comes back into focus as flesh and blood but, as always, only in bits
and pieces. Which is more than can be said for the literary fate of
Henry Miller, who, for all his attempts to bring sweating, greedy,
lascivious bodies copulating back into modern literature, became
immortalized as core-reaching, ethereal and without glands in
Anaïs Nin's journals.

The affair was to continue while Anaïs was also variously
involved with her cousin Eduardo, René Allendy, Otto Rank,
Joaquin Nin, Antonin Artaud, and Gonzalo Moré, who, as a
Peruvian Marxist activist, was possibly the most unlikely
candidate of them all, and it is hard to imagine what Gonzalo
made of Anaïs's stunning lack of interest in the outside world. In
sixty-five years of journal writing, Anaïs's political observations
can be summed up as this, written in 1934: 'What a mess the world
is in. I keep my face turned away as much as possible. It *stinks*. I
never read the papers. I refuse to worry about politicians.' [116] It is
unlikely that Gonzalo Moré was seduced by a journal that was
written almost daily in the 1930s and 1940s without a mention of
the Spanish Civil War (particularly when Anaïs was half-Spanish)
or the Second World War, choosing to focus instead on the far
more interesting task of compiling a list of admirers who were
lucky enough to have met Anaïs Nin (such as Norman Bel Geddes
and John Huston). Gonzalo was, however, grateful for the money.

As none of her lovers was known to the others, Anaïs's life was
for the next few years an exhausting bedroom farce and her journals
became as splintered as she was herself, with 'true' journals and
'false' journals being locked up and carted around from vault to
vault to 'record', rewrite, and edit every sensual moment with

monotonous uniformity. Her rich variety of lovers become one man, one voice, so that even the rumbling tones of Gonzalo are reduced to telling Anaïs parrot-fashion that her visionary being has rudely awakened him out of his life of meaningless politics. He is now humbly prostrate before her: 'Anaïs, what a force you are, spiritual and vital, though you are all wrapped up in myths and legends, you are like a whip on me. When I first saw you I felt a shock, you aroused my pride, for the first time I am shedding the fumes of alcohol; I want to *be*, Anaïs.'[117]

After Gonzalo came Edmund Wilson, America's man of letters and the recent ex-husband of America's grande dame of literature, Mary McCarthy. Anaïs could also add a youthful Gore Vidal to the chorus, and he would deeply resent her portrayal of him as a fawning sycophant who wanted to marry her, asking why he – young, beautiful, and homosexual – might want to marry a vain woman with a 'black upper gum' and rotten teeth who was the same age as his mother, and he sent Anaïs Nin up in *Two Sisters* and *Live from Golgotha*. Until she met Rupert Pole in the late 1940s, after which she centred down to a life of settled bigamy, Anaïs Nin recorded her affairs as if it were the same seduction that was taking place over and over again. Which in a sense it was, just as Henry Miller's many affairs were reduced to a list of anonymous 'cunts' he had known. The endless repetition and sheer predictability of Anaïs Nin's seductions add to the emptiness of her writing, that sense of loss in which Barthes locates bliss. For orgasm results in the blissful momentary loss of self, and while Henry Miller's continual search for a hard fuck amounts to no more than a reiterated desire to assert himself, in her own writing Anaïs Nin vanishes into a chorus of compliments and a crush of vague fumblings.

There is something 'embarrassingly static' about Anaïs Nin's journals, as Joan Bobbit, one of her non-cheerleading critics, has observed.[118] The journals describe an immobility that goes against her claim that they are a recording of an evolving self. The eleven-year-old child never changes, and in fact Anaïs Nin reveals herself to have a fear of change that verges on the catatonic. But maybe the self doesn't 'evolve' from innocence to experience to die enlightened with new-found wisdom, and this is what the journals reveal. Maybe all of our lives *can* be reduced to the endless repetition of one or two seductions, one or two phrases, which in Anaïs Nin's case are, 'read me' and 'desire me'. Reacting to the banal assumption that one's life consists of a steady progression from childhood innocence to the experience of adult maturity, Oscar Wilde said that only mediocrities develop, and it may be that Anaïs Nin's stasis is the least mediocre thing about her. In her preface to Rank's *Art and Artist*, Anaïs admired Rank's theory that 'all art is born of fear of loss and change',[119] and it is easy to see why she felt that this book described her. Ironically, Anaïs Nin's journals therefore destroy any myths of empathetic and exploratory romantic love they set out to explore, and what Rupert Pole calls her lifelong search for the 'one perfect love' amounts to nothing more than a repeated insistence that all love is narcissism, illusion and fantasy. Anaïs Nin's writing is one long unfulfilled seduction that never finds its object, just as Henry Miller's writing describes a fuck that never ends. Their writing describes what the French psychoanalyst, Jacques Lacan, sees as the giving of something you don't have to someone who doesn't exist.

IX

Henry Miller married three more times after the divorce from June, and both Janine Lepska and Eve McClure (who introduced herself to him in a fan letter), his third and fourth wives, believed they were marrying the 'Henry Miller' of his writing rather than this self-styled guru and 'monomaniac' (his term) with whom they found themselves. Henry, they discovered, was not 'able to give of himself verbally'[120] to a woman, which they thought surprising (surprisingly). Henry Miller's fifth wife, Hiroko Tokuda, a Japanese pop star, had never read him nor did she care to: she married him for a Green Card. Neither did she want to make love to a man in his late seventies (she was in her twenties), and when she left him their marriage was unconsummated. His final affair was an ideal epistolary one with a starlet called Brenda Venus. He wrote her over 1500 letters in four years, and his love of writing love letters was so great that he would often just write them for the fun of it and leave them undelivered.

The affair between Anaïs Nin and Henry Miller tailed off after the Second World War, when she settled in New York and he in California. In 1943 he sent Anaïs some money he had been given to help her pay for the hand press she had set up in Greenwich Village, on which she could print her own work, and he continued to encourage her to keep up the diary. This, he felt, was the least he could do after all the support she had given him, and his love of her work was to outlast the physical relationship that it inspired. 'I haven't the slightest doubt that 100 years from now this stupendous document will be the greatest single item in the literary history of our time . . . the thing to remember is that it was A woman, Anaïs Nin, by whom I was rescued and pressured and encouraged and inspired,' he wrote to Huntington Cairns.[121] Anaïs and Henry kept up their correspondence and met occasionally during the fifties and sixties. Henry Miller's writing remained silent about Anaïs Nin to the last. They saw each other for the final time in Cedars Hospital, when Anaïs already had the illness that was to kill her in 1977, three years before Henry Miller's own death. In recognition of her lifelong journal, Anaïs Nin became a member of the National Institute of Art and Letters in 1974, and she gave regular talks to university students on the craft of writing. While Anaïs ironically turned into something of a feminist celebrity, Henry – hated by feminists, despite the efforts of Erica

Jong – became a literary cult in the Californian beat era of the 1960s, finally making enough money from his writing to enable him to support his family.

Anaïs Nin's and Henry Miller's writing was never exhausted, there was never a point at which they realized they had said it all and could therefore put down their pens. Theirs was writing without limits and boundaries, a writing that could only have been produced before the advent of post-modernity's cynical refrain that everything to be said has been said, that literature is now exhausted, that the self is worn out with finding itself and is instead celebrating being lost. Their writing represents the death throes of Romanticism, a last blast at self-exploration before the fancy notion of even having a self to explore was exploded. There is one extraordinary moment in her journal where Anaïs Nin notes, without of course a trace of irony, a 'curious conviction about my writing, and it is that I say enough, I say the essential thing'.[122] Anaïs Nin wrote all day and every day but, like Henry Miller, she never said 'enough' to make her conclude her writing, she never said the 'essential thing'. To have said all that needs to be said suggests that her writing came to a finish, and she never finished in her aim to 'tell *everything*'.[123]

While Henry Miller's writing was a physical explosion, Anaïs Nin's was an endless expulsion; like a bulimic she was unable to contain the words she consumed. 'I could not stop writing even if I were mortally ill,' she wrote. 'I love my writing above *everything* . . .'[124] But mortality caught up with her, and she closed her journal eventually in 1973 when her body was too riddled with cancer for her to write another word.

THREE

Literary Consumption:
Laura Riding and Robert Graves

After, when they disentwine
You from me and yours from mine,
Neither can be certain who
Was that I whose mine was you.
To the act again they go
More completely not to know.

ROBERT GRAVES, 'The Thieves'

She doesn't 'speak', she throws her trembling body forward;
she lets go of herself, she flies; all of her passes into her
voice, and it's with her body that she vitally supports the
'logic' of her speech.

HELENE CIXOUS, 'The Laugh of the Medusa'

During the spring of 1929 Anaïs Nin's journals are full of the affair
she was having with John Erskine, her husband's old college tutor
and her favourite novelist. The two writers had what she called
'volcanic' sessions of 'talk' in which they congratulated one another
on their writing. Meanwhile, the gullible Hugo Guiler was busy
reading Proust and found himself regretting, not surprisingly in
the light of his wife's fetish for words, that 'instead of all that
successful banking he could have achieved a single poem'.[1]

As with her other seductions, Anaïs Nin's literary desire for John
Erskine expressed itself as sexual desire. Rather than feeling
possessed by Erskine during their relationship, Anaïs Nin says that
she was possessed by *words* and there is a nice ambiguity in her
phrasing here, making it unclear just who is possessing whom and

thus questioning whether she is writing or being written, swallowing or being swallowed: 'Just a day before leaving, writing comes to me in an irrepressible torrent. I feel myself wholly possessed by words – too late! Time to go. Paris and a million occupations will swallow me . . .'[2]

That same spring across the Channel in England, the American poet Laura Riding, two years older than Anaïs Nin, was also feeling possessed by words and so, with a 'doom-echoing shout' – the phrase is Robert Graves's – she leaped from the fourth-storey window of their West London flat. Laura Riding tried to find in poetry, her husband later said, 'an eventual solution . . . of the universal problem of how to make words fulfil the human being and the human being fulfil words'.[3] In 1929 this problem loomed large because, like Anaïs, Laura Riding was involved in a powerful literary seduction in which writing and bodies were rapidly filling one another's places, but she was filled so full of words that a sexual rejection was felt by her as if it were a rejection of poetry itself. She was also consumed by a literary collaboration in which it was increasingly difficult to tell who had swallowed whom.

In the seventh century, the woman poet Sappho of Lesbos leaped from the rock of Leucas into the sea. The apocryphal tale has it that she had been rejected by her lover, a boatman called Phaon, and in the story of Laura Riding's leap – which would become just as fabulous in her retelling of the event – she too was rejected by a man who was beneath her. For the poet Robert Graves, her lover and collaborator, Laura Riding's leap was the apex of her seductive force, and he delighted in the analogy between what he called Sappho's 'spectacular act of self-destruction'[4] and Laura Riding's own leap because Sappho, 'a woman of poetic genius', was possessed, according to him, by the Muse.[5] Possessed by the spirit of Sappho, Laura Riding was possessed by the Muse-goddess too, but not nearly so much as Graves was possessed by the poetic language of mythology and by, so his family and friends complained, Laura

Riding herself. Robert Graves's love for Laura was, he said, 'beyond anything thinkable' and when Laura leaped, Graves followed her, crashing on to the area at the back of the house from the window on the third floor. Poetry, they later agreed, came with them.

Following his own fall, Robert Graves seems simply to have brushed himself down before carrying Laura's broken body to the ambulance. Years later, when her love for him had flipped over into the vitriolic hate that would follow her to the grave, Laura Riding would unkindly suggest that Robert, a war-hero so badly wounded at the Somme that he read his own obituary in *The Times*, had not jumped at all but had used the fire escape in order to get to her. Graves's own jump was never alluded to in the narrative they both developed around the episode. Neither would Laura Riding ever relate what happened as being the result of her sexual rejection by Geoffrey Phibbs, the gentle Irish poet who looked like Yeats and became her 'poet against poems'. She was poetry incarnate, Laura Riding said, and this was why she swallowed poison and jumped.

In October 1928, six months before Laura's suicide attempt and two years after she set up home with Graves in London, Geoffrey Phibbs wrote to Graves from County Wicklow: 'Laura Riding's work has been getting more important to me . . . At present it is more important than anything else is.' Phibbs had recently discovered that his wife, Norah McGuinness, was involved with the Bloomsbury novelist David Garnett, and so when in early 1929 he was duly summoned by telegram to live and work with Laura Riding – whom he had never met – he packed his bags and went to London. While he loved Laura's writing, when Geoffrey Phibbs arrived he found that both she and Graves expected him to love her as well, and to his embarrassment, he told Norah, he simply wasn't up to the act: Laura Riding's body lacked the appeal of her books and he became impotent.

This was not the first time Laura Riding would have this effect on one of her seduced readers, but for the moment she wrote the event up as Geoffrey Phibbs's fatal rejection of poetry, pure and simple, and Graves – not believing that a derisive goddess could be resisted by anyone – was happy to agree with her. In a letter to Edward Marsh at the Home Office, whose help he badly needed to prevent Laura's being prosecuted (attempted suicide still then being considered a crime), Graves wrote that Geoffrey Phibbs

> dragged in the whole sex-complication quite gratuitously and vulgarly. I had merely emphasised L[aura]'s distress at his going off and leaving their joint work in the air. *Made it literary, merely*. (And the sex side *was* unimportant – to L. and to me at least).[6]

Making the seduction literary, merely, was what Laura and Robert immediately set out to do. Sappho's Leucadian leap was itself, after all, the construction of Greek dramatists; Riding's jump would also be given what Laura called in her poem 'John and I' 'the literary touch of his romance'. So in her 'official' account of the events of 27 April 1929 Laura said that she 'left that room, by the window of course, and poems came with me. Or rather I went with poems.'[7]

When Rosaleen Graves, Robert's sister, described the events surrounding Laura's jump as being like 'the most incredible Russian novel',[8] she used the wrong genre. What followed contains all the sorcery of high Romanticism, the violence of Greek drama, and the clutter and incest of the Gothic: the scenes and characters in the Graves and Riding story lack the attention to social and psychological detail that can be found in a Russian novel. Where one expects to find narrative realism in the subsequent account of events given by those involved and those observing, there is instead the abstraction of allegory and the grandeur of myth. Psychological and social intricacy are reduced by all to a shadowland of good and evil, and individual parts are played not by fully realized characters but by devils, witches, vampires, and goddesses.

So Laura Riding and Robert Graves did not live to tell the tale so much as tell the tale in order to find a way of living, for the ways in which they told it reveal how important tales were to their relationship and how certain narratives provided the structure they needed to interpret their lives. Robert Graves said that in her originality Laura Riding was like the mythical spider Arachne. But it was Graves who spun Riding out of Greek legend and she later said that his only interest in women, 'after our association began . . . was as a subject for professional literary treatment'.[9]

Geoffrey Phibbs became for them a demon, an image that suited both of their needs and that fitted into their private mythologies. For Robert Graves, who spent his life mining the language of myth from which poetry originated, employed a language of primitive symbolism while Laura Riding created a hierarchy in which she was not the Goddess desired by Graves so much as an unforgiving, all-controlling Old Testament God: I am infallible, she said, I am finality, and Geoffrey Phibbs was her beautiful fallen angel. But this is leaping ahead.

In America in 1924 the poet and critic John Crowe Ransom noticed that Laura Riding didn't concede the difference between 'literary relationships' and 'personal' ones, and she assumed that someone's liking her poetry was the same thing as 'burn[ing] with suppressed libidinous desires' for her.[10] Now she was settled in England, this difference no longer held, and Robert Graves's deification of Laura Riding as poetry incarnate was strengthened by her miraculous survival from her jump. When she rose from the concrete like a Phoenix from the flames they had the evidence they both needed that Laura was indeed a mythical being. Fearing, worshipping, and desiring to possess her to the point of willingly giving up all he had, Robert told his wife Nancy: 'I do not fear her or worship her or desire to possess her or anything that should not be.'[11] His remark is evidence less of lack of self-knowledge than of the difference between Laura Riding as the mortal Robert Graves neither feared nor worshipped and Laura Riding as the cruel pagan femme fatale they invented and whose image possessed them both. While Graves was possessed by the *idea* of Laura Riding, he saw her possession by the Muse as a literal incorporation, and he wrote it into his poetic mythology.

> [T]he real perpetually obsessed muse-poet distinguishes between the Goddess as manifest in the supreme power, glory, wisdom and love of woman, and the individual woman whom the Goddess may make her instrument for a month, a year, seven years or more.

The more prosaic reaction to Laura Riding was voiced by William Carlos Williams, who described her as 'a prize bitch'. For everyone else who came across the muse-poet and his White Goddess, they were the scandalous love-him, hate-her couple of the 1930s literary world.

'Since the age of fifteen,' Robert Graves wrote in *The White Goddess*, 'poetry has been my ruling passion and I have never intentionally undertaken any task or formed any relationship that seemed inconsistent with poetic principles.'[12] This is true in relation to Graves's extraordinary affair with Laura Riding and his observation goes a long way to explaining quite why he sacrificed so much for one person, including his children, his friendships and, for a while, his reputation. But what of his relationship with Nancy Nicholson, Graves's first wife, which appears to have had nothing to do with poetic principles? While Nancy neither wrote nor read in a way that seduced either her husband or herself, she played an important role in Graves's exploration of the femme fatale as a poetic principle. Nancy passionately believed in primal female power and Graves, who worshipped female powers as they have not been worshipped since Minoan Crete, agreed. She possessed none of the prerequisite qualities of ruthlessness and conviction, 'learning, beauty, and loneliness'[13], that Robert sought in a femme fatale, but he needed Nancy nonetheless as a foil to the 'exceedingly belle',[14] utterly unique, and dazzlingly intelligent Laura Riding, who would be his ruling passion for thirteen years.

When he first read one of Laura Riding's poems, in 1925, Robert Graves had been married to Nancy Nicholson for seven years and they had four children. Their two boys took on Robert's name and the two girls were called Nicholson: Nancy, a committed feminist, insisted on this. His mother, Amalia Von Ranke, was pious, unforgiving and domineering, and the mocking edge of her sadism is caught in the tale Robert told of her sending on the sandwiches left behind by guests.[15] In her son's imagination, Amy – as she was known – took on darker and more primitive endowments than this and her bossy officiousness became the idealized authority he would then project on to Laura Riding. For Robert Graves, who occupied a world in which Apollonian logic, reason, and purity battled against Dionysian fertility and lawless nature, the mother was a fatal figure, a taunting Medusa with castrating powers who both gave life and took it away. Graves's biographer, Martin Seymour-Smith, describes Robert's start in life as 'spine- chilling': 'The infant looked up into its mother's face and sensed that – without much ambiguity – she wanted to kill him, and not quickly.'[16] In *The White Goddess*, Graves described the muse who possesses women's bodies and is feared and desired by men as 'the Mother of All Living, the ancient power of fright and lust – the female spider or the queen-bee whose embrace is death'. The muse is the mother who kills her child, and Graves's feelings for Amy were caught between adoration and awe.

II

Robert Graves was born in Wimbledon, South London, in 1895, the third of his mother's five children. Amy Graves was forty years old and his father was forty-nine. Amy, who was not naturally maternal and whose high standards of morality dominated the household, was the second wife of Alfred Perceval, a widower with five children of his own when he remarried. The second Mrs Graves had none of the jollity of the first, Jane Cooper, and she knocked order into her husband as well as into their children; soon A.P., as he was known, was a teetotaller with rather less humour than he had previously enjoyed. Amy and A.P. were Victorian orthodox protestants while their eldest son, Robert, was a modernist and a bohemian, but rather than reject their influence on him, Robert sought much of his parents' stubborn bullying authoritarianism again with Laura Riding. It was his father's love of rules, however, found not only in his domestic management but also in the games he enjoyed inventing and playing with his family, that became vital to Robert and Laura's relationship. Because while Robert liked to obey rules – his interest in poetry was born of an exploration of linguistic rules and formal poetic structure – Laura liked making them. Word-games provided the couple with their major entertainment, but for Laura seduction itself was an elaborate game with rules of its own. Games are the sum of their rules and, as many would find out, there was cost attached to disobeying Laura's.

The Graveses and the Von Rankes had intermarried before, thus uniting two proudly illustrious families. The Von Rankes boasted amongst their pedigree the German historian of Popes, Leopold Von Ranke, and the Graves family, 'thin-nosed and inclined to petulance', could be traced, Robert said, 'back to a French knight who landed with Henry VII at Milford Haven in 1485'. A.P. inherited the family's 'persistent' literary strain,[17] and wrote lyrical poetry. He loved folklore and founded the Folk Song Society as well as being President of the Irish Literary Society (his father had been the Bishop of Limerick). It was one of A.P.'s popular verses, 'Father O'Flynn', which had been put to music, that attracted Amy and she said immediately on meeting her future husband how much she liked it. Graves's father had seduced his mother with a song and so

Robert was sung into existence. His origins lay in poetry, and going back to origins would be vital to both Robert and Laura in their search for the poetic.

His father's poetry, Robert said, 'saved me from any false reverence for poets'; an intriguing remark in relation to Graves's theatrical reverence for Laura Riding and the stunning effect that one poem of hers would have on him. But then, Graves's comments about Riding's *poetic qualities* far outweigh any discussion of her qualities *as a poet*. His normally measured critical vocabulary became curiously vague and grandiose when he discussed Laura Riding's literary achievement. Perhaps this is because Graves believed that the reader of poetry should be 'induced' by the words into a trance, 'which enables him to think in poetic terms'.[18] In this sense his muted voice and lack of objective judgement in relation to Riding's work are simply a dazed reaction to pure poetry. If the reader of poetry should be lulled into a state of semi-consciousness, Graves saw the task of the poet as one of seeking out and pursuing the 'poetic' rather than struggling over commas and metaphors. The 'poetic' will guide and inspire you, and Riding was the poetic.[19] Robert's brother, John Graves, recalled what must have been a fairly typical conversation with Robert in which he said of Laura 'that her work had first attracted him, and that she was the only poet who had reached all the historical levels – whatever that means. I said, "Do you mean that she is greater than Homer, Dante, Virgil and Sophocles?" Robert replied, "That wasn't the point." '[20] The point was, as he carefully explained once to the confused Jacob Bronowski, who had been banished from Laura's society after an intellectual dispute, that she must be understood as 'a great natural fact like fire or trees or snow and either one appreciates her or one doesn't . . .'

Saving his poetic reverence for Laura Riding, Robert directed his aggression to his father. He never acknowledged his father's love of poetry as an influence on him and claimed that Alfred Perceval

Graves, in turn, had 'never once tried to teach me how to write, or showed any understanding of my serious poetry; being always more ready to ask advice about his own'.[21] (None of this could be said of Laura, who never stopped teaching Robert how to write and rejected any advice of his to her.) 'Nor,' Graves said, did his father 'ever once try to stop me writing'. Nothing, however, could ever stop Robert Graves from writing; not his time in the trenches in France during the Great War or his subsequent neurasthenia, not the growing, unruly family he had to find a means of supporting, not the breakdown of his marriage to Nancy nor the suicide attempt of his lover, not his Majorcan houses full of guests falling in and out of love with Laura Riding, nor his eventual estrangement from Laura and his years without a muse.

Following his war experiences in 1918, Graves became determined that he was going to live by his pen alone. He believed, Miranda Seymour argues in her biography of Graves, that the war had spared him 'for a purpose. That purpose was to become a poet.'[22] So compelled was he to write that even when his ill health rendered him too unfit to fight he chose to return to the icy conditions of the Somme because it gave him poetic inspiration. Here, sitting up in bed he wrote through the night by candle-light – 'Isn't that a delightful – and unconscious – vignette of the authentic Robert?' his friend and fellow poet, Siegfried Sassoon wrote to Robert Ross.[23] Friends who stayed with Graves noticed how he was always absorbed by his work, utterly preoccupied with whatever topic it was he was now pursuing. He rose at dawn every day and went to his study where he was often working on two or three projects at the same time. When he was writing the *Sergeant Lamb* books, Graves would lay an extra place for Sergeant Lamb at the dinner table.

Robert Graves is one of the twentieth century's great compulsive writers and he wrote his way through it all: poems, criticism, stories, a biography and autobiography, plays, histories, novels, historical novels from antiquity to the modern period, biblical novels, rewrites of Dickens, social histories, translations, histories of poetry, letters, essays, and reviews. In sixty years he published fifty-five collections of poetry alone. The range of subjects covered in his forty non-fictional works stretched with easy confidence from Freudian dream theory to ancient Welsh ballads. His fifteen novels include the immaculately realized *I, Claudius* and *Claudius the God*. That he never suffered the agonies of self-doubt that produce writer's block is one of the oddest things about Robert Graves. Writer's block is as natural for writers as vertigo is for climbers: defeating the fear is part of the triumph. Graves felt too comfortable with writing, not sensing its strangeness, dangers, or pitfalls, and he consequently wrote too much. His best work was always his early love poetry, and he is most remembered for *Claudius*, his indispensable *Greek Myths*; and his bizarre, exuberant 'study' of the origins of poetic myth, *The White Goddess*.

When the glowing reviews of *I, Claudius* arrived at their home in Deyá and were proudly catalogued by Robert, Laura Riding cut them up. Graves had written the book in 1933, the year in which she stopped sleeping with him and perhaps Laura recognized in the castrating figure of Livia an image of herself, while in the quietly magnificent Claudius, who avenged himself on them all, she might well have seen Robert. But the violence of her action was more likely to have been inspired by envy and disappointment than embarrassment and indignation. Her later insistence that *The White Goddess* was 'derived appropriatively from my thinking'[24] was predictable, and while it is curious that she should want to lay claim to such a great white elephant of a book, there is no doubt that Graves's ideas here were derived from thinking about Laura Riding.

Robert Graves's poetic achievement is, as Paul O'Prey succinctly puts it, 'an eloquent and restrained account of a painful attempt to reconstruct a sense of identity after a severe breakdown'.[25] This is also the reason he wrote so much: the task he set himself was not an easy one. Identity was Graves's poetic subject and poetic inspiration was his great critical interest. Graves's understanding of the nature of inspiration led him to idealize poetry and the privileged role of the poet, and Harold Bloom suggests that he can never be more than 'a good minor poet' because of his 'distrust of figurative language, and his powerfully reductive tendency to historicize and literalize every manifestation of the Goddess he could discover, whether in life or literature'.[26] Seeing the Goddess as a *metaphor* for inspiration or the imagination would have made Graves's poetry risk more and given it a more tangled, thoughtful and savage beauty instead of its often exquisite fineness. Randall Jarrell sums up Graves's relative safeness as a poet when he places him next to Wordsworth or Rilke and compares 'a rearrangement of the room with a subsidence of continents'.[27]

When he was a schoolboy, Graves was advised to use verbs and nouns rather than adjectives and adverbs and this gives his prose the appearance of being low-key, non-literary, and rather like ordinary speech. For all his theories of muses and mothers – which have something of the obsessional about them – Graves's prose, with the exception of *The White Goddess*, which is as intellectually opaque as some of his poetry can be, has the bluff common sense and charm of a gentleman scholar. He is impressively erudite with a quick wit, as entertaining and full of story as your favourite uncle. In his criticism and fiction alike he is at his best when breaking off into anecdote: Robert Graves is a wonderfully gifted teller of tales. Even when he was under tremendous stress, Graves wrote with the self-deprecating irony that characterizes his work and wins him the sympathy of his readership. Aged thirty-three, while Laura was recovering from her jump in hospital, Robert rushed off his autobiography and he described himself in *Goodbye To All That* (a book in which the irony turned black and that lost him the sympathy of his family and closest friends) as looking like a modernist portrait:

96

My height is given as six feet two inches, my eyes as grey, and my hair as black. To 'black' should be added 'thick and curly'. I am untruthfully described as having no special peculiarity. For a start, there is my big, once aquiline nose, which I broke at Charterhouse . . . it was operated on by an unskilful army surgeon, and no longer serves as a vertical line of demarcation between the left and right sides of my face, which are naturally unassorted – my eyes, eyebrows and ears all being set noticeably crooked, and my cheekbones, which are rather high, being on different levels. My mouth is what is known as 'full', and my smile is tight-lipped: when I was thirteen I broke two front teeth and became sensitive about showing them. My hands and feet are large. I weigh about twelve stone four.[28]

Virginia Woolf said that Robert Graves had a 'crude likeness to Shelley, save that his nose is a switchback and his lines blurred' and when they were introduced she described meeting a 'bolt eyed blue shirted shockheaded hatless man in a blue overcoat standing goggling'. Woolf said that Graves was 'so thick in the delight of explaining his way of life to us that no bee stuck faster to honey',[29] and she mocked the pleasure he took in his and Nancy's unconventional household and his evident pride in 'despising' the Graves's grand family connections.

Nancy Nicholson was an artist from a family of distinguished artists: her father was Sir William Nicholson and her brother Ben Nicholson. Her mother, Mabel, also painted but sacrificed her talent to raise her family – at least this is what Robert Graves observed. When Nancy married Robert in St James's, Piccadilly in January 1918, she was a land-girl and he still a soldier. At the beginning of their marriage Graves was still badly shell-shocked 'with about four years' loss of sleep to make up', and if he 'saw more than two people in a single day', he couldn't sleep at all.[30]

Robert and Nancy's was an odd liaison, which they went into rashly, and it is easier to understand Robert's motivation than it is Nancy's. Until meeting Nancy, any sexual identity Robert Graves was beginning to realize, albeit unconsciously, had been homosexual: he was involved in a loving correspondence with a schoolboy at Charterhouse, his old alma mater, and his relationship with Siegfried Sassoon, whom he had met during the war, had all the jealousy and tension of an incipient affair. Graves's homosexual instincts may have been repressed – he was horrified when he discovered that his Charterhouse correspondent was in fact a homosexual – but he chose as his wife a tomboy with a mind of her own. When they met, in 1917, Robert was fighting in the trenches and dreamed of settling down to domestic comfort with a family, and Nancy's off-beat, strong personality seemed to fit the bill.

Nancy Nicholson was only eighteen and adverse to all forms of convention; she resented the marriage service and enjoyed only the champagne, changing back to her land-girl costume half way through the reception. 'Nancy Nicholson,' Laura Riding wrote sixty years after she broke up her marriage, 'was a staunch proponent of simple feminist principles of personal independence and political and social equality. Robert Graves accepted her ideas in automatic concurrence . . .'[31] Nancy's feminist principles were unacademic, it is true, and less abstract than Laura's, but having just fought in one of the most futile wars in history, Robert was inclined to agree with his wife's steadfast insistence that men had destroyed the world. He had just as automatically accepted his mother's ideas on purity and morality and he would later accept without question Laura Riding's views on everything, bar her insistence, when they reached Majorca, that time itself had stopped, on which occasion he kept his own theories to himself. Siegfried Sassoon soon got fed up of hearing his great friend 'talking through someone else's bonnet'.

In the early days of their marriage, when he was studying for his postponed degree in Oxford, Robert and Nancy rented a cottage at the bottom of the poet John Masefield's garden and Constance, Masefield's wife, noted in her diary that Nancy was 'a strange, shy, boyish girl, very clever with her fingers and quick in brain'. But she didn't, Constance perceptively wrote, have 'enough adventure in her to be a poet's wife'.[32] Neither, however, did Robert have the adventure in him to be the husband of an artist, and while Nancy was without the ruthless power that Robert needed in a muse, the crucial difference between herself and Laura was that Nancy worked with visual images and Laura with words. Within their relative fields, however, there seemed to be little difference in the two women's extremism. Nancy Nicholson had the artist's version of perfect pitch: Miranda Seymour tells a story of Nancy's returning a picture by her brother Ben, 'because it contained a displeasing colour'. Nancy would also 'walk out of a room she had painted if a guest wore a colour that clashed with it'.[33]

What Robert found in Laura was an erasure of the visual: there is nothing to see in Laura Riding's writing. In her verbally dense poetry, language replaces the visible and when Laura appears she is all blotches, parts, and fragments. She blocks out the sensuality of the visible as well as its Medusan terror – the Gorgon's look, remember, turned to stone. What is striking in the life of Laura Riding is her evident terror and distrust of vision and of relationships that *do not involve words alone*. Having all of her seductions through the written word, what did Laura think would happen without them? A clue lies in her childhood, when Laura Riding had watched her mother go blind. Because she could no longer be seen by her, Laura's relationship with her mother could only be verbal, and perhaps this explains her fear of *non-verbal* relationships in any form. Without words Laura Riding became – like Perseus in Athene's magic cloak – invisible.

Robert Graves also avoided the risks of looking. In his essay on 'How Poets See', Graves treats his subject curiously literally, discussing Keats's myopia rather than the range of his imaginative

99

scopic field. Robert Graves writes about vision in poetry as if he were Perseus himself, protected by his shield from Medusa's deadly gaze.

III

By the time Laura arrived Robert was thirty years old with twenty books of poetry and criticism to his name. A miniature edition of his poems had been made for the doll's house at Windsor Castle. He never had to struggle for recognition or publication; renown came as effortlessly for him as writing did. He had brought out three volumes of well-received war poetry whilst in the Royal Welch Fusiliers, which he joined on leaving school, and he published at least one book almost every year from 1916 until 1980. After the war Robert Graves, exhausted and bereaved, no longer used it as a topic for poems and he earned a reputation through his inclusion in Edward Marsh's popular anthologies of *Georgian Poetry*. Marsh's idea was to move away from the florid diction of the Victorian poets and support a group of poets who were tighter, sharper, and above all more realistic. Graves had lost his way poetically when Laura came along, and she was to make him completely rethink his relation to writing.

When Robert was seduced and diverted by Laura Riding's witty poem, 'The Quids', which he had been shown in a Nashville poetry journal, the *Fugitive*, he was living with his family in a cottage in the village of Islip, eight miles outside Oxford.

> The little quids, the monstrous quids,
> The everywhere, everything, always quids,
> The atoms of the Monoton,
> Each turned an essence where it stood,
> Ground a gisty dust from its neighbours' edges,
> Until a powdery thoughtfall stormed in and out –
> The celebration of a slippery quid enterprise.

'By God, she was superior, indeed supreme,' Robert recalled in the early years following the end of his affair with Laura. If 'the hairs stand on end, the eyes water, the throat is constricted, the skin crawls and a shiver runs down the spine', you are, Graves believed, in the presence of true poetry. Like a femme fatale, a good poem should terrify, even petrify, the reader, and Graves was stunned by this one. Laura, less dramatically but nonetheless sadistically, held that a poem should be cruel: 'harsh, bare, and matter-of-fact',[34] which is a good description of the effect 'The Quids' was to have on Graves's family, who were soon to be discarded in a somewhat matter-of-fact manner for the author of these lines.

Other of Laura Riding's poems were concerned with ideas as opposed to experience, and she was prone to dealing with vast subjects like the nature of Creation and the processes of thought, but she never produced another social satire such as this. A 'quid' is the substance of a thing or a 'quibble' and a 'monoton' is 'sameness' in writing, although Laura Riding extends and plays with these dictionary definitions throughout the poem. The comic busy-ness of these quids sends up the academic seriousness she was later to revere, while their sheer quantity parodies the sheep-like uniformity of a literary world that prides itself on its difference from the crowd.

If it seems astonishing that a reader could be seduced by a poem this impersonal, remember that seduction is an impersonal affair. The operations of seduction, according to Baudrillard, come closer to those of organized ritual than reckless desire, and ritual is dependent on rules, the observation of which far outweighs the importance of what they are to keep in place. Rituals are like games in this sense and Laura Riding loved games, of which seduction was her favourite. This is how 'The Quids' is best understood: as a game. It offers a haughty invitation to its readers to play, to react to the challenge of the poet. All Laura Riding's relationships operated as games in which the players were often unsure why they were playing or what exactly the rules were but they proceeded nonetheless. Her stakes were high, as those involved with her testify, but no one wants to be left out of a game, and although it was regarded as an honour to be asked to play in one of Laura's, invitations were not difficult to obtain. You simply had to pass the test of being right about how good her poetry was.

At home, Robert Graves had learned to be good at games, while at school and in the Royal Welch he was trained to be a good sportsman. Graves would play according to Riding's rules until the very end, investing in her as one would in a round of roulette. No stake was too high for him: when she leaped out of the window, he followed, and when she played her trump card ten years later, he departed with loser's dignity. By then it had become too easy for Laura to win with Robert and she found herself a new partner.

Robert Graves was drawn into what he called Laura Riding's 'teasing Quids' straight away, even though it took him several reads before he caught its rather smug irony, and he wrote to Riding's friends Allen Tate and John Crowe Ransom – both members of the group of Southern poets who called themselves the 'Fugitives' – about her. He was sent by them a manuscript of Laura Riding's poems, which he arranged to be published in England by the Hogarth Press. Laura could 'write like hell', Graves said when he was describing her to Edward Marsh, and his daemonic image anticipates the devils who would soon beset them both.

After a brief correspondence, Robert Graves requested that Laura come over from the States to join his family and to help him on a book he was planning to write with T.S. Eliot about modern poetry. Although Laura's friends thought she was invited to be Graves's secretary, she knew better. As she left America to sail for England in the winter of 1925, Allen Tate offered one of his uncanny predictions: 'I fear disaster: Laura is surely the maddest woman I have ever met, and if Graves isn't already mad – which I'm inclined to suspect from his issuance of a blind invitation to a lady read but

unseen – he will be a maniac before a month.'[35] On the morning of 2
January 1926 Laura Riding Gottschalk, as she then called herself, or
Laura Riding-Roughshod, as her friend Hart Crane called her, was
met by Robert Graves and his father-in-law at Waterloo station and
was taken that night to have supper with E.M. Forster.

There are various biographical accounts of this first meeting at
Waterloo, which agree insofar as Laura Riding is represented as
either too hot or too cold to be trustworthy, and either guilty or
innocent of her sexual effect. In one account, Graves takes one look
at Laura's 'small, tired, overly made-up figure' and gasps 'My God!
What am I going to do?' while Sir William left in 'robust horror'.[36]
Laura's rouge, lipstick and eyeshadow seemed inappropriate for a
young woman of twenty-five to be wearing at that time of day, let
alone for a single woman travelling alone. Laura seemed very
foreign: the fashion for English women was to have clean, fresh
faces. Nonetheless Sir William's reaction seems excessive in the
light of a woman Peter Quennel quietly thought of as being 'pale'
and 'mop-headed' while Tom Matthews, an American writer who
would play an important part in Riding's later life, confirms
Nicholson's distaste. Matthews said that when he met Riding a few
years later, she was 'very nearly ugly, or at least repellent – when
her deep sunk eyes went dead as stone (or a lidded snake's) and her
normal pallor faded to the tone of chalk'. She looked old enough to
be his mother, Matthews thought, which disturbed him because
they were in fact born on the same day. Another version of the
Waterloo meeting has Laura appear out of the crowd and the steam
in a smart and sombre long dark coat and a broad-brimmed hat,
'wearing the liveliest of expressions; her blue eyes were especially
striking, and she had brown hair which was swept backwards from
her forehead and fell on her shoulders'. So Laura Riding appears as a
range of types from downtown trailer-trash to college girl.
However, this first meeting between the poets evidently went
well and there were jokes all round about her make-up bag.

Sir William Nicholson had an appointment to go on to (so he said), leaving Laura Riding and Robert Graves to make the train journey back to Islip alone. They struck up an instant rapport: Laura wrote to a friend that the flood of lightning that filled their train compartment as they headed towards Oxford was a supernatural sign that struck them both dumb. Robert, who was still terrified of trains following his war-time experiences, may have been struck dumb for longer than Laura. Laura was treated like a vulnerable child by Nancy and Robert, and as soon as she arrived they made her a hot bath by the open fire. She was blissfully happy in the Graves and Nicholson household and her contentment was sealed when she quickly replaced T.S. Eliot as Graves's collaborator on his next book.

One week after Laura's arrival, she left for Egypt with Graves and his family. Nancy Nicholson and Laura Riding seemed to the other passengers on the boat like sisters: Laura had adapted her style to complement Nancy's bohemian flair and Nancy continued to make Laura's clothes long after Laura was sleeping with her husband. Robert had been offered a job teaching English at Cairo University, and this, apart from his time in the army, was to be the only salaried work he would ever do. As Robert grew increasingly bored by the teaching and frustrated by the students, the stifling heat became unmanageable and the children fell ill. His and Nancy's youngest son, Sam, contracted measles, which left him permanently deaf and then, to cap it all, Laura saw a ghost and convinced them all that their ill fortune had supernatural sources. So to the fury of Amy and A.P., Graves broke his contract and left Egypt after six months. Any pleasure he had got from the Cairo experience was to do with working with Laura. Graves's autobiography, *Goodbye to All That*, which was written to pay Laura's hospital fees while she recovered from her broken spine, closes at this point:

The remainder of this story, from 1926 until today, is dramatic but unpublishable. Health and money both improved, marriage wore thin. New characters appeared on the stage. Nancy and I said unforgivable things to each other. We parted on May 6, 1929. She, of course, insisted on keeping the children. So I went abroad, resolved never to make England my home again; which explains the 'Goodbye to All That' of this title.[37]

From June 1926, when Nancy, Robert, Laura and the children arrived back in England, until the summer of 1929 Robert resumed writing for a living but this time with Laura Riding firmly entrenched as his partner. To further the rage of A.P. and Amy Graves, the collaborators began to live and work together apart from Nancy and the children, moving to a flat in Ladbroke Square, West London, where they were chaperoned in a fairly ineffectual way by Rosaleen Graves: Robert said that this was when his sexual relationship with Laura Riding began.

For the bulk of this time, until Laura jumped, in the spring of 1929, the living arrangement had suited Robert and Nancy very well and there are tales of the three of them sitting in the cinema holding hands, with Laura glowing in the middle. When Laura had first arrived, Nancy had been ill with exhaustion and a thyroid condition (she had lost her hair and had ringworm on her scalp), so she welcomed the household help that Laura could provide. His wife had started to 'regret' her marriage, Robert said, and wanted somehow to be 'unmarried', so when Laura and Robert chose to live separately from Nancy, she in turn, he surmised, gained the freedom she had missed. In October 1929, after relations between the three had broken down, Robert and Laura followed the advice of their friend Gertrude Stein and went to live in Deyá, a small fishing village on the Spanish island of Majorca. It is paradise, if you can stand it, Stein warned them. They stayed there together for six years, until the outbreak of the civil war drove them back to England. But Robert returned with his second wife and lived there for the rest of his life.

IV

While they were writing in Egypt, Robert and Laura had fallen in love. A painfully sensuous panegyric written by Robert celebrates the seductive entwining of Laura's intellect and body and the erotic place and process of her thought:

> To speak of the hollow nape where the close chaplet
> Of thought is bound, the loose-ends lying neat
> In two strands downward, where the shoulders open
> Casual and strong below . . .

The sexual guilt Graves had inherited from his puritanical mother and that is apparent in his earlier poetry is notably gone; Laura, even more sexually liberated than Nancy, had liberated Robert. Laura was delighted that Robert's image in the opening line was taken from the title of her book, *The Close Chaplet*, which was published in 1926 by Virginia and Leonard Woolf's Hogarth Press. She dedicated this first collection of her poems to her half-sister Isabel, and to Nancy Nicholson. *The Close Chaplet* sold twenty-five copies.

The first book Robert Graves and Laura Riding wrote together was published in 1927, and *A Survey of Modernist Poetry* inspired William Empson's now classic study, *Seven Types of Ambiguity*. Graves's fluid and graceful prose combined with Riding's rigorously analytical mind to good effect and their collaboration sowed the seeds of the revolution in literary interpretation known as the New Criticism. The attention Graves and Riding paid to the details of the text itself, as a linguistic structure operating independently of the biographical details of the author, helped to find a way out of the dominant Browning's-a-Good-Chap school of criticism. *A Survey of Modernist Poetry* stressed the importance of close reading to help the 'plain reader' overcome the apparent difficulties presented by modern poetry, and the authors showed what could be achieved in examining the meaning of each word in poems by e e cummings and Shakespeare. Other poetic techniques, such as metaphor and metre, were seen as ephemeral to the art of interpretation. The book concluded that most so-called modernist poetry was doing nothing new at all, and that there were in fact only two truly modern poems, one of which was by Laura Riding (and the other by e e cummings). These line-by-line readings are the result, Graves and Riding stressed, of a 'word-by-word' collaboration, although this apparently simple phrase presents as many difficulties to the plain-close-reader as it later did to the writers themselves. Their struggle to redefine what they meant by the term, and to claim sole authorship of a work whose strength was its disempowerment of the author's authority, went on for many years after the book itself was forgotten.

The Graves family claimed that Laura had 'vampirised Robert from the first', but this is only a condemnation of Laura if you miss the vampire's mythic force that both she and Robert would have celebrated. The female vampire is the femme fatale par excellence, the truly seductive, powerful woman; Robert Graves's feminine ideal:

> The femme fatale can appear as Medusan mother or as frigid nymph, masquing in the brilliant luminosity of Apollonian high glamour. Her cool unreachability beckons, fascinates, and destroys. She is not a neurotic but, if anything, a psychopath. That is, she has a moral affectlessness, a serene indifference to the suffering of others, which she invites and dispassionately observes as tests of her power.[38]

This is certainly one of the personae of Laura Riding, but if anyone was really vampiric in the literary relationship between Graves and

Riding, it can hardly have been the inspirational Muse herself but rather the person who fed off her. When Laura left Robert in 1940 she had bled out her last word – 'Her almost incessant writing, which had poured from her like an issue of blood, was staunched to a few trickling drops'[39]– and Robert had to conjure her up again and again in future muses so as to maintain the level of masochistic pain he needed to write. In a description of the female poet as muse of the male, Graves gives us a monstrous mother: a woman who can discard the creature who feeds off her but can feed off no one herself. She is dependent on her own limited resources:

> At the worst this Muse, whom he loves in a more than human sense, may reject and deceive him; and even then he can vent his disillusion in a memorable poem – as Catullus did when he parted from Clodia – and survive to fix his devotion on another. The case of a woman poet is a thousand times worse: since she is herself the Muse, a Goddess without an external power to guide or comfort her, and if she strays even a finger's breadth from the path of divine instinct, must take violent self-vengeance. For a while a sense of humour, good health, and discretion may keep her on an even keel, but the task of living to, for, and with herself alone, will sooner or later prove an impossible one.[40]

What Laura gained in mythic power during her years with Robert, she lost in literary achievement. Her earliest poetry was her remarkable best and while she continued to write the occasional strong poem, none of the twenty-eight books she published while she was with Graves are worth reprinting, save *The Close Chaplet* and *Collected Poems*. Robert might have thought that Laura could 'write like hell', but to others her writing became increasingly hellish, and publishers only accepted her work when it came in a package with Graves's latest book or when he pressurized them to take it. Graves's own work went from strength to strength, precisely, Laura would endlessly claim, because he was stealing from her.

'There is one story and one story only/That will prove worth your telling,' Robert Graves wrote in a poem to his newborn son, called 'To Juan at the Winter Solstice'. Not only did Graves repeat his experience of his mother in his relationship with Laura Riding, but in his devotion to future muses he sought to repeat the story of Laura. And in his mythical representation of Laura, Graves limited her to a one-dimensional figure, ensuring that this was the only form of story that could describe her. The notion that we are each limited to giving a single narrative account of one another and ourselves was not even Robert's idea, Laura later claimed. He had stolen the 'key axiom' in these lines from her insistence, in a paper she had written and to which he had access, that there is only one version of the truth: 'There is only one story!' she had proclaimed. As Allen Tate wrote on first meeting Laura Riding in 1924, 'you get the conviction that the Devil and all Pandemonium couldn't dissuade her of her tendency'.

Laura's one story about Robert, the story she would tell again and again to describe their relationship, was to do with what she saw as his intellectual dishonesty. Robert had read Laura's story in classical literature before she came and had written the plot before they met. Much of his tale of Laura Riding is found in *The White Goddess*, written after she left him, and his other writings on the Muse, but his 'official' version of Laura's 'coming' is told in the dedicatory epilogue to the 1929 edition of *Goodbye to All That*, where Graves explains why she is not mentioned in his auto-biography itself. In this intensely personal love letter, Laura's catastrophic effect on Robert's family is evaded and her appearance is seen as a miracle defying representation. Laura is represented not as a woman but as an organizing, or 'centralising' force, as she would have it. Laura is represented as an idea:

by mentioning you as a character in my autobiography I would seem to be denying you in your true quality of one living invisibly, against kind, as dead, beyond event. And yet the silence is false if it makes the book seem to have been written forward from where I was instead of backward from where you are.

When Robert and Laura were no longer able to communicate, this epilogue was erased from subsequent editions. Writing backwards, writing over events, is what Robert Graves and Laura Riding both excelled at.

The abstract mysticism of Graves's style in his epilogue is in stark contrast to the dead-pan prose and black irony of the autobiography itself, which is a poke in the eye to his readers, whose intelligence he mocks with a disdain he picked up from Laura. The book, he said, is a hotch-potch of the styles and stories that readers indiscriminately love. He has 'deliberately mixed in all the ingredients that I know are mixed into other popular books' in order to make it sell.[41] Laura's arrival could not be contained in a simple narrative form such as this:

> For how could the story of your coming be told between an Islip Parish Council Meeting and a conference of the professors of the Faculty of Letters at Cairo University? How she and I happening by seeming accident upon your teasing *Quids*, were drawn to write to you, who were in America, asking you to come to us. How, though you knew no more of us than we of you, and indeed less (for you knew me at a disadvantage, by my poems of the war), you forthwith came. And how there was thereupon a unity to which you and I pledged our faith and she her pleasure. How we went together to the land where the dead parade the streets and there met with demons and returned with the demons still treading behind. And how they drove us up and down the land.[42]

One of these demons was Geoffrey Phibbs.

When Geoffrey Phibbs arrived on the doorstep of Laura and Robert's West London flat, 35A St Peter's Square, 'in a state of emotional lability bordering at times on psychosis',[43] Robert still believed his marriage to be intact and he failed to see why there might be a problem about his sexual involvement with Laura Riding. After all, Nancy no longer desired him and was therefore unable to be jealous or resentful. Robert didn't even see the potential time-bomb involved in inviting into the household of two emotionally vulnerable poets another emotionally vulnerable poet who was also seduced by Laura's writing. Three people were needed to play Laura's game, and so she was delighted that Geoffrey was joining them: Nancy could now be dispensed with. The presence of the rival poet was vital for Robert's game as well. His vision of Laura was as someone inaccessible and taunting: she had to be fought over, and he had to be sexually humiliated and punished. But if Robert's appetite for self-punishment seemed to know no bounds, it was nothing compared to Laura's.

V

Laura Reichenthal, as she was born on 16 January 1901, was the second child of a Polish Jew from Galacia. A committed socialist, he encouraged his gifted daughter to become another Rosa Luxembourg. Nathan Reichenthal had left Poland for New York when he was fourteen, and until Laura was born he worked in the clothing sweatshops of Manhattan. When he lost his job, long-term work was never easy to come by and his search for work took him and his young family all over the East and Mid-West. His adored first wife, Laura Lorber, died in 1894, leaving Nathan a young daughter called Isabel who needed looking after. He soon remarried, choosing as his bride the super-efficient Sadie Eder-sheim, who had been working in the sweatshops since she was a child in order to support her siblings and parents. As with Alfred Perceval Graves, Nathan Reichenthal had lost the woman he loved and married the second time for necessity; both idealized the dead woman and feared the living one. Laura and Robert were the children of bereft fathers and replacement mothers, and their relationship was dominated by this coincidence.

When she met Nathan, Sadie was twenty-five and going blind. She fulfilled her half of the bargain and raised his daughter, also bearing him another girl, Laura, and a son called Bobby. But marriage brought her none of the freedoms she had dreamed of. After years of unhappiness, Sadie finally separated from Nathan when Laura (named after her husband's first wife) had left home. All her life Laura would try to distance herself from Sadie's deep disappointment in her lot. Her mother's 'character was all dreariness', Laura unkindly said in a piece called 'Letter of Abdication',[44] and in a poem she wrote when she was twenty-one she referred to 'Mother Damnable, Mother Damnable'. Later, Laura would erase the existence of her parents but it was her mother's presence she found most intolerable. A family friend told Deborah Baker, Laura Riding's biographer, that Laura 'seemed to have *hated* her mother'.[45] Before she left America, Laura wrote these chilling lines:

> Mothering innocents to monsters is
> Not of fertility but fascination
> In women.

The mother was a fatal figure for Laura as well as for Robert, but not because of her alignment with nature; the mother in this poem is an *un*natural figure. Laura, who remained childless herself, would show a peculiar aggression to mothers in her future relationships while her passions were for their husbands, the fathers of young children.

As adults, Laura and Robert would prefer to have their relationships in triangles, and this was apparent in the ease they both felt sharing their lives with Nancy. Laura needed a man whose mind she could dominate and a woman she could compete with and Robert needed a muse, a male rival for his muse, and a mother to his children. The muse and the mother could not be incorporated at any emotional level for Graves, and he liked to set these two female principles in combat against one another. Both Graves and Riding reenacted their childhood conflicts again and again in these Oedipal triads.

Sadie Reichenthal was defeated by drudgery and poverty, and the Marxist literature that stimulated her husband and provided the earliest reading material for her daughter failed to either interest or enlighten her. In the Reichenthal family as well as the Graves family, intellect was associated with the father while the body was analogous with the mother: literature was synonymous with escape. Choosing to reject the closeness of the body and to align herself with the freedoms of the mind was a result of Laura's disconnection from Sadie and all she represented: 'I have lived far away from my mother, having no connection with her except to insist that she live far away from me . . .'[46] she wrote. But the job of separation was never this easy for Riding, who needed to work in close collaboration with another person all her life. In one of her early poems, 'Starved', she asked, 'Who owns this body of mine?' as if distinguishing her own person from that of her mother were still a problem, just as she would later find it difficult to distinguish herself from Graves.

From her father Laura received an education in ideas and the constant encouragement to *think*, to challenge the establishment. She was her father's daughter: it was Nathan who showed her how to channel her intellectual energies into reshaping her world. When Laura exchanged politics for poetry, in 1916, and therefore no longer fuelled her father's fantasy that she would be a revolutionary figure, she took with her all the radical fervour with which she had been imbued as a child and injected it into her poems. In fact, when Laura wrote about her life, it began for her with the 'discovery of poetry more than the circumstances of her birth and upbringing',[47] and her love of poetry was inherited from her elder sister Isabel, whose own poems were occasionally published. In poetry, Deborah Baker writes, was 'a charm to protect her from her mother's fate, from the sordid stench of poverty, and to release her into an "unlimited freedom of mind, knowledge, thought, utterance"'.[48] Poetry was also a way of competing with her sibling, whose literary skills as an editorial secretary had won her the hand of the company's editor.

Three years before Laura graduated from Brooklyn Girls' High School, Louis Gottschalk, the son of a Polish barber, left the boys' school. Like Nathan Reichenthal, Lou Gottschalk was a fervent socialist, and because he also chose politics and not poetry his relationship with Laura was destined to come to a similar end. Laura and Lou met at Cornell University where he was her History tutor, and when they married, in 1920, Laura dropped out of her degree and travelled with her husband to Urbana, where he had a job in the History Faculty at the University of Illinois. Lou had educated himself out of his background and was immensely proud of his achievement. While he lectured, Laura wrote, pouring out novels and poems regardless of her lack of formal education; hence the startling newness of her earliest poetry, whose autodidactic quality shows in her imaginative and linguistic strength as well as in her naïveté. Lou thought she was undereducated; Laura's point was that she had already seduced her educator and would continue to seduce those more educated than herself.

By 1925 Laura Riding had published some fifty poems in journals ranging from the *Fugitive*, *Nomad*, *The Stepladder* and *Contemporary Verse*. When she was twenty she wrote a long poem, *Voltaire: A Biographical Fantasy*, while Lou worked on a biography of Jean-Paul Marat. Laura's lifelong need to work in unison with someone else began in her marriage, where she chose to write on a subject related to her husband's, and in Lou's *Marat* it is evident from his acknowledgement to Laura – 'whose time and efforts have been devoted to this book to a degree only second to my own' – that she liked to see herself as his collaborator. Laura's fear of writing on her own bespeaks less a dread of intellectual isolation than a desire for incorporation in another's writing and for a closeness so intimate as to make the two hands indistinguishable.

In 1924, 'Dimensions', which Laura Riding had sent to the *Fugitive* magazine, won the Nashville Poetry Prize for the best poem of the year. Laura's poem objectified her body and mythologized her death – themes that would recur:

> Measure me for a burial
> That my low stone may neatly say
> In a precise, Euclidean way
> How I am three-dimensional.

The Fugitives thought she was their find of the year and Laura Gottschalk took her award extremely seriously: here was the break she needed to get out of a marriage that ceased to interest her, and she wrote to Allen Tate, one of the judges, that she was planning to live alone and to support herself. It now struck her that she was only interested in the company of poets and that Louis had no understanding of the importance of poetry. Laura's ex-husband always cited poetry as the reason for their divorce.

In her excitement at the new world now opened up by the Fugitives, Mrs Gottschalk arrived uninvited at their headquarters in Nashville in order to introduce herself to the entirely male fraternity of Southern poets and to read them more of her poems. Laura Gottschalk seemed 'frighteningly intense' to Allen Tate, John Crowe Ransom, Robert Penn Warren, and Donald Davidson, and they found her urgent desire to join the gentlemen's fellowship inappropriate and overbearing. That Laura's poetic ideals were not their own is clear from the direction that her work was to take, but the aesthetic doubts expressed by the Fugitives disguised their fear of her iconoclasm as well as their latent misogyny, and Laura was not made welcome. Undeterred, as Louise Cowan laconically puts it in her history of the Fugitives, 'Miss Riding tried to assume leadership in the project and ended by causing some little dissension . . .'[49] A more violent description of what happened is in a letter from John Crowe Ransom to Allen Tate, in which he says that Riding is 'a deep and mischievous person' who tried to set them up against one another fighting for her as prize: 'I was Agamemnon and you were Achilles, and she, it follows, was the fair Briseïs.'[50] Robert Graves would be put in similar epic positions with his rivals, but it was all grist to the mill for him.

Realizing that she would not be invited to run the Fugitives, Miss Laura Riding Gottschalk, as she now called herself, none-theless left her dejected husband and went to New York in 1925 where she met up with Allen Tate, who had also left the South, and they had a brief affair. However, in 1924 Allen had married Caroline Gordon, who was expecting their child, but neither of these facts stopped Laura from wanting to join the Tate household, and while Caroline was in labour Laura busied herself reorganizing their furniture and tidying their cupboards. This was to be the first of her triangular relationships with parent figures, and Caroline Gordon found it unbearable. How convenient then, that just as the Fugitives were running out of reasons for rejecting the flood of poems she sent them (nineteen out of twenty of which were worthless, they said), and Allen Tate and his wife were feeling embarrassed by her presence in their lives, Laura was to receive an invitation from the established English poet, Robert Graves, suggesting that she join him and his wife in their household. Denouncing her 'American fellow poets' as 'combining something less than complete poetic seriousness with something less than complete poetic seriousness',[51] Laura got on a boat to Southampton.

Lou Gottschalk – who would see his wife only once more, when she was wrapped up in complete poetic seriousness with Graves in London – paid for her ticket.

VI

When Laura Riding was told by the Fugitives that her poems went on for too long she responded, surprised that this was a criticism, by saying that she just couldn't stop writing. Laura's writing was compulsive and continual. 'That young lady has more energy than a phalanx of dynamos, with seven billy-goats thrown in,' Tate wrote of Laura's drive.[52] 'I had never met anyone who worked as she did,' Tom Matthews, Laura's sometime collaborator wrote after staying with Graves and Riding in Deyá:

> She wrote for most of the day and often late into the night – stories, poems, criticism, letters. She always had two or three books going at a time. Besides her own work, and collaborations with Robert, she had a hand in many other pies, helping, advising, 'straightening out the muddle', in someone else's poem, picture, sculpture, novel.[53]

Taking out the references to poems and to Robert, Tom Matthews' account of Laura at work in the early 1930s describes Anaïs Nin as well. For both Laura Riding and Anaïs Nin, existence in writing was more real than existence off the page. Or as Laura Riding put it, 'existence in poetry becomes more real than existence in time – more real because more good, more good because more true.'[54] Anaïs Nin preferred to be edited and odourless on a sheet than fleshly and perspiring between them, and she thus spent much of her time translating the latter existence into the former. But putting aside their shared drive to turn into their writing and their capacity to captivate and seduce their readers, their megalomania and the discomfort they felt with their bodies, the mythologization of their femininity and their dislike of other women, their need to be desired by men and their refusal to accept criticism, their extravagant and theatrical costumes and the care they took over their appearance, their determination to achieve literary greatness and the belief that their writing was breaking new ground, the generous support they gave to other writers and the cultish followings they both inspired, their thirteen-year partnerships with male writers more commercially successful than themselves and the marginal status as 'mad' women they each have today – putting aside these coincidences, Anaïs Nin and Laura Riding could not have been more different.

This is because Laura Riding saw herself as an intellectual terrorist of the first order. While Anaïs Nin seduced her male readers and then sought continual reassurance that her writing had neither unsexed her nor castrated them, intimacy for Laura took the form of writing with someone and in this she went for the jugular, cultivating a ruthless intelligence quite terrifying to her collaborators. Tom Matthews wrote a book about his experience of Laura Riding called *Under the Influence*, in which he details his unhappy obsession with her. The memoir is a testimony to Riding's love of games and to her Medusan effect. Before he became editor of *Time* magazine, Matthews 'collaborated' with Riding ('or, more accurately . . . Laura wrote, using me as a pencil')[55] on a bad novel called *The Moon's No Fool*, and writing with her left him, as it had left Geoffrey Phibbs a few years earlier, drained of sexual energy: 'This intense time with Laura did leave its mark on me, however (or should I say, her mark?), like a bruise. For a month I was impotent.'[56]

Laura's next collaboration with Tom Matthews, published in her journal *Epilogue 1*, was set up as a question-and-answer session. Tom-the-castrated-schoolboy asked the questions, which were along the lines of 'Does God exist?' and Laura-the-Goddess provided the answers. Reading this dialogue has the effect, as does much of Riding's prose, of making one feel suddenly very tired; she had the knack of turning what was of potential interest into a topic of almost inhuman dreariness. Another collaborator, the Oxford poet Norman Cameron, admitted after a fatal dispute with her about the meanings of 'fake' and 'fluke', that he had developed a 'kind of horror' of Laura, and he returned from Deyá leaving the house he was building there unfinished. As far as Laura was concerned, by disagreeing with her, Cameron had broken the rules.

VII

'I hope you will understand about poems,' Laura Riding wrote in her account of her leap from the window,[57] and in order to understand about Laura Riding it is important to understand what she meant about poems because, she said, 'My poems then are instead of my life.'[58] Like Graves, Laura Riding was 'religious' in her 'devotion to poetry',[59] but Julian Symons, the thirties writer and critic, noticed that Laura could not separate her drive to purify language and poetry from her 'close finickiness in personal relationships'.[60] The ideals of poetry dictated her way of life, her communication with family and friends, her sexual relationships, the country she lived in, and in this she was also like Graves. 'To live in, by, for the reasons of, poems is to habituate oneself to the good existence,' Riding argued. 'So read, so exist.'[61] Graves agreed with her in this too, and they were also in agreement that character and style mirrored one another: if you were a good person then you were a good poet. That Robert Graves managed to square this belief with his abandonment of his four young children in the name of poetry is testament to the power of believing. But what distinguished Laura was her obsessional belief that once language is perfected then a perfect self will emerge out of poetry: literally. What Riding meant by a 'perfect' language was one in which the exact, 'true', meanings of words are located and documented, and the perceived relation between this clinically pure language and the ideal self is what makes Laura Riding's work and life both fascinating and difficult.

For Riding, ultimate 'truth' – and this is what concerned her – could only be found in poetry and only then when words were used 'literally, literally, literally, without gloss, without gloss, without gloss'.[62] If words can attain literal perfection, and Riding dedicated her life to purging language of linguistic parasites and impurities, it follows that the written self can be perfect too, because language and identity are simply the same thing. Laura Riding's writing life was an attempt to turn herself into this clinically pure poem: 'A poem,' she held, 'is an advanced degree of self.'[63] Riding tried to strip herself of all consciousness except what she saw as being 'poetic' because poetry is the consciousness of 'what is self'.[64] What was 'self' increasingly became to her no more than a walking dictionary of semantically correct signifiers. Her version of the human subject and the story of her life left no room for fantasy, irrationality, the unconscious, or desire, and therefore bore no relation to identity as it was simultaneously being explored by Freud, who also revered the word.

Freud and Laura Riding were both interested in the self as a narrative structure and each explored the unlocking of words as revealing a truth about human identity. But for Freud this verbal disengagement as it was performed in psychoanalysis was an endless activity, where words opened up further words in an associative chain that led to and then circled around the unconscious mind, a bottomless pit in which censorious distinctions between truth and falsehood, reality and fantasy, no longer hold anyway. The Freudian subject is a desiring subject, which means that he is never satisfied, never finished. What Freud ironically called 'his majesty the ego' referred to a self fractured and incomplete, a product of the ceaseless layers of stories we tell about ourselves. Mental life is for Freud intimately related to the coherence of our plots: we lose the plot when we lose our place in the tales we tell, for – as Graves and Riding were keenly aware – a coherent narrative is party to psychological health.

Laura Riding, on the other hand, saw language as a *finite* structure and she looked towards the origins of words and stories in order to fashion a perfectly contoured self rooted in a bedrock of 'truth'. Truth for Riding was not at all the unstable and fluctuating affair it represented for Freud, while 'reality' was less an abstract idea for her than something that had four corners and a ceiling. 'In truth there are no kinds,' she wrote; 'Truth is the result when reality as a *whole* is uncovered by those faculties which apprehend in terms of *entirety*, rather than in terms merely of parts.'[65] For Laura Riding, words led not towards but away from the irrational self, and their precise use fulfilled the human being, replacing rather than reinforcing the need for bodies and the urges of desire. Words and stories have a clear beginning, ending, and literal meaning for Laura Riding: *ergo*, she does too. Laura embodied, so she informed Geoffrey Phibbs and Robert Graves, 'Finality'. Given these parameters, the seductive appeal of her writing was thus a strange and devastating affair for those who came under her sway.

VIII

After she had thrown herself and her poetry out of the window, and Robert Graves had said goodbye to all that and gone to Majorca with her, Laura's sexual desire for him ended: all that was said goodbye to as well. What was resurrected from the paving at the back of 35A St Peter's Square was the word, and it was not, to Robert Graves's disappointment, made flesh. Sex, Laura claimed, was a distraction to mental life: 'I like men to be men and women to be women, but I think that bodies have had their day . . . Physicality only postpones judgement.'[66] In her reincarnated form Laura became a virgin and her body sought the same purity aspired to by her language. In a goddess this was to be expected, and Robert wrote the script: 'Though a woman so fated cannot help feeling physical desire for a man, she is forbidden by her identity with the Goddess from worshipping or giving herself wholly to him, even if he desires to worship and gives himself wholly to her.'[67] Robert did desire this, sorely, and their physical relationship was replaced on his part by affairs with house guests and on hers by writing almost everything in collaboration either with Robert or another good-looking heterosexual man. On occasion, Robert would be having sexual relations with the wife while Laura was writing with the husband. When George Ellidge was collaborating with Laura on *14a*, her ghastly dramatic novel about the events that led up to her leap, Mary Ellidge was consummating her relationship with Robert, and Laura and Robert wanted to repeat this arrangement with Tom Matthews and his wife Julie. They were turned down by the Matthewses, although Julie Matthews and Robert Graves had previously declared their love for one another.

But if collaboration was a kind of consummation, it was also a kind of consumption of the other person. So for all Laura's talk of language perfectly realizing the self in its clarity, through their word-by-word collaborations Laura and Robert were so thoroughly incorporated in one another that it was hard for them to tell who was who, and this produced endless disputes over authorship. Robert Graves's poetry became preoccupied with the theme of losing himself 'in damned confusion of myself and you' ('The Reader over my Shoulder'). Less aggressive was an earlier celebration of Laura, 'To Whom Else', in which he thankfully consented 'To my estrangement/From me in you'.

Who consumed whom in the Graves and Riding collaboration, and when does literary collaboration not involve consumption? Consuming someone, you obtain the qualities possessed by *them* even though they are a product of *you*. Devouring a person is another means of identifying with them, but in doing so you destroy precisely what it is you desired. Part of the pleasure of possession is the knowledge of the theft involved, and Graves and Riding would both begin to accuse one another of thieving as they tried to disentangle themselves.

In *A Pamphlet Against Anthologies* (1928), Graves and Riding's next book after *A Survey of Modernist Poetry*, they included a foreword in which they listed and chastised the 'vulgar' critics who had given priority to Graves in their reviews, despite the authors' statement that the book was a 'word-by-word' collaboration. This next work was also a 'word-by-word' collaboration, they declared. Robert Graves was adamant that in the writing they did together Laura's contribution should not only be recognized but her name should appear first, regardless of alphabetical rules of precedence. 'Graves and Riding,' he argued, was like 'Sullivan and Gilbert' or 'toast and tea'. Typical of Graves's defence of Laura's superiority was his exchange with Michael Roberts, the editor of T.S. Eliot's *Faber Book of Modern Verse*, who invited him to contribute some poems. Graves, irritated that he had been approached independently of Riding, as if he had a poetic identity separate from hers – which he insisted he did not – agreed to Michael Roberts' request on the condition that Riding be included too. And unless she be given more pages than Graves (she was originally given fewer) he threatened to withdraw his own poems. Finally, Laura wrote to say that she would only accept Michael Roberts' request for her poems if he wrote to her saying that he 'honestly' wanted seventeen pages of her work, and wasn't giving her this amount of space because he felt cornered and bullied. The anthology eventually contained thirteen pages of Riding's poems, followed by ten pages of Graves's.

When the couple separated, and 'the beast with two backs' was 'a single beast' no longer – as Graves put it in 'Sea Side' – the division of the words began. Laura Riding was outraged by William Empson's acknowledgement of Robert Graves's influence, and not her own, on his *Seven Types of Ambiguity*, and over twenty years later she began a squabble with Empson about her claim to the authorship of Chapter Three with its brilliant comparison of the original and the modern versions of Shakespeare's sonnet 'Th' expense of Spirit in a waste of shame'. Empson later confirmed his belief that it was Graves who had inspired him, only not in this particular work. His debt to Graves lay in two earlier books that explored the idea of ambiguity, and to Riding's fury Empson stated that 'modern literary criticism was invented by a number of people, but by Graves as much as any other individual'[68] – and this *before* she had come along.

In *Modern Language Quarterly* Robert Graves then confirmed his belief that he was the motor behind the chapter, but both he and Riding seemed to be more concerned to resurrect identities that had broken down than to claim academic kudos. As Graves wrote in 'Callow Captain':

> A wind ruffles the book, and he whose name
> Was mine vanishes; all is at an end.
> Fortunate soldier: to be spared shame
> Of chapter-years unprofitable to spend,
> To ride off into reticence, nor throw
> Before the story-sun a long shadow.

A long shadow was cast behind the next story on which they were to embark. In 1931 Jonathan Cape commissioned Robert to write a novel called *No Decency Left,* which Cape was determined would be a best-seller like *Goodbye To All That*. Robert drafted a plot but Laura, disliking it, kept the plan and rewrote the novel, claiming that she could turn it around into a money-spinner (having never made a penny out of her writing while Robert supported them both on his). So convinced was she the book was a winner that Laura wanted it published in her name only, conceding reluctantly when Cape insisted on the pseudonym of Barbara Rich. When *No Decency Left* was a dismal flop, Laura publicly disowned it and claimed it was by Robert, which in a sense of course it was.

Another pseudonym Laura had employed with Robert was 'Madeline Vara', and articles written under this name appeared in the multi-authored *Epilogue* series she was editing in Deyá. The object of *Epilogue: A Critical Summary* was to continue the search for the ultimate truth and to deal 'in an uncompromising authoritative way with the value of things'. The fourth and final edition was turned into a chaotic book, *The World and Ourselves*, in which Laura laid out her personal solution to the 'international problem'. In each edition a variety of articles was written on a range of subjects by the 'inner' group of people who frequented their homes in Deyá, and Robert claimed that the pseudonym was a 'house' name, used by any of the contributors who desired anonymity. Laura sometimes claimed it was her own personal *nom de plume* and at others that it was used by 'everybody and nobody'. Evidently, collaboration had gone too far for clear distinctions between authors to be made, and Laura found it hard to remember what she had written as Madeline Vara and what had been written by Robert. In a furious article published in 1973 called 'Some Autobiographical Corrections of Literary History', she claimed that an essay on Nietzsche in Graves's collection, *The Common Asphodel*, was by herself writing as 'Madeline Vara' and not by Robert, who had stolen the credit. Robert summed the problem up in 'To Bring the Dead to Life':

> Subdue your pen to his handwriting
> Until it prove as natural
> To sign his name as yours.

Writing with Laura was a matter, Tom Matthews said, of trying to 'survive the clutch of that octopus brain' of hers, and Robert clearly enjoyed the pain.

Collaboration for Laura was a game of possession and she never doubted that her way with words had not left her co-authors seduced. Robert Graves's abject kowtowing to her every literary whim was all the confirmation Laura needed of her phenomenal power. While they were writing *The Moon's No Fool* together, Tom Matthews arrived one morning to find the usually punctual Laura absent. Instead there was a long and complicated letter addressed to him, which needed to be read twice before he could grasp its meaning:

> As I read, my alarm deepened. The gist of it was that she knew the effect she made on me; that if I could master my feelings I was to remain in this room, she would come back and we would go on with our work as before; if, however, I could not be sure of controlling myself I was to get up and go, now; she would understand, she would not hold it against me, but we must not continue to work together. She would return to the room in fifteen minutes (five had already elapsed) for my answer.[69]

'What possessed me to stay?' Matthews still asked himself when he remembered this event thirty years later. He stayed because he was, as he says, possessed. You were no more likely to leave Laura Riding or to question her than you were to leave a game of poker in the middle or to question its rules. The point of Laura's game was that it had to be played to the bitter end, and 'to enter a game,' Baudrillard says, 'is to enter a system of ritual obligations'.[70]

Laura Riding's possession of him impaired Tom Matthews' reason as well as his potency, and when he described Laura's charms, Matthews meant it literally. As if he had been spellbound, he found himself believing that she was some kind of virago:

> Her brilliance, or mental force, was so dazzling and lightning-like that there was something frightening about it. Julie and I agreed that Laura's mind was supernormal but that she used her extraordinary powers for good, not evil. The way

we put it was: 'She's a witch, but a good witch.' We *believed* that.[71]

He later believed that 'Her literariness made [her] seem inhuman. It stripped her of her humanity.' The writer Robert Nye also saw the effect on him of Laura Riding's poems as being 'like spells'.[72] It was only when their relationship was breaking down that Robert tried to coerce an embarrassed friend into agreeing with him that Laura looked like a witch.

On the eve of the Spanish Civil War, Laura and Robert left Deyá, taking with them one suitcase each. Laura never came back, but when Robert returned ten years later with his second wife, he found his work as he had left it on the desk. After an unhappy time as exiles in London, Robert and Laura went for a year to France with a group of friends including a young recently married couple called Alan and Beryl Hodge, and Laura got them all working together on a *Dictionary of Exact Meanings*. Then, in January 1939, a copy of *Time* magazine arrived on the doormat containing a review of Laura Riding's *Collected Poems*, which had been published in America and without Robert's influence. Laura Riding, who had claimed when she left the States that she would never return, then decided that she wanted to go back that spring. There, with Robert, the Hodges and another friend, David Reeves, they would continue the dictionary plans. Even though the civil war was now declared over and they were free once more to go home to Deyá as they had planned, Robert didn't question the logic of this next move or the motives behind it, although at some level he knew that a seduction had taken place between reviewer and reviewed. When their boat docked in New York in April, it was exactly ten years since Laura Riding had jumped out of the window of 35A St Peter's Square.

The *Dictionary* was vital to Laura but she was also working on another group project called the 'Protocol', which was a continuation of her previous 'First Protocol of the Covenant of Literal

Morality', in which she attempted, by means of publishing letters from 'inside people' like herself, to inform the world's leaders of the immorality of their actions. The reason this leaden-sounding project attracted contributors at all may have been because Laura's certainty in the strength of her powers of reasoning was reassuring in the face of a second world war, and Robert for one needed reassurance.

Given that these dictionaries and protocols were the direction her writing now took, it should not have come as much of a surprise to Robert that shortly after they arrived in New Hope, Pennsylvania, Laura renounced him, poetry, and seduction altogether, in order to farm grapefruit in Wabasso instead, at the side of the handsome and athletic *Time* reviewer of her poems, Schuyler B. Jackson II. Laura married Schuyler in June 1941 and in her new life, which was marked by a change of name to Laura (Riding) Jackson, she concentrated all her energies on writing a *Dictionary of Related Meanings,* with Schuyler as her collaborator. The seductive Sapphic Goddess had become, as Samuel Johnson defined the lexicographer, a harmless drudge.

She gave up poetry, Laura said, because it had personally failed to reach *her* standards and not because she had failed as a poet. In her tangled accounts of why she stopped writing poems, Riding suggests that they had not managed to save her from herself: 'My kind of seriousness, in my looking to poetry for the rescue of human life from the indignities it was capable of visiting upon itself, led me to an eventual turning away from it as a failing of my kind of seriousness.'[73] Tom Matthews believes that Laura 'must have been ordered and enforced' by Schuyler B. Jackson to stop writing and he recounts a story told to him in which Laura was seen standing next to a stoical Jackson, weeping while she fed copious notes into a large bonfire. Another version of what happened to Laura is found in Graves's 1953 essay, 'Juana de Asbaje', which is haunted by the presence of his former muse. Here Robert mourns the fact that 'a possessed woman poet will rather subject herself to a dull husband or ignorant lover, who mistrusts her genius and may even ill-treat her physically, than encourage the love of a Catullus or Alcaeus, which demands more than it is hers to give'.[74] That was his story, and he was sticking to it.

'Would anyone practise literature for the sole purpose of sacrificing it?' the essayist Maurice Blanchot asks. 'We can only sacrifice what we believe exists. Thus one must believe in literature to begin with, believe in one's literary vocation, realise it – in other words, one must be a writer and nothing but a writer.'[75] Laura Riding's sacrifice was immense: renouncing literature was a mark of its seduction of her, as nothing is sacrificed that could be given up easily. The celibate writer gave up writing in order to return to the physical world. And yet her explanations for the sacrifice are curiously inadequate, being more than ever inarticulate and surprisingly lacking in analysis. For Laura Riding the case is a simple one: poetry failed to reach her level of High Seriousness. It is as if the 'truth' that poetry could not reach was something Very Serious Indeed, and this sense of her 'kind of seriousness' defines Laura Riding's work.

Riding's preoccupation with issues 'important' and 'serious' and her division of the serious from 'trivial' pleasure (as if serious thought cannot be enjoyable or as if pleasure can have no serious thought behind it) are also responsible for her increasingly legalistic and precise use of language. Laura's kind of seriousness is singular in the absence of pleasure it affords her reader: never has seriousness had such a bad press as in her descriptions of poetry. This example of Laura Riding Being Serious is chosen at random (it is hard to distinguish between passages let alone chose between them) from the introduction to *Poems: A Joking Word*, published in 1930. It is Laura's account of why she threw herself out of the window:

Before anything can be that has got to be, it has got to be preceded by something that hasn't got to be. These poems have got to be. Or rather, when they weren't, they had got to be. Or rather, I had got not to feel myself and think doom but to think myself and feel doom.

That is, what has got to be has got to be preceded. My preface has got to precede these poems, though it hasn't itself got to be. And I had got to write these poems, though I hadn't myself got to be. I had only got to precede. I had only got to write. I had only got to be as to the writing of these poems that had got to be, I had not got to feel myself and think doom but I had got to think myself and feel doom.[76]

The pity is that Laura Riding did not renounce prose instead. The same meditation on the exact meaning of the word 'doom' goes on in a similar vein for page after page: 'I had only got to feel doom . . . doom is where I am . . . And by doom I don't mean the destruction of me . . . Made into doom I feel made . . . Doom is what has got to be . . . But doom can't mean dooms because doom means complete doom . . . Poems are particularly to feel doom . . . Doom is . . . Poems are doom like doom coming up last and therefore at first like poems . . . But you haven't the word dooms . . .' What Riding is trying to represent stretches to snapping point the possibilities of what can be either written or read, and the more she argues for the clarity of the literal truth in writing, the more opaque her writing becomes. It is as if after her jump Laura Riding no longer felt as if language belonged to her: she is speaking a foreign tongue here. Either way, doom sets in for the reader as well. Reading Laura Riding becomes as enjoyable as reading the telephone directory, and the only viable response to her prose is to throw oneself out of the window in sympathy.

'This was the road by which I travelled in the making of a dictionary,' Laura Riding later explained. 'The meanings of words,

I had come to feel, had to be known with perfect distinctness before they could be used with perfect truthfulness.'[77] Work on the dictionary she devoted herself to after 1939 had in fact been going on in various forms since 1933, when she had discussed the idea with Jacob Bronowski, then a brilliant Cambridge undergraduate, who had been invited to visit Laura and Robert after he wrote a pleasing review of *Poems: A Joking Word* (the friendship lasted for several years, until he defied Laura's authority). Laura's initial plan was to purge 24,000 words of ambiguity and improper meaning, and she was never to give up on this project. Oxford University Press was unattracted by the rigidity of Laura's proposal, while Schuyler B. Jackson II thought it was worth marrying her for, and twenty years later, when she was still struggling with Schuyler to define 100 words a day, Little Brown, who had given them a contract, gave up the ghost and retracted. The dictionary was abandoned, and in its place Laura and Schuyler wrote an account of the difficulties they had encountered in writing it, *Rational Meaning: A New Foundation for the Definition of Words*. Laura finished the book seven years after Schuyler's death, but it has never been published in full.

Having seen herself when she was with Robert Graves as *full* of poetic words, after she left him, in 1939, Laura Riding dedicated her time as a dictionary-maker to *emptying words out*, to unloading language and displaying it in all its homonyms, synonyms, etymology, and various usages. Her preoccupation was with fixing meaning, screwing it to its sticking point, as if she feared it might easily become unfixed and run amok, taking the writer with it. There was something essentially satisfying for Laura in her attempt to show at once all the meanings and potential directions of words; to say, with clinical objectivity, everything that it is possible to say, and without involving *herself* at all. This mighty task was taken on by someone who, as John Crowe Ransom said of Laura when she was first published in the *Fugitive*, 'had neither birth, subsistence, place, reputation nor friends, and was a very poor little woman indeed'.[78] Reaching further and further back into the English language, it is as if Laura Reichenthal, Gottschalk, Riding Gottschalk, Riding, Jackson, (Riding) Jackson, who adopted an English accent, was shedding her own layers and trying to find her own origin.

'Seriousness,' Allon White has argued, 'always has more to do with power than with content. The authority to designate what is to be taken seriously (and the authority to enforce reverential solemnity in certain contexts) is a way of creating and maintaining power.'[79] Seriousness aligns itself with social prestige and its attendants: Good Taste, High Culture, Importance, and Difficulty. But there is nowhere that seriousness is taken more seriously than in a dictionary, where serious words assume the upper hand and define the frivolous, where a naturalized 'official' language defines the unofficial and different languages of dialects, regions, and 'lower' orders. It is here that the division between sober and thoughtful 'high' language and trifling 'low' language, the language of common usage, is authorized and reproduced. If Laura Riding had turned to poetry because it was a way of being elite, she now renounced it, she said in the introduction to the 1980 revised edition of her *Collected Poems*, precisely *because* it was elite. Poetry revealed its sacred truths in a 'high' language whose 'word-use' 'speaking-range' and 'meaning-effectuality' are not employed in 'common', ' 'low' usage. 'Poetry bears in itself the message that it is the destiny of human beings to speak the meaning of being, but it nurses it in itself as in a sacred apartness, not to be translated into the language of common meanings in its delivery.'[80] Poetry's exclusivity came as something of a surprise to her, but the fact that Laura Riding then went on to carve in stone the differences between serious high and trivial low language types suggests that she wanted to be taken more seriously than her poetry could even begin to allow for.

As a dictionary-maker, Laura moved from being a modernist to being a Victorian. Not only was her exchange of poetry for grapefruit and etymology Jamesian in its scale of aesthetic sacrifice (think of Milly Theale falling silent and turning her face to the wall, or Isabel Archer marrying that charlatan, Osmond) but Laura Riding's dedicated belief that the key to truth could be found in the origins of words was quintessentially mid-nineteenth-century. The *Dictionary of Related Meanings* is as heroic as Richard Burton's search for the source of the Nile, as visionary as Darwin's desire to trace the origin of species, as flawed as Casaubon's 'Key to All Mythologies', and about as seductive. George Eliot's *Middlemarch* is typical of the nineteenth-century novel's concern with the vexed question of origins, which articulates itself most obviously in the Victorian leitmotif of orphans not knowing where they have come from and thus not knowing who they are, as if knowledge of the former ensured certainty of the latter. While Laura Riding is closer to the rootless Will Ladislaw, with his Polish father and restless disposition, she would clearly identify herself with Edward Casaubon, the taxonomist whose genuis went unacknowledged. Like Casaubon, Riding chose for herself a project that could never be completed.

For every Casaubon there is a Dorothea Brooke to believe in him, and Laura found hers in Schuyler B. Jackson. Schuyler achieved what Dorothea, who had only ever wanted to do the filing, had only dreamed of. He became a fully-fledged equal in the research that would dominate his and Laura's marriage. Laura's final book, *The Telling*, published in 1972, four years after Schuyler died and Laura took up her pen again, is dedicated 'To Schuyler, my husband, my partner in the endeavour to take words and oneself further . . .' Robert Graves, who was thought to be Laura Riding's butler when they first arrived in Deyá, was never granted such privileges. But then with Graves, Laura had taken words and herself no further than the concrete slabs outside the window from which she fell.

The weighty 'seriousness' of Laura Riding's mission was her seductive lure, her siren's song. Laura's gravity was her appeal and it exercised fantastic power over those around her, making fools of them all. When, in 1939, she persuaded Robert Graves and their dictionary entourage to go with her to America she argued that their trip was not in order to escape the Second World War but so as to prevent it. The party stayed with Tom Matthews and then with his friend Schuyler Jackson – who was building a house, no less, for these people he had never met – and as ever Laura turned their family homes into her official HQ, reorganizing the furniture and the domestic routine, disciplining the children, having everyone rushing about on errands for her while insisting that she be given the best bedrooms, breakfast in bed, and total privacy when she needed it. In the evenings Laura would lead group discussions about the world situation, which were characterized by deafening silences; the other discussion point was everyone's love for Laura, which they were required to reiterate before they could belong to her group: 'Our visitors dwindled to none as word got about that something was going on at our house – something that felt like sitting up with a dead body,' Tom Matthews said.[81]

The war was to be impeded by Laura's 'Protocol', and during its production she consummated the affair with Schuyler Jackson that had begun with the review of her poems. Physicality was no longer thought to postpone judgement (oddly, in the circumstances) and after they had been locked in Schuyler and his wife's bedroom for two days, Laura emerged to announce to the rest of the household: 'Schuyler and I do.' While Schuyler's rejected spouse, Kit, was subsequently falling to pieces in a mental hospital, leaving her four children abandoned, her clothes and belongings were burned in one of Laura's ritual purgings. The degree to which Robert Graves was oddly complicit in Laura's game to win Schuyler is evident by his inhumane behaviour to the warm and welcoming Kit Jackson. Unsupportive and unsympathetic to the last towards her plight,

Graves acted as if all were fair in love and war, and he stood by and watched as Laura supplanted Kit at the dinner table and then in the bedroom. Miranda Seymour suggests that in his 'melodramatic glee' it may even have been Graves who gave the hint to Laura that Kit was a witch. He certainly spread it around his friends that Kit had tried to seduce him one night by climbing into his bed. The result was that during her stay with the Jacksons, Laura Riding seduced six educated adults into seriously believing not only that their close friend and hostess practised black arts because a pile of sanitary towels had been left on the bathroom floor in a cryptic manner, but that together they could write enough to avert the Holocaust. She convinced Schuyler anyway, who had long felt his life to be devoid of purpose and his talents to be wasted.

Laura was back to square one: she gave Schuyler the kick-start she had given Robert Graves back in 1926, and as Robert had done before him, Schuyler left his wife and four young children for a life of words with Laura. Laura's game had started all over again and with a new set of players.

IX

Schuyler B. Jackson had been told about Laura Riding by his college friend Tom Matthews. Matthews had also talked about Schuyler to Laura: he adored Schuyler and thought he had the most brilliant mind of any man he knew. He was convinced that the two of them would like one another. Schuyler was not at all the hero Tom Matthews made him out to be. Disappointed in his marriage and his ambitions (he had failed in every career he had attempted so far), Schuyler Jackson was drinking heavily and dreaming of an alternative life. Meanwhile his empty affair with a figure skater had now come to an end. He saw himself as a serious contender whose life had been reduced to mundane trivia, and when, aged thirty-eight, he opened Laura's new book, he found just these issues of seriousness and triviality discussed in her introduction. Given his state, Laura therefore felt that in taking Schuyler away from his family she had only done what any committed literary critic in her position would do: she was saving his soul with words. Schuyler also read in her preface to the *Collected Poems* Laura's reassurance to her readers that with her, as 'with few other poets . . . readers [are] safe from being seduced into emotions or states of mind which are *not poetic*'. Laura's readers are only seduced into *poetic* states of mind, but then Laura Riding is poetry itself and so the reader is seduced into a state of mind in which he or she is entirely possessed by her.

This is what happened to Schuyler Jackson. A jobbing reporter, he was occasionally given work in *Time* by Tom Matthews, and when he read Laura's *Collected Poems* he identified himself as one of her elite readers and set out to review her book. The review, which would eventually bring Laura Riding back to America from thirteen years in Europe, was no easy task. Finding her poetic philosophy very difficult to understand and thus to write about, Schuyler turned to Tom Matthews for help, and Matthews, himself baffled, turned to Graves for advice. Given the composition of the collaborative group working on the reception of her *Collected Poems*, Laura had a hand in her own review: everyone quite consciously wrote what she wanted to hear and so she was seduced by herself. Schuyler was seduced by his 'own' writing too, and he thought the published review a landmark in literary criticism. Up to this point, Schuyler's only claim to literary fame had been when he met W. B. Yeats in Ireland and was championed by him in the Irish Parliament as the next great poet, Yeats having not yet read any of Schuyler's poetry.

Schuyler's poetry was unread by Laura as well and she didn't much mind that his review was not his own: literary seductions occur through the word and not through the writer. His review was the high point of Laura's career, and he lavished praise on her for taking on the 'responsibility' to make 'words make . . . sense'. Rilke and Riding were the only true poets, Schuyler said, and Laura Riding was thus the only great living poet: no one had said this about Laura since she said it herself in *A Survey of Modernist Poetry*. Her book was 'the book of books of the mid-twentieth century'. The review was so adulatory, so *grateful* – so like the letter Geoffrey Phibbs sent to Robert Graves about Laura's work ten years earlier – that when it was passed around the table, Dorothy Simmons, a sculptress and guest at the Graves and Riding home, exclaimed: 'I think the man's in love with you.'[82] She was ticked off by Laura for being vulgar (a favourite word), but four months later Laura went to Pennsylvania to meet her perfect reader. Schuyler never read another poem of Laura Riding's because she never wrote one again: Laura had indeed become 'Finality'. It is appropriate that someone obsessed with rewriting origins should give herself such a clean literary ending – before starting out on a renewed search for beginnings.

That was the last time Robert Graves would ever see Laura Riding, and he returned to England in 1940 without her. Laura went to Florida with Schuyler and she stayed there until she died in 1991. They lived in misanthropic isolation; Schuyler gradually became estranged from his children and when he died in 1968 it was because, his ex-wife Kit believed, 'the shock of facing the enormity of his error was more than his heart could stand'.[83] Following Schuyler's death, Laura occasionally put pen to paper to write something furious about Robert Graves stealing from her. In her indignant rage there is an echo of June Mansfield's fury with Henry Miller, for Laura had also been invented by her partner and then plundered, although perhaps not in the literal way she believed.

Initially, after she had got together with Schuyler, Laura had suggested that Robert go back to Nancy and he thought about it enough for Nancy to believe it was a possibility. Instead he asked her for a divorce (which she gave him ten years later) and in 1940 Graves set up home with the homely Beryl Hodge, who left Alan for him, and he quickly became a father again. Graves and Beryl had begun to fall in love when they were living with Laura in France, and Laura, noticing that Robert was no longer recording her jokes in his diary, took him aside to tell him how incompatible he and Beryl would be as a couple. When Nancy divorced him, Graves married Beryl and he stayed married to her until his death in December 1985.

While Beryl briefly tried to impersonate the awesome Laura Riding by attempting to intimidate her guests, with her love of cats and hedgehogs and her quiet decency she was no muse. Neither did she write and because he had to work in sexual triangles, Robert began their life together by collaborating with Beryl's husband, Alan Hodge, on a study of social history in England between the wars called *The Long Weekend*. Robert Graves was later that year to receive a letter from Schuyler Jackson that severely chastised him for his relationship with Beryl and gave him news of Laura's well-being. She was now recovering, Robert would be glad to hear, from the 'miraculously held-together heap of human wreckage that Laura became in attempting to save your soul with words.'[84]

X

Which brings us full circle back to Geoffrey Phibbs, because this salvation is precisely what he wanted from Laura as he held together the heap of human wreckage he had become when his wife had her affair with David Garnett. And Graves described in much the same terms as Schuyler Jackson the mess that Phibbs had reduced Laura to when he rejected her writing. Before he joined Laura Riding and Robert Graves, in the spring of 1929, Geoffrey Phibbs had moved in the same Dublin circles as A.E. and W. B. Yeats. Hogarth Press had recently published a collection of his poems with the remarkably apt title – if we recall the effect on both him and Tom Matthews of working with Laura – *The Withering of the Figleaf*. But Phibbs is better known today as Geoffrey Taylor, under which name he later collaborated with John Betjeman on an anthology of English Love Poems and one on British landscape. He also went on to write books about insects and Victorian gardens. The writer Frank O'Connor, a friend of Phibbs in Ireland, described him as 'lov[ing] poetry as no one else I have ever known loved it', and while Laura Riding was his favourite poet, it was her two 1928 collections of critical essays, *Anarchism Is Not Enough* and *Contemporaries and Snobs*, that inspired him to correspond with Graves and to enclose some poems of his own to be passed on for Laura's approval.

Laura Riding had always been under the shadow of Robert Graves, who was taken seriously, who got whatever he wanted published by the best publishers, and who knew every literary personage in England. She was therefore delighted by her impact on Geoffrey Phibbs. So much so, in fact, that she barely responded to the poems he sent her, just as she had been uninterested in any of the work produced by the Fugitive group in Nashville. Laura Riding was interested in being seductive and not in being seduced and in every case of literary seduction she was seduced by men who found *her* work seductive. Rather than doing as most writers would who were offered a compliment, simply thanking Geoffrey Phibbs for his kind remarks and giving a few of her own, Laura Riding invited her admirer to come and live with her and Graves in London. Which was precisely what Robert Graves had done three years earlier when he read Laura's 'The Quids'. And just as Geoffrey Phibbs had communicated his seduction by Laura vicariously through Robert Graves, Robert had communicated his own earlier seduction through Allen Tate and John Crowe Ransom. Later, the seduction between Schuyler and Laura was mediated by Tom Matthews, who was possessed by them both, but rather than ask

Schuyler to come and live with her and Graves in Europe, Laura opted to go to him instead. As Graves – or was it Laura? – wrote, 'There is one story and one story only, That will prove worth your telling,' and they repeated theirs over and over again.

After he received Laura Riding's telegraphic summons in February 1929, Geoffrey Phibbs – seemingly in the trance Laura had reduced Robert to – packed in his journalism and left Ireland, accompanied by his more sceptical wife, Norah McGuinness. He introduced himself to Laura at her flat where he (and only he), Norah remembered, 'was received with open arms'. Laura described her first impression of Phibbs in her novel, *14a*, as 'very black-looking; his face seems dark and hot. His eyes are blue, but these too seem dark, as if intensely preoccupied with something that had just happened to him.' The ignored Norah was, Frank O'Connor (who loved her) wrote to Geoffrey Phibbs, 'the finest woman in Ireland' and in the same chastising letter O'Connor correctly anticipated that 'in three months time you will be the most miserable man in Ireland'. In three months time Phibbs was indeed to tell Laura, 'I did what I did and am terribly terribly unhappy.' To Robert he would write: 'I'll never see the end of my own futility,' that even though he now no longer wanted to be a part of it, Laura 'still had the greatest mind and all that . . .' Geoffrey's rather pedestrian character is gloriously apparent in his muddled letters to Laura, Norah, and to Robert Graves, who made him 'so bluddy nervous that where I spoke afterwards I think I put things wrong'.[85]

While he was clearly a lightweight, hardly able to make up his mind or to hold his own in a conversation, in every account of Geoffrey Phibbs he is seen as powerfully 'satanic' or demonic. This is how he is described by Frank O'Connor ('There was something about him that was vaguely satanic') and by Frank O'Connor's landlady (who asked that Phibbs stop calling as 'he was the Devil'[86]), as well as by Laura Riding herself, and with such numbing repetition that one wants to hand her a thesaurus. She described the events around her jump in allegorical terms, and for the Virgin Mary read Nancy Nicholson. This is from the preface to *Poems: A Joking Word*:

> Once upon a time I was standing in a room with the Virgin Mary who was also Medea and so on, and the Devil who was also a Judas and so on . . . And the Devil and so on, though pretending to be with doom . . . He was only the Devil and so on. And he knew it . . . And as he was the Devil and so on and therefore could behave only underhandedly . . . The Devil and so on might be called a poet against poems. But standing in that room the quick result was that he was only the Devil and so on.[87]

And so on. The prosaic Geoffrey Phibbs sits uneasily alongside these cloven-hoofed reports, and reminds one of Henry Miller's and Anaïs Nin's descriptions of the tiny June Mansfield as a towering inferno. In another version of her jump, a short story called 'Obsession', Laura Riding called Geoffrey Phibbs and Nancy Nicholson 'the Nunquam' and 'the Pridem'; Phibbs was 'of old the Devil', denouncing Laura Riding as 'only a witch'.

Shambling and impoverished when he arrived in London, the 'Irish Adonis' – as Wyndam Lewis called Geoffrey in the stories about 'free love corner' with which he entertained New York literary circles – had brought with him only £6, borrowed from his parents. Laura's first move in 'shedding' him of the past (because this was essential in proving his loyalty to her and to poetry) was to burn the few clothes he possessed in order to remove their contamination by Norah, just as she would burn, ten years later, the possessions of Kit Jackson when she fell in love with Schuyler. Robert Graves was left to lend Geoffrey items from his own wardrobe, including underpants and socks, each of which was itemized in an inventory that he sent to Phibbs when relations broke down irretrievably several months later.

What is interesting in Laura's destruction of others' property and the repetition of expunging inconvenient people is the *ritual* she established in order to achieve these ends. The routine of ritual again conforms to the logic of the game, where the ceremonial observation of rules and repetitions takes on a pleasure and a purpose of its own. Rituals represent a desire to remember as opposed to an exorcism, and the repetition of Laura's behaviour implies that whatever she was trying to get rid of wouldn't go away but that she needed to commemorate the act of expulsion. In burning the possessions of a lover's wife, or the possessions of a lover that have been touched by his wife, or even her own poetry, Laura was endlessly getting rid of the third party in the way of her relationship, whilst she needed this third party in order to have the relationship in the first place. Robert Graves, who routinely invited a muse into his marriage to ensure the presence of a third person, called this game of Laura's 'wiping the slate clean' when he wrote about her in *The Long Weekend*. Laura performed this act of erasure again and again, eventually wiping out all traces of her partnership with Graves. Rewriting was the story of Laura Riding's life.

When Robert was living with Laura at 35A St Peter's Square, Nancy and their four young children shared a barge on the Thames at a nearby mooring point. Graves and Riding romanticized, or rather mythologized, their set-up by calling it 'The Holy Circle', the 'three-life', and 'the Trinity', and by drawing analogies between their own way of living and the lifestyle of Percy Bysshe Shelley, apparently missing the fact that the Romantic poet's domestic ideology made every woman he would ever encounter utterly miserable. So the flat at 35A was optimistically known as 'Free Love Corner', which suggests that there was both a shared philosophy of freedom and a relaxed attitude to sharing, neither of which Norah McGuinness was to find when she arrived there with her husband. Norah later described how, having reached St Peter's Square,

I was unimportant, an outsider and must be got rid of. Laura, as cold as the cheap sparkling trinkets with which she was covered, accompanied Geoffrey and they brought me to the Regent Palace Hotel – thrust a bottle of Brandy in my hand and said 'Drink this and forget your tears.' Then they left me in the desolate bedroom. I had practically never drunk Brandy in my life and, not knowing how to drink it, swallowed half a bottle. I could have killed myself. On the third day I went down to the Lounge – and a nightmare which still haunts me was the constant crying of room numbers by the page boys.[88]

Norah soon returned to Ireland, however, allowing room for the inevitable affair between her husband and Laura Riding to begin its near fatal course. During his short time with the Holy Trinity, which now included Nancy and became the 'four-life', Geoffrey was educated in the use of Riding and Graves's printing press, called the Seizin, and he took Robert's place as Laura's intellectual ally. Geoffrey had moved from a state of 'non-conscious, non-happiness to a state of conscious happiness', he said, but before eight weeks were up his interest in Laura Riding was exhausted, not least because it involved sleeping with Robert Graves as well. He learned that Laura would not contemplate leaving Robert for him; at this stage in her life she was unable to conceive of having a relationship with one person alone, so if Phibbs wanted her at all he would have to stay in the group.

Living at 35A was exhausting in other ways too, and it seemed that Laura's desire for the 'literal truth' was a fairly relative affair. Geoffrey gave Norah an account of a day spent by Laura locked in the lavatory because he had said that she was smaller than his wife. She only came out when he conceded that Laura was the taller of the two (which she wasn't). When her brother Bobby was born – thus threatening another happy couple – Laura had locked her mother in the lavatory until the initial horror had gone away. Another illustration of Laura's behaviour is given by Frank O'Connor, who describes visiting Phibbs on March 29 and being

> shaken when Phibbs told me that the Woman poet was at work and must not be disturbed, because even I was observant enough to see the unfinished sentence in her handwriting on the paper before me, with the ink still wet. I was even more disturbed when I lit a cigarette and he told me that she did not like smoking. She disapproved of ashes – and of crumbs, so we would smoke and eat on the barge.[89]

Laura Riding's chain-smoking was in fact so bad that it made her ill. This was not 'farce', Frank O'Connor said, but 'tragedy', and he accused Phibbs of exhibiting 'Satanic pride' in his actions. During this period Laura also, as Richard Perceval Graves puts it, 'revealed to Phibbs (as presumably she had already done to Graves) that she was more than human. They could think of her, if they liked, as a goddess.'[90]

While Robert Graves masterminded the mythologizing of Laura Riding, Geoffrey Phibbs missed living with someone who could be treated as a human being. After a conversation on Nancy's barge between Geoffrey and Robert, in which Robert said that his own relationship with Laura was threatened by Geoffrey's presence, Phibbs began plotting his escape. Graves would never be allowed to recover from the guilt of his complicity in Laura's rejection, and the fact that it almost cost her her life explains the shift in power-relations between the couple after her jump. Borrowing the necessary money from an aunt who lived nearby, on 1 April Geoffrey ran away from St Peter's Square to Paris, where he met up with Norah, and they went together to Rouen for a second honeymoon. Just as Phibbs had been too weak to tell Laura that he wanted to leave her, she was too cowardly to respect his decision (possibly because of the feeble love letters he continued to send), and she planned to chip away at his evident frailty until he was back in her power.

A search party was therefore dispatched for Laura's erstwhile lover and when Phibbs was located in France, she went herself on 6 April, accompanied by Robert and Nancy, to retrieve him. Laura grudgingly suggested to Geoffrey that they could turn the 'four-life' into a 'five-life' by inviting Norah McGuinness into the fold, but not surprisingly, this tactic failed. Not even the promise of all writing a dictionary together would tempt Norah. '[N]othing, not even losing Geoff, would induce me to go to what I thought was the mad house of Hammersmith,' she remarked. 'So I just said "No." '[91] When Phibbs proved the stronger for being apart from her and he and Norah refused to return to England, Laura Riding had an hysterical attack on the floor of the hotel foyer, where she collapsed screaming with her legs in the air. Robert Graves managed to dignify Laura's behaviour by romantically referring to the episode as the time when she 'seemed to die'. Her convulsions, he said, were like his own experience of being severely wounded in the trenches thirteen years before and at a spot nearby.

Geoffrey Phibbs went from France to the family estate in Sligo where Laura, who, as Allen Tate observed, would not be dissuaded of her tendency, sent him strange coded messages in the form of bus tickets, odd coins, and bits of twisted wire. When these also failed to retrieve him, Nancy Nicholson was promptly dispatched to Lisheen, the Phibbs family house. It was his father's rudeness to Nancy when she arrived – believing she was Laura, he ordered the whore off his grounds – that resulted in Geoffrey's changing his name to Taylor. Geoffrey had now lost his wife, his job, his clothes, his books, his father, and his name. Nancy, however, was in love with him, and she persuaded Geoffrey to return to Hammersmith. He had no sooner made than he broke his promise and went instead to see David Garnett, whose recent affair with Norah had driven him into the arms of Laura Riding's poems in the first place. It was at Garnett's house that Graves finally tracked Phibbs down, having hired a special train in order to do so. Geoffrey Phibbs was dragged out of bed by Robert Graves, and the pursuer and the pursued returned to Laura late in the evening on Friday, 26 April.

An argument between Geoffrey Phibbs, Laura Riding, Robert Graves and Nancy Nicholson ensued immediately the men returned. Phibbs, at the end of his tether, still refused to continue the 'four-life' or to construct a 'five-life', and the following morning, as he proved less and less tractable, Laura bid 'Goodbye chaps' and slipped off the window ledge on which she had been sitting. Phibbs, 'saying that he couldn't stand it',[92] also left the room, with much the same indecent haste as Laura and without discovering whether she was dead or alive. Robert Graves bolted down the stairs to reach her but, realizing that there was nothing much he could now do, left the building also, from the third-floor window. It was left up to Nancy to phone for an ambulance. Later that day, after he had informed the police – who suspected him guilty of attempted murder – that Laura was a vampire, Geoffrey bumped into Nancy in a West End cinema and spent the night on the barge where she was living with her children. There they stayed in harmony for five years until Phibbs left to marry someone else. Nancy's children always looked on him as a father figure and Laura and Robert would never forgive him his betrayal.

XI

In *14a*, Laura's novel about the events at 35A – which is so narcissistic that it could have been written by Anaïs Nin – she describes Geoffrey's crime as being his attempt to control the story they were co-authoring. When Geoffrey suggests that the two of them might run off together, Laura (or 'Catherine') has to patiently explain to Phibbs (or 'Hugh') that 'You can't cut others out of the story just to simplify it. It's not only your story, remember . . .'

Geoffrey Phibbs forgot that they were collaborating; stories, like babies, are the product of two people. In Laura's rewriting of events, Phibbs pleads with his lover to let him have one more harmless collaboration for old times' sake, and her will eventually gives way:

HUGH: . . . Oh, Catherine . . . Have you really forgiven me?
CATHERINE: It's not a question of forgiving, Hugh. If we can only quiet down now, all of us.
HUGH: We must, Catherine. And we'll do that book together, about the knowledge of good and evil? That would keep me quiet.
CATHERINE: Why, yes, Hugh. Whatever you like . . . I don't want to *write* – but if we do it as you said: you asking me questions, and I answering them, and you putting it all down . . .
ERIC: And we could all work on it. There are so many questions to ask that only Catherine can answer.
CATHERINE: Oh, you'd soon get the trick of answering them yourselves.[93]

Laura's revenge on Frank O'Connor for being Phibbs's friend and for loving her rival, Norah, is to have him (in the guise of 'Andy') say to her, 'Catherine, I want to tell you to your face that you are the spiritual Medusa of the age . . . It's like being inside a book – a cruel, tragic book.' Looking Medusa in the face and becoming involved in one of Laura Riding's books have the same effect, as Geoffrey Phibbs and Tom Matthews discovered to their cost. Norah McGuinness meanwhile, who appeared as Maureen the thief, sued the publisher for libel and *14a* was withdrawn.

But it is through the figure of Athene and not Medusa that the tale of Robert Graves and Laura Riding's literary consumption can best be understood, as they had both swallowed Athene's story whole. In his *Greek Myths*, Graves gives an account of the extraordinary birth of the virgin warrior who was also the Goddess of Wisdom and of Crafts, and Athene's biography reads much like the rewriting of her own life history by Laura Riding.

> Zeus lusted after Metis the Titaness, who turned into many shapes to escape him until she was caught at last and got with child. An oracle of Mother Earth then declared that this would be a girl-child and that, if Metis conceived again, she would bear a son who was fated to depose Zeus . . . Therefore, having coaxed Metis to couch with honeyed words, Zeus suddenly opened his mouth and swallowed her, and that was the end of Metis, though he claimed afterwards that she gave him counsel from inside his belly. In due process of time, he was seized by a raging headache as he walked by the shores of Lake Triton, so that his skull seemed about to burst, and he howled for rage until the whole firmament echoed. Up ran Hermes, who at once divined the cause of Zeus's discomfort. He persuaded Hephaestus, or some say Prometheus, to fetch his wedge and beetle and make a breach in Zeus's skull, from which Athene sprang, fully armed, with a mighty shout.[94]

With Robert Graves, Laura Riding had a collaboration of the sort enjoyed by Zeus and Athene. Like Zeus, Graves created a war-like female born of his wisdom. Athene and Laura Riding both burst forth ready-formed from the masculine mind rather than the feminine body. Athene was 'possessed' by Zeus but, as with Graves and Riding, it is unclear who inhabited whom. Athene was incorporated in her father and no more than an extension of him, but in carrying Zeus around and serving as his 'obedient mouth-piece' he became an extension of her too. Like Laura Riding on 27 April 1929, Athene was possessed by a man from whom she leapt with a doom-echoing shout. Later, Tom Matthews described experiencing another of Laura's Athenian births when he collaborated on a writing project with her and found that 'the effort of continuous concentration was so intense that at times I experienced an almost physical sensation that my head was actually splitting'.[95]

Once Laura Riding had given up poetry there was no further role in her life for Robert Graves. Like the cruel Goddess she was, Laura rejected her poet, and like the Muse-obsessive he was, Graves found another incarnation to consume, and then another, and then another. But none of his future muses was a warrior like Laura, who spat him out and left him riding roughshod. So when Laura Riding went back to her origins in Wabasso, Robert Graves began searching for copies in Deyá, but they both continued to battle over their story. Thirty years later Graves was still writing about the literary femme fatale whose poem pushed him as far as he could go. Like Laura, he was looking for the final word.

> The pride of 'bearing it out even to the edge of doom' that sustains a soldier in the field, governs a poet's service to the Muse. It is not masochism, or even stupidity, but a determination that the story shall end gloriously: a willingness to risk all wounds and hardships, to die weapon in hand.[96]

FOUR

Literary Containment:
Osip and Nadezhda Mandelstam

The house was quiet and the world was calm.
The reader became the book; and summer night

Was like the conscious being of the book.
The house was quiet and the world was calm.

The words were spoken as if there was no book . . .

WALLACE STEPHENS

27 December 1938. Schuyler B. Jackson II's review of Laura
Riding's *Collected Poems* is in the post, and will reach her in six days'
time. Four months later she will return to America, lured into the
arms of her seduced reader. When she arrives she will discard
Robert Graves and her possession by his muse to begin a poetic
silence that will last for the rest of her long life. Meanwhile, on his
way to do five years forced labour in Siberia, Russia's celebrated
lyric poet, Osip Mandelstam, dies for one of his poems. He is in a
transit camp near Vladivostok, nearly 6000 miles from Moscow
where, four months ago, his journey began. His defeated health –
'I'm . . . utterly exhausted, emaciated, and almost beyond
recognition,' he wrote to his brother shortly before he perished –
was precisely the result of his refusal to be silent at a time when to
write as he was writing was suicidal.

   Not that this particular poem had ever been written down, at
least not by Mandelstam himself, nor even by his wife, amanuensis
and greatest reader, Nadezhda Yakovlevna. But then the story of
Osip and Nadezhda Mandelstam extends our understanding of the
processes of writing and reading and of the secret dialogue between

the writer and the reader until these terms and positions adopt an entirely different range of meanings. Their story also extends our understanding of literary seductions, because literature – in the sense of writing, manuscripts, letters – hardly exists here, and Mandelstam's poetry had Nadezhda most firmly in its seductive grip in the years after his death, when she turned herself into his living archive, trading her flesh for his words.

The subject of Mandelstam's writing was, he said, 'philology', which means literally the 'love of the word' (*philia* is 'love' and *logos* is 'word'). This intense concentration on the etymological echoes of the language is typical of Mandelstam, and it is one of the reasons why translations of his poetry are so unsatisfactory, appearing so unlike the poetry he describes writing and Russian speakers describe reading. 'They are like dreams,' the great Symbolist poet Alexander Blok said of Mandelstam's early poems, 'but dreams exclusively from the field of culture.' Because he spoke his poetry out loud during composition rather than silently writing it down, Mandelstam's words have a 'distinctive sound quality', his translator Richard McKane says. 'Not only do Mandelstam's poems rhyme, but also sounds and roots evoke other sounds and roots. Form and content unite in an unsplittable whole in the Russian.'[1] 'The English speaking world,' the poet Joseph Brodsky wrote, 'has yet to hear this nervous, high-pitched, pure voice shot through with love, terror, memory, culture, faith – a voice trembling, perhaps, like a match burning in a high wind, yet utterly inextinguishable.'[2]

While the conditions he was writing under were vastly different from those of the other writers encountered so far, writing for Mandelstam was every bit as necessary as it was for Henry Miller and Anaïs Nin, Robert Graves and Laura Riding. In fact, precisely because of the extreme circumstances under which he worked, writing became more urgent for Mandelstam: 'The integrity of man is evident from his attitude to the word,' Leo Tolstoy said, and for Mandelstam to have given up on the word would have been a mark of political as well as of personal defeat. Writing became for Mandelstam an ethical act in a society that had become ethically moribund, and it represented hope when the best one could hope for was to be buried with a headstone. Theirs was not a normal era, Nadezhda Mandelstam wrote, 'when each person lives out his life to his own separate and individual death and poems lie quietly about in desks or in the forms of books, awaiting the hour of unbiased judgement'.[3] Theirs was an era of mass destruction; of the extermination of books, manuscripts, and human beings.

Writing for Mandelstam no more involved pushing a pen along a sheet of paper than Nadezhda's reading of his work involved passively perusing the pages of a book. 'I have no manuscripts, no notebooks, no archives,' Mandelstam proclaimed. 'I have no handwriting because I never write. I alone in Russia work from the voice, while all around the bitch pack writes. What the hell kind of writer am I!?'[4] And what the hell kind of reader was Nadezhda Mandelstam? Her reading of Mandelstam was so close that it knew no barriers or resistances; it was a reading in which she devoured the words and incorporated the writing, making it a part of herself. Nadezhda Mandelstam read her husband like an open book and she took the activity literally. Her reading of Mandelstam became a parody of reading as it is defined by Sven Birkerts in *The Gutenberg Elegies*: 'We bring the words, set in the intensely suggestive sequences and cadences of the writer, into ourselves. We engulf them in our consciousness and then allow ourselves to be affected by them.'[5] So what kind of reader *was* Nadezhda Mandelstam, next to whose undying commitment to Osip's writing other seduced readers pale by comparison? Her containment of Mandelstam's words became her *raison d'être*, replacing any life lived for herself alone. But first, the fatal poem.

'We none of us doubted that for verse like this he would pay with his life,' Nadezhda Mandelstam later said of the poetry reading that took place in November 1933, probably in the apartment of the poet and novelist Boris Pasternak.[6] Here Mandelstam recited to five nervous listeners – although he would later read it to many more – his poem about Stalin:

> We live, deaf to the land beneath us,
> Ten steps away no one hears our speeches,
>
> But where there's so much as half a conversation
> The Kremlin's mountaineer will be mentioned.
>
> His fingers are fat as worms
> And the words, final as lead weights, fall from his lips
> His cockroach whiskers leer
> And his boot tops shine.
>
> Around him a crowd of thin-necked leaders –
> Fawning half-men for him to play with.
>
> The whinny, purr or whine
> As he prances and points a finger.
>
> One by one forging his laws, to be flung
> Like horseshoes at the head, the eye or the groin.
>
> And every murder is a treat
> For the broad-chested Ossete.

This was the perverse logic of Mandelstam's times: his poem to Stalin was delivered to the wrong address in the certainty that it would reach its destination. One of his listeners, whose days were already numbered, denounced Mandelstam to the authorities, repeating to them the poem's content word by word. The first time Mandelstam's poem was ever written down was therefore by a Kremlin official. Nadezhda Mandelstam later worked out who the informer was but felt no vengefulness towards him and never disclosed his name. She realized that he'd had little choice: in

Stalin's attempt to eradicate the human intellect he was a great leveller, making victims alike of writers and readers, speakers and listeners. Had it been discovered that the informer had heard the poem – treated as an 'unprecedented criminal document' – and said nothing, his fate would have been worse. As it was, he perished before Mandelstam did himself.

This poem's 'straightforward, uncomplicated quality' was disliked by some of Mandelstam's readers.[7] It is as untypical of his high lyricism and intellectual felicity as 'The Quids' is of Laura Riding's oeuvre, but its majesty and solemnity are pure Mandelstam. The effect the poem had on Stalin was no less violent than the effect of Riding's poem on Robert Graves, and it functioned like a literary seduction in reverse. In literary seductions the reader would give up his life for the writer, but in this case the writer was expected to die for the reader. In its own horrific way, Stalin's reaction to this 'lampoon', as he described it to Pasternak, was as great a testament to the power of poetry as is possible. If poetry didn't matter, if it was no more than the effete musings of the bourgeoisie, if it didn't engage with the present and past of a language and its psyche in some vital way, then why should Stalin have bothered about the verse of this frail and middle-aged Jewish poet who only published nine slim editions of his work in his lifetime? 'Poetry is respected only in this country,' Mandelstam used to say; '– people are killed for it. There's no place where more people are killed for it.'[8] And no poetry was more threatening to the state than the lyric, with its intense focus on the self. People are killed for poetry because they are still capable of living by it, Nadezhda wryly observed.[9] Three months after reciting his Stalin poem, Mandelstam went walking in Moscow with his friend, the poet Anna Akhmatova. 'I'm ready for death,' he told her, as if he had now written his last sentence. But his best poetry was yet to come.

The force of Stalin's reaction to the poem was not to do with the dictator's hurt vanity nor even the poem's political dissension.

Neither of these points mattered. Mandelstam's writing was dangerous to Stalin, Brodsky rightly points out, because of his 'linguistic, and, by implication, his psychological superiority'.[10] In this sense, Mandelstam touched a much deeper nerve in the state, because his poetry showed that language will not be put in order in the way that institutions can be, that the Russian language will not be amenable, and that so long as this 'magnificently inflected language capable of expressing the subtlest nuances of the human psyche'[11] continues to exist, 'its sound casts a doubt on a lot more than a concrete political system: it questions the entire existential order.'[12] To arrest the meanings of words once and for all is what Terror wants, the French philosopher Jean-Francois Lyotard has argued. Also recognizing this, Mandelstam told Anna Akhmatova that poetry is power (Akhmatova hardly needed telling: she was to believe that a visit by the Oxford philosopher, Isaiah Berlin, to her apartment one evening in 1945 resulted in the Cold War). A poet, Mandelstam said, is one who 'disturbs meaning',[13] and this is why poetry in his case – language at its most powerfully disturbing, its most disobedient – both threatened the state and destroyed the poet.

This never stopped him writing as he wished. Mandelstam had long abandoned self-preservation for the word, and he had already been warned, at a public reading, 'you are taking yourself by the hand and leading yourself to your execution.'[14] Nor did the suicidal quality of his writing ever provoke him into churning out the officially stamped civic verse he despised, the type of jargonized anti-poetry prescribed through the state publishing houses. This poetry should be written in Soviet new-speak and conform to the Kremlin's requirements that it be ideological, objective, and forward-facing; that it embrace the bright future of the Soviet Union proletariat while condemning the dark and slavish past. 'People who had voices,' Nadezhda Mandelstam acidly remarked, 'were subjected to the vilest of tortures: their tongues were cut out and with the stump that remained they were forced to glorify the tyrant.'[15]

Mandelstam's obstinate preoccupation with the arts, with classical form, mythical subjects, and other irrelevancies like church architecture and Charles Dickens's novels – 'dreams exclusively from the field of culture' – was making him a liability. His Stalin epigram was therefore in part an ironic attempt to write verse that was unambiguously and directly political as opposed to the outmoded bourgeois nostalgia he was accused of writing: 'They need to have everything said straight out,' Nadezhda Mandelstam explained, 'and I think that is why M[andelstam] wrote this poem in such plain language – he was tired of the deafness of his listeners who were always saying: "What beautiful verse, but there's nothing political about it! Why can't it be published?".'[16] As if Mandelstam's preference for the aesthetic above politics in his poetry (and in his life) was not in fact the problem for his publishers, the very reason why he stopped being published after 1928, when the Party increasingly took charge of literary activity. For twenty years after his death Mandelstam's work was confiscated when it was found. Osip doesn't need Gutenberg's invention, Anna Akhmatova used to say to console Nadezhda; it doesn't matter that you will never see his poetry come out in this country. We live in a time when poetry is read not on the printed page but on manuscripts that circulate around the readers, and is stored not in books but in the memory. Full publication of Mandelstam's writing has only been available in Russia since the Glasnost years.

II

The four greatest Russian poets of the twentieth century were born one after another at the end of the nineteenth century: Anna Akhmatova in 1889, Boris Pasternak in 1890, Osip Mandelstam in 1891, and Marina Tsvetaeva in 1892. They each began writing in the twilight years of Imperial Russia and experienced the difficult transition to the Soviet system. Together they helped to produce the astonishing cultural renaissance of the 1920s, described by Isaiah Berlin as 'an extraordinary upward curve in European civilisation',[17] and Akhmatova, Pasternak and Tsvetaeva would all play a part in Mandelstam's fate. Boris Pasternak helped to save Mandelstam's life; Marina Tsvetaeva was at one point his lover; Anna Akhmatova was his friend and stuck by him through everything. 'The lifelong friendship between these two terribly ill-fated people was perhaps the only consolation for the bitter trials they both endured,' Nadezhda wrote of her husband's relationship with Akhmatova.[18] But Mandelstam resisted the power of these poets' work and they resisted the power of his. Mandelstam was typical in fighting against what might seduce him because he saw seduction as a kind of spell or a form of hypnosis. The seductions in this story are between poets and readers and not poets and poets, and seduction in the case of the Mandelstams takes on its literal meaning of diverting from the path, drawing aside from the party. As Mandelstam wrote of himself, 'little was straight about him.'

Little was straight about Anna Akhmatova either, and it is typical of her seductive appeal that she provides such a diversion in my story of the Mandelstams. An example of her diverting effect is an anecdote of the reading Mandelstam gave in 1933, at which he was asked by the 'loyalists' who were inevitably present in the crowds who would still turn up to poetry readings to 'express his opinion about contemporary Soviet poetry and evaluate the older poets who came down to us from before the Revolution'. Mandelstam was furious; he was being interrogated in front of a waiting audience and he had somehow to deal with this loaded question. He 'strode up to the edge of the stage,' an observer recalled, 'his head thrown back as always, his eyes ablaze. "What do you want from me? What sort of answer?" Then he said, in an adamant, melodious voice: "I am Akhmatova's contemporary." '[19]

With the mention of her name the house erupted in thunderous applause.

This was the year in which Anna Akhmatova said that Mandelstam had literary Leningrad at his feet, but her own celebrity came sooner. 'At present,' Mandelstam said of Akhmatova in 1916, 'her poetry is increasingly becoming one of the symbols of Russia's greatness.'[20] Anna Akhmatova remained the icon, muse and femme fatale of her exhausted country throughout her seventy-five years. As early as 1925, a collection of some of the poems that had been written about her was published as *The Image of Akhmatova*. There were to be considerably more by the time she died, forty years later. She moved like a stately galleon through twentieth-century Russia, stubbornly refusing to leave her motherland while other writers were fleeing to Europe, and she epitomized Russia's grief and grandeur both in her poetry and in her life:

> No, not under the vault of alien skies,
> and not under the shelter of alien wings –
> I was with my people then,
> There, where my people, unfortunately, were.[21]

Anna Akhmatova was so revered during the Second World War that she was asked to address the women of Russia by wireless, an astonishing position for a poet to be placed in. She was seen as Russia's tragic heroine, but Akhmatova was the first to cast herself in mythical terms: she was Cassandra, the prophetess of doom, an image that Mandelstam took up in one of the poems he wrote for her. She later became, her biographer Roberta Reeder says, like Antigone, staying behind to bury the dead. But she was also Demeter, the grieving mother searching for her stolen child lost in hell: Akhmatova's only son, Lev Gumilev, spent eighteen years in concentration camps because he was the offspring of two pre-Revolutionary poets. Her lyric poetry had cult status amongst its readers, and her second book of poems was memorized by its entire readership. A popular game used to be to recite the first line of one of Akhmatova's poems from her second collection, *Rosary*, and challenge someone to complete it. When Akhmatova read her poems to the huge audiences who came to hear her, should she ever search for a word the crowd would prompt her. What is astonishing is that they knew by heart not only her published but also her unpublished work, the poems that circulated in manuscript form or 'samizdat' in what Anna Akhmatova called these 'pre-Gutenberg' times.

Anna Akhmatova's story weaves its way in and out of the Mandelstams'. She was Mandelstam's oldest friend and she later became the friend of his widow, who memorized Akhmatova's verse as well as her husband's. 'How did it happen that three self-willed individuals, three nitwits with heads of straw, three incredibly frivolous people – Anna, Osip, and I – maintained and preserved throughout our entire lives our Triple Alliance, our indissoluble friendship?'[22] Nadezhda asked, and it is a question that needs exploring, not least because Osip's and Anna's friendships with Nadezhda were entirely concerned with preservation and dissolution. Akhmatova was a vital third person in the Mandelstam's relationship, much as June Mansfield was for Henry Miller and Anaïs Nin, and as Geoffrey Phibbs was for Laura Riding and Robert Graves, although her role in the triangle was markedly different.

In her short book on Mandelstam's and Akhmatova's creativity, *Mozart and Salieri*, Nadezhda described herself as the medium between the two poets; Mandelstam had his 'conversation with Akhmatova through me'.[23] But they were mediums for Nadezhda as well; she lived vicariously through them both, their forms gave her substance: 'If my life had any meaning at all,' she wrote in her old age, 'it was only because I shared all the tribulations of Akhmatova and M. and eventually found myself, my own true self, through my closeness to them.'[24] After Mandelstam died,

Nadezhda revealed: 'I never for one moment paid the slightest attention to what befell me personally . . . The only real thing during the whole time was my meetings with Akhmatova – and then only if we were alone.'[25]

III

On 15 January 1891 Osip Emilievich Mandelstam was born in Warsaw. His childhood, however, was spent in Tsarist Russia and he lived through the revolutions of 1905 and 1917, the First World War, the Civil War, the death of Lenin, collectivization, the first of the five-year plans, and the start of the Terror. His widow was left to experience the Second World War, the Cold War, the climax of Stalin's reign and the mass exodus of prisoners from the concentration camps in the late 1950s following his death. He grew up in the classical city of St Petersburg and went to the famous Tenishev school, leaving four years before the novelist Vladimir Nabokov entered as a student. Mandelstam's father was a skilled leather merchant and his mother a music teacher. Emil Veniaminovich and Flora Osipovna Verblovskaya, non-religious Jews, were cultivated and intelligent people, and it is not clear why Mandelstam chose to say so little about them in his adult life, or why he chose to say nothing at all about his two brothers. When he left school, in 1907, he went to Paris, principally to read and to think about poetry, and for a short period, from 1909 to 1910, he studied in Heidelberg, before returning to enrol in St Petersburg University in 1911. He never took his degree, and two years later his first collection of poems appeared, establishing his reputation.

For some unknown reason Mandelstam was exempted from the war and in the middle of the war years, in 1916, he had an affair with the poet Marina Tsvetaeva. Mandelstam, Nadezhda said, 'fell in love with poets, with their books, with one poem, or just a single line', and the romantic, wild, overwhelmingly gifted figure of

Marina Tsvetaeva was the first poet he fell in love with although he claimed never to have liked her poetry. In which case he was alone. When she published her first poems, in 1910, she won instant acclaim, and her autobiographical writings, critical reviews and literary portraits are also stunningly good, making her a master of prose as well as of verse. Once Anna Akhmatova, who jealously guarded her position as Russia's literary seductress, had asked a critic what Tsvetaeva was like. When she was told 'Oh, remarkable!' Akhmatova had snapped, 'But can one fall in love with her?' 'It's impossible not to,' was the critic's reply.[26] Tsvetaeva, who had a genuine passion for Akhmatova's writing –

> At a sleepy, morning hour,
> – it seems as if it was four fifteen –
> I fell in love with you,
> Anna Akhmatova

– was delighted by this anecdote and hoped that it meant that Akhmatova might return her love.

Marina Tsvetaeva's adoration of Anna Akhmatova is the only straightforward literary seduction – if that is not a contradiction in terms – to occur between this particular group of 'silver-age' poets. 'Oh, how I love you, how I rejoice in your existence, how I suffer for you, how elated I am because of you!' Tsvetaeva wrote in a letter to Akhmatova. 'It's such a pity that all this is just words – this love – I can't bear it – I would like it to be a real bonfire on which I was burnt.'[27] It was not until 1940, the year before her death, that Tsvetaeva at last met Akhmatova. She was in a deep depression but, a mutual friend said, in her conversation with the Muse Marina had sparkled.

Nothing like this occurred between Marina Tsvetaeva and Osip Mandelstam. When she knew Mandelstam, Tsvetaeva was married to Sergey Efron, a soldier fighting in the White Army. 'Tsvetaeva wrote monarchist poems,' Ilya Ehrenburg dryly observed, 'so Efron joined up – what, you may wonder, could the White Army mean to a Jew like him?'[28] Efron's action was typical of the Tsvetaeva effect: her poetic force was so strong that it could lead a man to battle and to books. Her husband struggled to keep up with the passionate demands of Tsvetaeva's poetry, until eventually he gave up and began writing as well, just her sister had done before him and their daughter would do later. Over the year of their affair, Tsvetaeva exerted her influence on Mandelstam too and she taught him to write love poetry, to love Moscow and gave him, Nadezhda said, 'his capacity for spontaneous and unstinting love which so much struck me at the very beginning'.[29]

Tsvetaeva and Mandelstam had met before at the summer residence of the artist Max Voloshin, and passed each other by without interest. Their relationship began at a public reading in Petersburg when they heard one another's verse. Tsvetaeva watched Mandelstam 'half-closing his camel eyes, declaim . . .

> Let's go to Tsa-arskoe Se-elo,
> Where there are smiling Uhlan Lancers,
> Free and happy, free and drunk,
> As they leap up into their stout saddles.'[30]

In the poems Marina Tsvetaeva subsequently wrote celebrating her affair with Mandelstam she addresses him only as a poet and never as a lover. Her prose, however, is the reverse, and she leaves us a wonderful portrait of the young love-struck Mandelstam in which his poetry is ignored. Her fond, comic account of Mandelstam in 'Story of One Dedication' throws into sharp relief the extent to which Nadezhda Mandelstam's later memoirs of her husband will never represent him as a lover and only deal with him as a poet. The man who appears so vividly in Tsvetaeva's prose fades away in Nadezhda Mandelstam's. The Mandelstam Marina Tsvetaeva describes, written in response to what she saw as the false accounts of him given by émigré opportunists, is child-like, impetuous, vulnerable and histrionic. In the following extract, Tsvetaeva's nursemaid, Nadya, is complaining to her about Mandelstam after he has turned up for one of his typically 'Mandelstamian' visits:

> 'Miss, what a queer one that Osip Emelich is! I'm feeding Andryusha his kasha just now and he says to me, "How lucky your Andryusha is, Nadya. He always has kasha enough ready for him, and his socks have all been mended. But as for me," he says, "no one feeds me kasha, and there's no one to mend my socks." And it was so-o sad, the way he sighed, the poor orphan . . . And I says to him, "But Osip Emelich, you ought to get married. Why, any girl would be glad to marry you. You want me to arrange it? There's a priest's daughter . . ."'
>
> 'But Nadya, seriously, do you really think that any girl would . . .?'
>
> 'Oh, get along, Miss . . . I just told him that to make him feel better. He made me feel so sorry for him. There's not a one that would marry him, let alone *any*, unless it be some girl with only one arm. He's so peculiar!'[31]

When Osip did take his bride to meet Marina Tsvetaeva seven years later, Nadezhda was left, like Norah McGuiness when Geoffrey Phibbs met Laura Riding, standing in a dark box room while Tsvetaeva and her eldest daughter greeted Mandelstam in another part of the flat. He was wary of introducing his wife to his old friends after this.

Marina Tsvetaeva's youngest daughter, Irina, did not survive the Revolution and died in the orphanage in which her mother had placed her in the winter of 1919. These were the hungriest years in Russia's history and Tsvetaeva was no longer able to feed both her children. She was out of sympathy with the Revolution and, in 1922, having not seen her husband since 1917, Tsvetaeva emigrated to France where she continued writing. In 1939, now separated from Efron, who had been exposed as a double agent, she made the fatal mistake of returning to Russia. When she arrived she discovered that her husband had been shot and her daughter was in a labour camp. In August 1941 she hanged herself in her lodgings in Elabuga, in the Tatar Autonomous Soviet Socialist Republic, where she had been evacuated.

IV

'A *raznochinets* [intellectual] needs no memory – it is enough for him to tell of the books he has read, and his biography is done,' Mandelstam wrote in his autobiographical essay, *The Noise of Time*.[32] Mandelstam was without need of a memory anyway because Nadezhda did his remembering for him, and she thus became one of the books who spoke his biography. 'I believe that M. was always intent on showing me things he wanted me to remember,' she said,[33] and she would later serve as Russia's memory as well when she wrote her own account of the Stalin years and the collective amnesia they inspired.

As a child, Osip Mandelstam had been a passionate reader, consuming Ibsen, Tolstoy, Hauptmann, Knut Hamsun, Rozanov, and Verlaine. He also learned to love the colour, size, and feel of books, to love books as objects: 'the colours of the spines are . . . the colour, height, and arrangement of world literature itself.'[34] Mandelstam's vivid account of the family bookcase in *The Noise of Time* is one of the rare occasions on which books will appear as tangible and tactile matter in the story of the Mandelstams, and the reverence Osip shows towards the books that formed him stands in marked contrast to the disinterest he would have as an adult in the material process of writing. 'The bookcase of early childhood is a man's companion for life,' he wrote, and Mandelstam's description of the bookcase serves as a metaphor for what he called 'the Judaic chaos' of his family life in general. Nancy Pollak argues, in

Mandelstam the Reader, that in his account of the bookcase Mandelstam identifies the poet as reader in a Judaic tradition. Here 'the book is central: [it is] a tradition based on the conception of the universe as text, and as created out of text; a tradition sustained by reading and commentary.'[35] Mandelstam's experience of childhood reading comes close to 'the Jewish notion of inexhaustible revelation through words and their exegesis',[36] and he works on the word like a rabbinic scholar.

> I always remember the lower shelf as chaotic: the books were
> not standing upright side by side but lay like ruins: reddish
> five-volume works with ragged covers, a Russian history of
> the Jews written in the clumsy, shy language of a Russian-
> speaking Talmudist . . . Above these Jewish ruins there
> began the orderly arrangement of books; those were the
> Germans – Schiller, Goethe, Kerner, and Shakespeare in
> German – in the old Leibzieg and Tübingen editions, chubby
> little butterballs in stamped claret-coloured bindings with a
> fine print calculated for the sharp vision of youth and with
> soft engravings done in a rather classical style . . . Still higher
> were my mother's Russian books – Pushkin in Isakov's 1876
> edition . . . The colour of Pushkin? Every colour is accidental
> – what colour could one choose for the purl of speech? Oh,
> that idiotic alphabet of colours by Rimbaud . . .! Lermontov
> had a greenish blue binding . . .[37]

Mandelstam's own collection of twenty-three poems, *Stone*, published at his expense in 1913, was small and slim with a green cover. In 1916 a larger edition of *Stone* appeared with a rust-coloured cover. Then another edition appeared in 1923, subtitled 'First Book of Poems'. In 1922 he published his second collection of poems, *Tristia*, which was republished in 1923 as 'Second Book'. *Stone* and *Tristia* were published together in 1928 in an edition simply called *Poems*; and this is the sum total of poetry published in

Mandelstam's lifetime. From 1910 onwards he produced a body of essays on writers and writing and reviews of contemporary culture, and in the 1930s he wrote his substantial prose works 'Fourth Prose', 'Journey to Armenia', and 'Conversation about Dante'. The poems he wrote between 1930 and 1934 were confiscated by the police during Mandelstam's first arrest, to be reproduced from memory by Nadezhda Mandelstam and published as *The Moscow Notebooks*. The poems he wrote in exile between 1935 and 1937 were saved at Nadezhda's request by the Mandelstams' friend, Natasha de Shtempel, from an evacuation of Voronezh in 1944, and are known as *The Voronezh Notebooks*. These two ghostly collections of notes, which are in effect his posthumous works, remained unpublished until recently.

V

In the desolate sub-zero conditions of the concentration camp, Osip Mandelstam died of 'heart failure', the authorities later informed his widow. Which is tantamount to being told that her husband had died of dying, as the failure of the heart is the exact definition of death. Mandelstam believed that the food he was given in the camp had been poisoned, and Anna Akhmatova thought he was right. She was later convinced that for a period Stalin had ordered her food to be poisoned as well. Nadezhda Mandelstam told Anna Akhmatova that she would not be at peace until she knew that her husband was dead, and she was informed of his death on 5 February 1939, when a money order she had sent him was returned to her 'because of the death of the addressee'. It was a long time, however, before she was able to discover the date on which he had died and even now the 'official' date of 27 December 1938 cannot be verified. 'He vanished into space and time with less trace than Hart Crane,' Mandelstam's biographer, Clarence Brown, writes, 'more anonymously than the victims of Dachau.'[38] He was forty-seven, but the toll of the previous few years made him look much older; his hair was grey and thinning and his skin sallow and drawn over a skeletal face. 'My health is so bad,' he wrote to his father two years before, 'that at forty-five I see signs of eighty-five.' Mandelstam was one of 1500 writers who perished under Stalin between 1924 and 1953, writers whose numerically tagged bodies were thrown naked into mass graves in the middle of nowhere. When he had been well enough, he would recite his poetry to the other prisoners in the camp, and Nadezhda believed that copies of Mandelstam's verses were compiled into albums, which circulated around other camps. Once he heard that a line from one of his poems had been scratched by someone on to the wall of a death cell: 'Am I real and will death really come?'

'Yes, I am lying in the ground but my lips are moving,' he wrote in his *Moscow Notebooks*. This image anticipates the miraculous survival of his voice through years of silencing, both before and long after his death, and it also describes the last few years of Mandelstam's life when, with Nadezhda, he was forced to live underground, exiled from Moscow where he could get work, begging food and money from the friends who would still acknowledge him, at physical and mental breaking point, and yet still composing his verse. (Mandelstam always spoke of 'composing' rather than writing his lines, and this term comes closest to his technique.) His amused neighbours would watch him at work, stalking proudly through the town, his head thrown back and his face transformed with rapture as he murmured his lines. Three years before his death, when he was in exile in Voronezh, S.B. Rudakov – another exiled poet – recalled observing with astonishment Mandelstam's 'frenzy of work':

> I have never seen anything like it . . . I am beholding a
> working machine (or perhaps it is more accurate to say
> organism) of poetry. *There's no man left*: it's Michelangelo. He

sees and remembers nothing. He walks around and mutters:
"a black fern in a green night." For four lines he pronounces
four hundred. I mean this absolutely literally. He sees
nothing, he doesn't remember his lines . . .[39]

Mandelstam knew that he was writing against a time bomb and in
Voronezh he produced a third of his total poetic output: ninety
poems in two years.

There's no man left: Mandelstam himself had disappeared and
turned into his poetry. By all accounts, there was very little of the
man left following his first arrest anyway; for the last few years of
his life Mandelstam was physically and psychologically shattered
and the poems – until they eventually killed him – were what held
him together. After he was arrested in May 1934 for his Stalin
poem, Mandelstam was tortured so badly in the Lubyanka's inner
prison that he slashed both his wrists rather than suffer further the
hours of interrogation and lack of sleep, the salted food and lack of
water, the blinding light and the straightjacket. The interrogation
involved asking Mandelstam to give a line by line explanation of
his poem and a justification for its poetic achievement. While his
self-defence was clearly dignified, claiming that his hatred of
fascists was what motivated the poem, a Soviet writer, Pyotre
Paulenko, who hid in the cupboard during the interrogation,
spread stories across Moscow about how pathetic Mandelstam had
been under pressure. Emma Gerstein, a friend who saw him when
he was released, remembered that, 'Osip was in a numbed state. His
eyes were glassy. His eyelids were inflamed, and this condition
never went away . . . his eyelashes had fallen out. His arm was in a
sling.'[40] Mandelstam's 'camel eyes' had been his defining feature; if
his widow ever came across a reference to long eyelashes by one of
his contemporaries, she said that she knew that they were talking
about Osip.

Three days after his release from the torture chambers, Mandelstam was taken by special convoy to Cherdyn, in the Ural mountains, where he was to be exiled for three years. Stalin had been 'compassionate'; as well as letting the poet live he allowed his wife to go into exile with him. Hallucinating and demented, convinced that because Anna Akhmatova had not been at the station to wish him goodbye she had been murdered by the secret police, and fearing that he was about to be rearrested, Mandelstam threw himself from the high first-floor window of the deserted hospital ward in which he was recovering his senses. His wife, who rushed to the window when she saw him climb over the ledge, 'reached out desperately with both hands and managed to grab the shoulders of his jacket. He wriggled out of the sleeves and dropped. I could hear the sound of his falling – a dull thud and a cry. His jacket was left hanging in my hands.'[41] Like Laura Riding, Osip Mandelstam leapt because of poems and survived to write about it: 'A leap, and I am back in mind.' His jump, he believed, had made him whole again, but he still searched for Akhmatova's body in the ravines.

Mandelstam's fate following his first arrest would have been worse had it not been for the intervention of Pasternak and Akhmatova. Akhmatova went to the Kremlin to plead on Mandelstam's behalf, and Pasternak was telephoned at his home by Stalin, who asked him whether he had heard Mandelstam's 'lampoon about himself' and whether Pasternak thought that Mandelstam was a genius. Pasternak replied that neither of these points was relevant, that the only thing that mattered to him was that he was speaking to Stalin and that a meeting between the two of them to discuss life and death was vital. 'If I were Mandelstam's friend I should have known better how to defend him,'[42] Stalin said before he hung up. Pasternak was haunted by that remark and felt that he could have done more to help his fellow writer, although Nadezhda Mandelstam and Anna Akhmatova said that he deserved four marks out of five for his treatment of the situation.

Mandelstam never revealed what went on in the Lubyanka, but in the first weeks of exile his mental health was so bad that Nadezhda was forced to persuade the Kremlin her husband would die if he had to stay in Cherdyn. It was at this point that Stalin telephoned Pasternak. Mandelstam was far more dangerous to Stalin dead and defiant than alive and compliant, and so the dictator allowed the poet to choose his own place of internal exile: anywhere outside the 'compound area' of Leningrad or Moscow. Stalin's policy with Mandelstam at this stage was to 'isolate but preserve', and this way he hoped his victim might better come to terms with Soviet Reality. Nadezhda was invited to be with her husband because his preservation seemed more likely if he was being looked after than if he was left alone. Little did Stalin know how true this was. Mandelstam opted to go to the town of Voronezh, in southern Russia, remembering that a friend had recommended it once. Here, in their drab slum, he became the working organism of poetry described above by Rudokov. After a year and a half of silence, the poems he produced were written down and saved by Nadezhda and now comprise *The Voronezh Notebooks* – which goes to show how little poetic inspiration has to do with external experience.

After Voronezh, barred from Moscow and refused work everywhere, Mandelstam wrote about ten final poems and these were confiscated during his last arrest. Nadezhda was too distressed to memorize them and never managed to remember them subsequently.

The Voronezh exile succeeded in breaking but not in bending Mandelstam. Rather than helping him to find his place in the Soviet system, it proved to him that he had no identity anywhere. At the beginning of 1937, as his three-year term was coming to an end and he was barely surviving on what Akhmatova called 'half translations, half reviews, half promises', he was forced to turn for money to Korney Chukovsky, a literary historian, essayist, translator and critic who is most celebrated for his children's books. As there is so little extant material documenting Mandelstam's life, the letter is worth quoting at length:

> What is happening to me cannot go on any longer. Neither my wife nor I have the strength left to prolong this nightmare . . . This has not turned out to be a "temporary sojourn in Voronezh," an "administrative exile," or anything of the kind. I'll tell you what it is: a man who has suffered from a very critical mental illness (a bleak and exhausting madness, to be more exact) goes back to work physically maimed, right after this illness, after an attempted suicide. I said those who judged me were right. I have found historical meaning in everything. Fine. I rushed headlong into my work. For this I was beaten, rebuffed, and subjected to a moral trial . . . After a year and a half I became an invalid. About that time, although I had done nothing else wrong, everything was taken away from me: my right to life, to work, and to treatment. I was put in the position of a dog, a cur . . . I am a shadow. I do not exist. I have only the right to die. My wife and I are being driven to suicide . . . The illness. I can't remain 'alone' for a minute . . . If I am left alone they'll have to put me in a madhouse.[43]

This is one of the very few surviving letters in which Mandelstam is desperate. The majority of his letters, like his essays and poems, show a defiant refusal to be beaten and to lose hope. Mandelstam detested it when writers complained about their conditions and used their homelessness, hunger, or poverty as an excuse for not writing. He was furious when Pasternak once remarked of his and Nadezhda's new apartment in Moscow that, now he had a home, Mandelstam would be able write some poetry. He could write it very well before, he believed. Why should he need four walls and a ceiling in order to hear the music of the Russian language in his head?

VI

What the hell kind of writer am I!? What the hell kind of writer *was* Osip Mandelstam, this 'little Jewish boy with a heart full of Russian iambic pentameters'?[44] And what the hell kind of 'writing' *is* poetry when it is not physically 'writing' itself, when it is not born of building a linguistic structure in which words appear on the page in their most vivid and self-conscious state; when it is not about committing to paper visual and verbal patterns, or lines dense with imagistic reference? Mandelstam was uninterested in the act of writing, which he saw as simply copying the poem down. Poetry, he believed, should be as close as possible to the lips of the poet and it belongs either in the poet himself or in the person of his reader.

What kind of writing results, not from the desire to 'draw' language or to record thought, but instead from a deafening humming noise invading and taking over the poet against his own volition? This is what Nadezhda Mandelstam described her husband as experiencing. His poetry, he said, established itself in an extraspacial field of activity. The poem began as

> a musical phrase ringing insistently in the ears; at first inchoate, it later takes on a precise form, though still without words. I sometimes saw M. trying to get rid of this kind of 'hum', to brush it off and escape from it . . . But it was always louder than any noise, radio or conversation in the same room.[45]

It was the same for Anna Akhmatova. When her cycle 'Poem without a Hero' came to her, 'she was ready to try anything just to get rid of it, even rushing to do her washing. But nothing helped. At some point words formed behind the musical phrase and then the lips began to move.'[46] When the poem is being formed, Nadezhda observed, 'nothing can stop the inner voice, which probably takes complete possession of the poet'.[47] Each poem begins as a 'sonorous moulded shape of form', Mandelstam wrote, which then has to be converted into words. It eventually reaches fruition without having seen the motion of the poet's hand: 'The mouth works, the smile nudges the line of verse, cleverly and gaily the lips redden, the tongue trustingly presses itself against the palate.' Once complete, Nadezhda noticed, the poetic sounds seem 'to fall away from the author and no longer torment . . . him with [their] resonance. He is released from the thing that obsesses him.'[48]

What Mandelstam wrote in his head, Nadezhda read with her body. After Mandelstam's release from the possession and obsession of the poem, Nadezhda's involvement with it began. But 'possession' seems too violent a term and 'obsession' too clinical to describe her steady, unswerving, and – as she tells it – oddly rational incorporation of Mandelstam's poems. This is not a tale of possession by words, as with Henry Miller and Anaïs Nin, or of mutual consumption, as with Robert Graves and Laura Riding. This is a tale of *containment*; of enclosure and not occupation. Containing Mandelstam was clearly vital for both of his most powerful readers: not only was it Stalin's object to contain Mandelstam within the bounds of Russia – 'isolate but preserve' – in order that the power of his language be restrained, but Nadezhda held each poem within herself. Her containment of her husband became the story of her life. 'There are many women like me who for years have spent sleepless nights repeating the words of their dead husbands over and over again,'[49] she said. And while that is undoubtedly the case, few would pay the price that she did.

'All night I expect important guests, / Gently rattling the door chain fetters,' Mandelstam once wrote. They came for him on the night of 16 May 1934, six months after he read the Stalin poem in Boris Pasternak's flat. The Mandelstams were living in an apartment on Nashchokin Street in Moscow and Anna Akhmatova had just arrived to visit them from Leningrad; she had no money, but so urgent was Mandelstam's need to see her that she sold a statuette of herself to a museum in order to afford the train fare. Finding that they had no food to offer their guest, Mandelstam borrowed an egg from their neighbour. When the Cheka, or the secret police, arrived it became clear to the Mandelstams that another guest of theirs, an acquaintance who had been with them all evening and had long out-stayed his welcome, had been planted on them to ensure that Mandelstam did not leave the building. Now that his job was complete, he was ordered by the police to go. Their flat was searched and a total of forty-eight papers, including phone numbers and addresses, were taken away and confiscated, but the Cheka couldn't find what they were looking for. Throughout the search a ukelele was playing on the other side of the wall. Akhmatova's egg was left uneaten.

Before he was taken away, at seven in the morning, Nadezhda packed her husband's belongings in a bag while he selected some books to have with him. The Cheka laughed at the couple's precautions, saying, as they usually did following an arrest like this, that the prisoner would not be gone long enough to justify them. Mandelstam was gone for three years, and when he and Nadezhda returned to Moscow, their apartment was being lived in by another tenant, who denounced them to the secret police: they were no longer permitted to live in Moscow. Every address they ever had collapsed beneath them and Mandelstam spent the last year of his life homeless. 'Nowadays all you need is an ashtray and a spittoon,' Anna Akhmatova said.[50]

An hour after Mandelstam was taken, Akhmatova's son, who had been living with Osip and Nadezhda, arrived at the flat and was quickly told to go away. 'People sensed the dynamic strength in him and knew that he was doomed,' Nadezhda said of Lev Gumilev. 'Now our house had been stricken by the plague and become a death trap for anyone prone to infection.' The Cheka came back later that morning to raid the flat a second time. Anticipating this, Anna Akhmatova told Nadezhda Mandelstam not to put the papers they had left on the floor after the first search back in the trunk. That would make it look as if they were hiding something. The police didn't bother looking at anything written in prose; they wanted only the Stalin poem, which had never been written down. It was then that Nadezhda Mandelstam realized her task, 'the one for which I have lived ever since. There was nothing I could do to alter M.'s fate, but some of his manuscripts had survived and much more was preserved in my memory. Only I could save it all, and this was why I had to keep up my strength.'[51]

It was at Nadezhda's repeated request that Mandelstam agreed to have his poems written down at all. During their first few years together he recorded nothing and in 1923 he put together his *Second Book* from memory. 'It was easier to save a manuscript than a man,'[52] Nadezhda reasoned, and then it was she who transcribed the poems in her own hand, writing at his dictation what Osip had heard while 'listening in to himself'. As paper became increasingly dangerous, Nadezhda hid the poems she could in saucepans and cushions (until cushions became a thing of the past) and distributed other poems into safe hands, while committing everything, poems, his autobiographic prose, and all of his essays and articles, to memory. 'Twenty years went by between the time of M's death and the moment when I was able to take from their hiding-place all the poems I had managed to save and put them openly on the table.'[53] One of these hiding places was the 'inner darkness' of her own mind, an infinitely superior place in which to hold a poem, Mandelstam believed:

> When you've destroyed all the rough drafts,
> and you hold a sentence in your mind
> steadfastly, without tedious references,
> integral in inner darkness,
> when that sentence stands up on its own,

opening its eyes, that were squinting in concentration,
then its relationship to the paper
is the same as that of the dome to the empty skies.[54]

Writing 'strengthens the ties between people', Nadezhda held, and poetry 'flows from one person to another, from the living and the dead to other people'.[55] This is exactly what happened in her case, where the tie between the living reader and the dead poet became indissoluble.

Nowhere is there an image of a literary seduction more haunting than that of Nadezhda Mandelstam, the invisible woman, cradling for twenty years the saucepan containing the scraps of her dead husband's verse while the body of his writing was stored in her mind. These years of waiting and hiding she called 'my life in the tomb',[56] and like this, with Mandelstam's words entombed inside her, the poet's widow wandered across the largest space on earth in her ceaseless journey from one dull town to another: a living book. 'We always associate the word "book" with printing, and think of it in terms of format and typographical convenience,' she wrote of the way in which the book was being redefined by Mandelstam's example,[57] and there is no stronger example of the pre-Gutenberg era Russia had been thrown back into than the person of Nadezhda Mandelstam herself.

What stands out in this scene is the way in which, when all else falls away – their poverty, their homelessness, their persecution, the continued, defiant joy they took in their lives – writing and reading, the flow of poetry from one person to another, were the most significant aspects of the Mandelstam's relationship and what gave the couple their strength. There is nothing else Nadezhda chose to preserve from her marriage save Mandelstam's position as a poet and her own as his reader par excellence. 'Some of M.'s poetry and prose is lost, but most of it has been preserved. How this happened is the story of my battle with the forces of destruction, with everything that conspired to sweep me away, together with the poor scraps of paper I managed to keep.'[58]

Nadezhda's widowhood recalls the closing pages of Ray Bradbury's futuristic novel, *Fahrenheit 451*, beautifully filmed by François Truffaut, in which a small community of book-lovers escape from a society in which the possession of a book is a crime that, if discovered, will result in the book's being burnt. 'There must be something in books . . . to make a woman stay in a burning house,' the hero, Montag, muses as he watches a woman choose to burn with her books, like Joan of Arc at the stake, rather than live without them. The rebels live in a forest where they have each memorized a book by which they then become known; one person might become *Pickwick Papers*, another *Paradise Lost*, and so forth. The story ends with the exiles repeating their chosen book, word for word, as they circle around, weaving in and out of one another, each oblivious to their surroundings, aware only of the words they must preserve. With the survival of the books the continuation of some kind of civilization can be relied upon, but only at the expense of one's personal identity, one's selfhood. The author's name vanishes along with the reader's: only the book lives on. ' "Books aren't people," ' one of Bradbury's characters protests. ' "You read and I look around, but there isn't *anybody*!" ' As in the best reading, the author and the reader each dissolve and the book takes on a life – a body – of its own.

The only time that Mandelstam ever deliberately sat down at a desk to write a poem from scratch, a poem that did not announce itself to him first as a wordless noise, was during the desperate period in 1937 when he wrote the above letter to Korney Chukovsky. Determined to achieve an antidote to the epigram whose death sentence was hanging over his head, and to see an end to his 'homeless wandering existence, poverty, humiliation and the constant surveillance of the secret police',[59] Mandelstam struggled with pen on paper to produce something that would pacify the dictator. He wrote his 'Ode to Stalin'. While the 'Ode' failed to save Osip's life, Nadezhda believed that it helped save her own and, in saving her, the poem therefore inadvertently gave Mandelstam a voice beyond the grave. 'It is possible . . . that without it I should not have survived either – their first impulse was to destroy me, too, . . . By surviving I was able to save his poetry . . .'[60] And herein lies the dynamic between the Mandelstams: Osip was busy writing himself to death, both actually and metaphorically, while these same poems breathed life, both actual and metaphorical, into Nadezhda. 'When he went out of my life, I would have died too but for the joy breathed by his verse . . .'[61] Poetry was a matter of life and death for the Mandelstams, their means of preservation. It was a form of mouth-to-mouth resuscitation.

With Osip and Nadezhda Mandelstam a certain merging of identities took place and it would often be unclear who was breathing for whom. While his verse was posthumously breathing life into her grieving spirit and, by recording and repeating it, she was putting breath and body back into his verse, without Nadezhda Osip could not breath at all. In a letter to her mother written in 1937, Osip confided:

> As soon as Nadya [Nadezhda] goes away I am stricken with an agonising psychosomatic illness which has the following symptoms: in recent years I've developed an asthmatic condition. *Breathing is always difficult*. When I'm with Nadya I breathe normally, but when she has to leave I literally begin to suffocate. Subjectively speaking, it is unendurable: I sense the end. Each minute seems like an eternity. When I'm alone I can't take a single step by myself. It's impossible to get used to. The last time she was gone (7 days) I grew worse by the day . . .[62]

Elsewhere in his work, Mandelstam used 'breathing' as a metaphor for the physicality of poetry – 'an individual formula for breathing'

178

– which was always for him an oral performance, one of inhalation and exhalation. Walking, 'taking steps', was also a metaphor for poetry. According to Nadezhda, Mandelstam couldn't compose without walking. 'He either paced the room (unfortunately we never had very much space for this) or he kept going outside to walk the streets.'[63] In his dazzling essay, 'Conversation about Dante', Mandelstam elaborated on his theory: 'Both the *Inferno* and, in particular, the *Purgatorio* glorify the human gait, the measure and rhythm of walking, the footstep and its form. The step, linked with breathing and saturated with thought, Dante understood as the beginning of prosody . . . The metrical foot is the inhalation and exhalation of the step.'[64] Not able to breathe or to walk without Nadezhda, his poetry would die without her presence. *'The illness. I can't remain "alone" for a minute.'* For her own part, without the life Mandelstam's poetry breathed into her, Nadezhda 'would have died' herself. By keeping Mandelstam's poetry alive, she was investing in her future. 'Read in order to live,' Flaubert commanded, and this is exactly what she did.

VI

She lived until 1980, forty-two years after her husband's death. It was not long enough to see the official rehabilitation of Mandelstam's name in 1987, nor long enough to see published in the Soviet Union her two magnificent memoirs *Hope Against Hope* and *Hope Abandoned*, in which she describes the couple's relationship with Mandelstam's poetry. Her concern in the books, written in her mid-sixties, 'is with a man long since dead, who for more than thirty years has been lying somewhere in a mass grave – though he still manages, without the aid of Gutenberg, to be a thorn in the side of all "true Soviet writers" '.[65] She waited most of her life to write and once she had begun, it poured out of her. Nadezhda Mandelstam emerged as one of Russia's considerable writers: *Hope*

Against Hope and *Hope Abandoned* have all the sweep and grandeur of the great Russian prose of the nineteenth century, and like that prose they seemingly appear from nowhere. As an account of living under Stalinism her books are an invaluable and courageous historical document, but it is in their tale of the exchanges that take place in a literary seduction that their shocking originality lies.

Nadezhda Mandelstam's prose is urgent and rapid and the focus of these huge books – which, at 1200 pages, amount to more words than Mandelstam produced in a lifetime – is on her husband's work. While she wrote only about Mandelstam, the only reference he ever made to Nadezhda can be found in the last writing he ever saw published in his lifetime, *Journey to Armenia*. So until her books appeared no one had ever heard of the poet's widow. Even Gleb Struve and Boris Filippov, émigré scholars who in 1955 edited the three-volume edition of all the known works of Mandelstam (in the original Russian but published in New York) and were therefore the world experts on him, were unaware of the existence of a wife. And when, in the 1960s, Anna Akhmatova suggested to the young poet Joseph Brodsky that he call on her friend Nadezhda Mandelstam if he was passing her way, he did not know who she was.

Nadezhda Mandelstam's work must rank alongside Henry James's profoundly unsettling autobiography, *A Small Boy and Others*, as the most self-effacing account of the self yet written. For having at last told in *Hope Against Hope* the story of her life with Mandelstam, Nadezhda Mandelstam realized in *Hope Abandoned* that she had left herself out. 'This happened quite spontaneously, without any conscious intention: it was simply that I still did not exist.'[66] She came back to life when her writing – 'my main task' – had been achieved. *Hope Abandoned* then becomes her attempt to tell her own story – 'I feel my pain keenly now, and am going to write about myself alone' – [67] but after a few paragraphs of describing her adult life at the time she met Osip, Nadezhda fades out of the text once more, never to return. Typical of the book is Chapter 28, called 'Three stages in my life', which documents three stages in Mandelstam's life instead. Nadezhda Mandelstam's books describe a kind of horror of the self and reveal a desire, not to turn into her writing, like Laura Riding, but, like Anaïs Nin, to write herself out – much as all traces of Mandelstam were written out of existence for two decades after his death. Nadezhda had become like her husband: a 'non-person'.

Hope Against Hope and *Hope Abandoned* focus intensively on the last five years of Mandelstam's life, detailing his thoughts and actions with remarkably recalled precision. And yet, like the portraits of George Barker and Byron produced by their seduced readers, Elizabeth Smart and Caroline Lamb, they tell you almost nothing about Mandelstam *the man*, who he was when he wasn't *being a poet* or before he wrote poetry, who he was when he wasn't suffering for writing or being read by Nadezhda. The briefest comparison with Marina Tsvetaeva's earthy memoirs of Mandelstam in 1916 reveal the strangeness of Nadezhda's representation. Tsvetaeva's petulant Mandelstam groans, 'Jam, jam, the whole day I eat jam. I don't want any of your jam! What a house – no chocolate!' and resents the privileges afforded to Tsvetaeva's young son, 'Andryusha's! Andryusha's! The jam's Andryusha's, the chocolate's Andryusha's, yesterday I wanted to sit in an armchair and that was Andryusha's! . . . Now, just break off a piece . . .' Nadezhda's Osip Mandelstam, on the other hand, whilst being the all-consuming object of her books, never himself eats or drinks: the only time his body's needs are mentioned is in relation to breathing, and even here Nadezhda can respire for him. What the hell kind of writer did Nadezhda think he was?

Because of his privileged role, Nadezhda Mandelstam believed that the poet was better able to preserve his 'self' in a culture in which the human being no longer had value. This is in a sense true, but Mandelstam's preservation took place not as a result of anything innate in his poetic identity but because Nadezhda stored him inside *her* self. *Hope Against Hope* and *Hope Abandoned* tell the story of Mandelstam's consumption by poetry and by Nadezhda. While the books are tributes to selfless love and testaments to the indomitable drives of desire, it would seem that sexuality for the Mandelstams was less an affair between male and female – as it was between Osip Mandelstam and Marina Tsvetaeva – than a dangerous liaison between writer and reader. It was through writing and reading that the sexual drama of the Mandelstams was acted out, and implicit in Nadezhda Mandelstam's long account of storing her husband's words is the seductive pleasure she experienced in the process.

Reading with the body – for this is what Nadezhda did – invites what Barthes calls 'jouissance', or bliss, a carnal pleasure akin to orgasm but produced by the grainy physical signifiers of the text. Experiencing this textual bliss the reader is responding to the body of the writing with her own body; the pleasure has nothing to do with what the text *says* or *means*; this is the eroticism of language itself. Jouissance lies outside culture and ideology and beyond the self; like orgasm, it observes the temporary dissolution of time, place, and selfhood. The language of bliss, Barthes writes in *The Pleasure of the Text*, is 'lined with flesh, a text where we can hear the grain of the throat, the patina of consonants, the voluptuousness of vowels, a whole carnal stereophony: the articulation of the body, of the tongue, not that of meaning, of language'.[68] There is no better place for this language to be found than in 'writing aloud'; 'vocal writing' epitomizes the Barthesian theory of textual pleasure: '*Writing aloud* is not expressive . . . it is carried not by dramatic inflections . . . but by the *grain* of the voice, which is an erotic mixture of timbre and language.'[69] The voice is an art form and writing aloud catches the texture of speech in close-up, much like cinema, whose focus on the face, and on the fleshy lips specifically, records the materiality of language, its sensuousness, its breath and spittle. Mandelstam *only* 'wrote aloud' and Nadezhda, who said that in preserving his poems she was containing not just the words but the tone and texture of his voice, sank down into the movements of his tongue until she had quite melted away.

The Mandelstams' is a love story but of a very different sort, a story of the preservation of words in which bodies serve only as linguistic shrines, as the sources and repositories of poems, and in which passions are a 'philological' experience. Nadezhda Mandelstam's books are only ostensibly about the writing and reading of a poetry that shaped the writer and reader, forming itself inside the poet and fleshing itself out in the reader. The other tale that emerges from *Hope Against Hope* and *Hope Abandoned* is the stranger one in which the writer and reader are not shaped by Mandelstam's poetry so much as *unshaped* by it, in which the figures of writer and reader, serving only as mediums for words, dematerialize and fade out, leaving only the poems in their stead. Nadezhda was married to her husband's verse and it was this to which she was widow. Her childless state was compensated for, she wrote, by Mandelstam's poetry: planted by his seed, the poems were nurtured in her womb.

In an attempt to explain why 'in my first book I excluded myself', Nadezhda Mandelstam wrote of the Stalin years: 'In the midst of such general misery and doom, the word "I" lost its meaning, becoming shameful or taboo . . . wasn't it something of a feat to keep a grip on one's own personality and a true sense of identity in our era of wholesale slaughter and death camps on such a vast scale?'[70] Maintaining an awareness of self in a 'depersonalised world where everything human was silenced'[71] is certainly one of the subjects of her books, and yet this other tale suggests that it was not only the politics of Stalinism that led Nadezhda Mandelstam to replace her own identity with her husband's poetry. This was a continuation of the drama that started when the couple first met in carnival time back in Kiev, when Osip began his task of 'mold[ing] me in his own image',[72] and where Nadezhda 'agreed to become his shadow'.[73]

It was May Day 1919 when Osip first spoke to her, telling how the Bolsheviks reacted to the murder of a comrade with a 'hecatomb of corpses'. The couple finally parted on May Day 1938 (it is Nadezhda who remembered the date as 1 May; in fact they parted a week or so later), when their conversation was interrupted mid-sentence as Osip was 'led away, pushed from behind by two soldiers'.[74]

Nadezhda Yakovlevna Khazina had been eighteen years old when they met, ten years younger than Osip. He preferred younger women, Nadezhda said, because they were easier to dominate. She had been born in 1899 in Saratov but brought up in Kiev; nothing is known about her father, but her mother was a physician. Her parents were Jewish, highly educated, and ensured that their daughter was educated too. Nadezhda became a superb linguist with a first-rate knowledge of European languages, including English; a skill that she would need when the only work the Mandelstams could get was translating.

She was what Anna Akhmatova would later describe as being 'laide mais charmante' – ugly but charming. Compared to Akhmatova's statuesque beauty, her six-foot frame with her tragic, hooded grey eyes and high cheekbones, any other woman would look bovine. Akhmatova's stunning face, unforgettable profile and sinuous physique were painted, sketched and sculpted all of her life, an iconographic process that began on her honeymoon in Paris when she met the artist Modigliani and he drew her languorous form in one continuous line. In contrast there are only a few photographs of Nadezhda Mandelstam, but one taken in 1922 does not show an ugly face. On the contrary, she had a very sensual appearance. Her hair was dark, and her skin pale and soft. Her features were strong, rich and generous with large rather pronounced eyes and very wide full lips. She seems attentive in the picture; she is as usual sitting still, listening and watching.

Osip, on the other hand, *was* ugly but charming. He had an elfin face, and looked, one contemporary said, like the airbound figures in Chagall's paintings. Mandelstam was small and wiry with a receding quiff of hair, a high forehead, and large ears on a head that everyone describes as being comic and bird-like. He always seems animated in photographs, and his dark eyes shine. Nadezhda said that when they met they 'already shared the two qualities which were to remain with us for the rest of our lives: light-headedness and a sense of doom',[75] and it is these qualities that photographs of the couple capture.

Mandelstam was agile, restless, excitable, and jumpy, but this child-like exterior belied his gravity and wisdom. Ilya Ehrenburg remarked how, in the political climate of 1918, Mandelstam's 'profound understanding of the grandeur of what was taking place astonished me'.[76] 'During our early days together,' Nadezhda recalled, 'in the Kiev of 1919, M. was perhaps the only person I knew who pondered the meaning of events, as opposed to their immediate consequences . . .'[77] He was a fidget and could never keep still, yet he listened with startling intensity when people spoke. 'Here was a creature more perfect than most people,' wrote Nikolai Punin, Anna Akhmatova's third husband, on meeting Mandelstam. 'He listened to his interlocutor with his lowered long lashes, as if listening not to words but what was hidden behind the words . . . A conversation between him and other people very often turned into a poetic improvisation in a special, spiritual space.'[78] When he read his poetry the audience held their breath: 'I have never seen a human face so transformed by inspiration and self-forgetfulness. Mandelstam's homely, insignificant face had become the face of a seer and a prophet.'[79] Another contemporary remembered how 'Mandelstam's reading was more than rhythmical. He didn't just scan or pronounce his lines – he sang them like a shaman seized by visions.'[80] When Nadezhda first heard Osip recite his poetry in Kiev he was sharing the stage with Soviet poets who 'read verse suitable for the occasion: loud, brash, peppered with slogans, and altogether in the spirit of a variety show'.[81] Mandelstam's laconic reading of a poem from *Stone* was out of tune with the trumpeting mood, and confirmed Nadezhda's belief that she had met a visionary, someone whose lead she must follow. She memorized the poem and her aim became 'to justify M's existence by preserving the things that gave it meaning'.

Nadezhda Yakovlevna Khazina was an art student, mixing with a 'herd' of left-wing painters. Her life was 'a round of pleasure', and every night the bohemian group would meet in a basement night-club for artists, musicians, and writers, called the Junk Shop. It was here that she met Osip, who was visiting Kiev and staying in the Hotel Continental above the club. The mutual attraction was instant. Osip said their meeting was fate, and Nadezhda remembered that they 'took up with each other as though it were the most natural thing in the world . . .' After *Stone* was published in 1913, Mandelstam had acquired a considerable reputation amongst the other poets of St Petersburg and Moscow, but it is not known whether Nadezhda had heard of him or had read any of his poems prior to meeting him. This kind of detail is left out of her memoirs, and there is too little information about either Nadezhda's or Mandelstam's early lives for us ever to find out.

Not that it matters. While it was vital for their future relationship that Robert Graves had read Laura Riding before meeting her and unnecessary for Anaïs Nin and Henry Miller to meet at all, so preoccupied were they with themselves and one another as writing, whether or not Nadezhda had come across Mandelstam's poetry is irrelevant for their particular literary seduction. This is because as far as Nadezhda is concerned, 'My life really began when I met M.,'[82] and so anything that happened before was without significance. Mandelstam wiped her slate clean, erasing the trace of any previous influences, which presumably would have included any earlier readings or misreadings (which amounted to the same thing) of his poems: 'he stubbornly trained me not to read but to *listen* to poetry, learning to appreciate it by ear . . . I felt like a horse in the hands of a trainer.'[83] Reading print on pages was not what he wanted for his wife. Mandelstam wanted Nadezhda to learn 'close-reading' in the fullest sense of the term, reading that gave you maximum proximity to the person of the writer so that you exchanged your identity for his:

> From me he wanted only one thing: that I should give up my life to him, renounce my own self, and become a part of him. That is why he so stubbornly dinned his own ideas into my head, getting me to see things his way . . . I not only belonged to him but was a part of his own being . . .[84]

In those first few weeks in Kiev, Mandelstam began the process of educating Nadezhda in his poetry and taking over her art. Loving separate things, Nadezhda said, 'was the same as separating' for Osip, and separation from his woman was something he feared: 'All his efforts were directed to isolating me from other people, making me his own, breaking me in and adapting me to himself.'[85] He was jealous and possessive, not letting her out of his sight, and he genuinely failed to understand why Nadezhda 'could not remember a poem he already had in his head, or why I did not automatically know what he knew'.[86] Mandelstam 'literally read my thoughts and was astonished if I didn't know what he was thinking at a given moment'.[87] This made the process of dictating his poems and prose seem more like telepathy, and Nadezhda had often to remind her husband of the difference:

> The first few phrases he dictated so quickly, as though he remembered them by heart, that I could scarcely keep up with him. Later the pace slowed down, but I often got confused by the long sentences. He just failed to understand why I

couldn't get them down at one go, but at the same time I found him leaving out one or even several words, as though he thought I would hear them without his having to utter them . . . "Do you think," I snapped back at him, "that I am sitting in your head and reading your thoughts?"[88]

Which is exactly what Mandelstam did think. After all, Nadezhda observed, he and Anna Akhmatova were telepathic, both with one another and with her. 'It's witchcraft,' she used to say of the way Akhmatova finished off sentences Nadezhda had not yet spoken out loud.

Having been with Nadezhda exclusively for four months, Osip left Kiev in August 1919 and didn't see her again for a year and a half. He joined a band of actors on their way to the Crimea, packing his bags when he realized that the local Whites suspected him of being a Bolshevik sympathizer. Nadezhda said that she would join him, but 'with all the bloodshed in the streets outside I just couldn't bring myself to move'.[89] While he was away he initially wrote to her, the same sentimental, doting letters he would send her until he died: 'Your childish little paw, all charcoal-smeared, your dark-blue smock – I remember everything . . .'[90] This is how Mandelstam liked to see women. They were, 'by their nature subordinate, even rather inferior beings who needed care and attention – frightened, wide-eyed, shrinking creatures given to telling fibs and – even more to his liking – a little brainless'.[91]

The political unrest in Kiev made communication between the two increasingly difficult and they lost touch. Then, in 1921, Osip heard from a mutual friend that Nadezhda was still in Kiev but at a new address and he immediately went south to find her. He was just in time: her parents had been evicted the day before and the apartment had been allotted to a Soviet official. Mandelstam arrived simultaneously with an army of women prisoners who had come to scrub the floors in preparation for the new tenant, but Osip and Nadezhda were immune to the obscenities that were levelled at them by the cleaners, who wanted the trespassing couple out of their way. During the next two hours, 'M. read me a lot of poems and said he would certainly take me away from here.'[92] He took Nadezhda north, and they married because it made travel easier. This was only a formality: Nadezhda felt that they had been married since 1 May 1919.

What gives seduction its strength is the enactment of weakness on the part of the seducer, and so for all his promise of leadership what brought Nadezhda round to Mandelstam was his need for her.[93] But what is astonishing in this case of literary seduction is the *confidence* Osip had in Nadezhda's role; while his jealousy belied his initial security with her, Osip otherwise gave himself up to Nadezhda as his container without a flicker of a doubt. Less explicable, however, than his dictatorial rule over the woman he regarded as his 'only property' is Nadezhda's complicity in this arrangement, for she was certainly not spineless.

They had their first row when Nadezhda went off flying for the day so that she could learn how to 'loop the loop' and Osip – who panicked at the prospect of difference – 'simply could not understand how I could develop a taste for something if he did not share it. He wanted me to look to him and only to him . . . But neither meekness nor forbearance was in my character, and we were constantly colliding head-on . . .'[94] Joseph Brodsky confirms this. When he met Nadezhda Mandelstam as an old woman he described her as lacking humility, as being 'terribly opinionated, categorical, cranky, disagreeable, idiosyncratic'.[95] Mandelstam's biographer, Clarence Brown, gives us a picture of 'a vinegary, Brechtian, steel-hard woman of great intelligence, limitless courage, no illusions, permanent convictions and a wild sense of the absurdity of life'.[96] Not someone who lacked personality, then. Her staying power and thus her ability to preserve her husband for posterity came from her Jewishness, Nadezhda said. Where else could she have got such 'maniacal obstinacy bred only by centuries of disaster, persecution, pogroms, and gas chambers'?[97]

'But who shall be the master?' Diderot asked. 'The writer or the reader?' It would be too simple – and also simply not true – to say that the Mandelstams' relationship was a case of male aggression and female submission in which he triumphed and she suffered. And not only because they shared the aggression, submission, triumph, and suffering, or because while he acted like he owned her it was she who was containing him. Nadezhda's account of her interaction with Mandelstam suggests that this was a case of the poet creating his reader and not of the husband repressing his wife, and the relationship between reader and writer was by no means straightforward.

Just as it was difficult to tell who controlled or contained whom, the Mandelstams' case made it hard to define which was the writer and which the reader. While Mandelstam, who would always read his poetry aloud, was *literally* the reader of his works, Nadezhda, who wrote the poems down, memorized them, and reproduced them, became literally their writer. Mandelstam always considered his first reader to be a vital contributor to the poem; the reader or listener 'rounds off' the writing process. So while the writer reads, the reader completes the writing. But reading and listening are two different activities: being read to is a violent experience, it silences one's own interior voice. Reading his poems aloud to his wife, Mandelstam became both their writer and their reader: Nadezhda was seemingly left with no position. But as the poems' scribe, she was in the same privileged position in relation to the word as Mandelstam's revered Dante, whom he described at length as also writing to external dictation, as also being 'a copier'. Further, as the guardian of her husband's words, Nadezhda was firmly in the hallowed Jewish tradition. 'No other tradition or culture has ascribed a comparable aura to the conservation and transcription of texts,' George Steiner says. 'In no other has there been an equivalent mystique of the philological.'[98] So any authority available to the writer belonged by rights to Nadezhda.

In Russia as nowhere else, the Romantic notion of the writer as hero was and still is taken seriously and for good reason: writing was and is heroic. Part of Mandelstam's hold on Nadezhda was that he represented to her the qualities of the rebel hero: the defender of freedom against tyranny, of the individual against the state, a belief in something beyond the drab (at best) reality on offer. Mandelstam was more than a writer or a writer of poems: he was a Poet in the full sense that the word has acquired, and everything he did was integral to this. While a Poet is more than someone who writes poetry, not everyone who writes poetry acquires the status of Poet. Take Thomas Hardy, for example; he will always be known as a novelist and yet his poetry is thought superior to his prose. Compare with the mythologies around the word 'poet' the associations we have with writers known as 'novelists', 'essayists', and 'journalists', and it is easy to see that the poet's craft is not the most important thing about him. Byron, the most popular poet of the early nineteenth century, remains famous not for his poetry but for playing the role of the poet par excellence, and while that might have involved the writing of some superb poetry, he is remembered principally for his position as a political idealist, for his domination of women, and for dying in the name of liberating an oppressed country. Byron is not, in any of these senses, dissimilar to Mandelstam. A novelist is not credited with having a 'novelistic lifestyle' in the way that a poet is thought to live 'like a poet'; an essayist does not have, as a poet is thought to, a specific 'look' or temperament; no other style of writer is assumed to be outside the humdrum, above the material, and beyond the law. A novelist simply writes novels, but a poet is an iconoclast. Next to poetry, prose seems not only law-abiding but law-enforcing; 'It is as if prose in its true state were, finally . . . the State,' Susan Sontag writes.[99] For Nadezhda Mandelstam to give herself up entirely to Mandelstam was a mark of her Romantic belief in the Poet as hero; and in this sense she sacrificed herself for an ideal and a cause, not for any wifely obedience to her husband.

The poet is a spokesman for his readers, Mandelstam taught Nadezhda, and he must never lose sight of the responsibility of his role. Therefore, 'What he must not do on any account is to seduce people. The poet is only human, like his fellow men, and thus he cannot know more than others. For this reason, if he sets himself up as an authority or preaches, he is a seducer.'[100] The seductive power of leadership was terrifying in Stalin's Russia, but the hold Mandelstam held over Nadezhda was nothing like this. Nadezhda followed Osip's lead not because of his authority but because she was *already* seduced, and her seduction by his poetry had nothing to do with him. Mandelstam's poems had an objective existence for them both, and it was for the sake of the poetry that they would each sacrifice themselves. 'We can consider verbal representations not only as objective data of consciousness, but as human organs, just like the liver or the heart,' Mandelstam wrote in his essay, 'On the Nature of the Word'. Regardless of the intimacy and closeness to the word involved in his way of reading and writing, Mandelstam treated his poems as objects entirely independent of the poet: they interrupted him with their presence, they spoke *through* him. He merely gave voice to what could not be heard; he was as lured and seduced into singing as his wife was towards the song.

Osip didn't wield seductive power over everyone in Kiev that summer of 1919. In Nadezhda he had found his ideal audience, but she discovered that their relationship 'annoyed everyone for some reason . . . My brother used to say to [Osip], "Nadia doesn't exist – she's just your echo." "That's how we like it," he replied glee-fully.'[101]

Echo was not an inappropriate figure for Evgeni Yaklovlevich, a writer himself, to refer to here: Ovid's tale of Echo and Narcissus is another version of the story of the Mandelstams. In *Metamorphosis*, Echo has lost the power of speech and sees the beautiful Narcissus in the forest. Doomed to return his last words, she transformed his rejection of her love into its confirmation, "May I die before I give you power o'er me," he says. "I give you power o'er me," she echoes. Echo pined away for love of Narcissus until 'only her voice and her bones were left, till finally her voice alone remained; for her bones, they say, were turned to stone'. Except it was not *her* voice that remained, but the echo of someone else's. Narcissus, meanwhile, drowned in his own reflected image. Ovid's tale is tragic because Echo's containment of the words of Narcissus is seen as being devoid of pleasure or reward. This was not so in the case of Nadezhda Mandelstam.

VIII

Who was Nadezhda Mandelstam when she was echoing her husband? What state was she in when she was repeating to herself over and over again Mandelstam's poetry? *Where* was she when his lines were pouring out of her? She was not thinking; she was not dreaming; she was not, in the fullest sense of the word, *herself*, or in communication with herself, and yet she felt that this echo was her purpose, that this was what defined her, and that these lines not only spoke for her but *spoke her*. She is a troubling figure because she inhabited two realities, neither of which was strictly her own. Externally, she went through the motions of living in Soviet Reality (an ideological construct) while internally, she secretly nurtured the antidote to this deadly, philistine drudgery. From the age of eighteen until her death she lived suspended in someone else's language, and the reason why the strangeness of this image is hard to put away is that it is also uncannily familiar. We have each been in her position ourselves, and have yearned to be there again. For is this not what happens in all reading? Is this desire to cast ourselves adrift from the material world and suspend ourselves in words not the reason that we read at all? 'Where am I when I'm reading?' Sven Birkerts asks. 'Isn't this another way of asking what happens to the buzz of consciousness when the writer's language takes possession of us?'[102]

Nadezhda Mandelstam's containment of her husband is only a radical extension of what is involved in any deep or close engagement with a text. If reading plays a part in constructing the self, then she showed that it did the reverse as well. 'I can forget myself only when I am alone, and only in a book, over a book!' Marina Tsvetaeva said.[103] But when Nadezhda forgot herself in a book she did it literally: if the reader reads to lose herself so that she may then return to herself with greater knowledge, Nadezhda Mandelstam's experience of reading was to lose herself and find that she had no self to which she could return. In her hands, reading might therefore be seen as a parody of the passive, introspective and escapist gesture it is represented as being in countless paintings and writings, in which the solitary reader is seen dissolving into the page, disengaging from the represented world and sinking into the invisible world of the book. And yet this is not the case, and not only because very little of the reading Nadezhda Mandelstam described *was* isolated and silent.

'There was not the slightest hint of quiet in our time,'[104] she said. And this included reading, which for Osip Mandelstam was active not passive, and was noisy like dialogue. He deliberately never used the word 'reader', preferring instead to speak of the 'sobesednik', which means a figure with whom to converse.[105] When Mandelstam met with his friends they would read to one another, from their own poetry and the poetry of other people. Anna Akhmatova was the same and the two read one another every line they wrote and they always read immediately, before they exchanged their news.[106] When Akhmatova and Mandelstam discovered that they had both been absorbed in Dante, they recited him to each other,

and Mandelstam wept to hear 'just those words, and in your voice'
as Akhmatova read to him.

Reading, like poetry, was a conversation for Osip, but for
Nadezhda reading led to writing, making it not quite the end in
itself or the disappearing act it might at first seem. In their
approaches to reading, Osip and Nadezhda Mandelstam represent
the differences between the reading styles of Ruskin and Proust.
Proust's introduction to Ruskin's *Sesame and Lilies* argues that
Ruskin, along with Descartes, held a dry view of reading: 'the
reading of all good books is like a conversation with the worthiest
individuals of past centuries who were their authors.' For Ruskin,
the reader is taken over by the author during this exchange. Proust,
however, saw reading not as a 'conclusion' but as an 'incitement' to
the reader to 'think for himself'. Proustian reading is not an
exercise in self-discipline but an invitation to access one's own
inner life. Reading makes one more alert to one's 'deep self' and in
this sense it is a profoundly lonely activity, with none of the clutter
of conversation about it. Ruskin's theory had 'not tried to go to the
very heart of the idea of *reading*', Proust thought.[107] Reading, he
argued, is

> the exact opposite of conversation in consisting for each one of
> us in having another's thought communicated to us while
> remaining on our own, that is while continuing to enjoy the
> intellectual authority we have in solitude and which
> conversation dispels instantly, while continuing to be open to
> inspiration, with our mind yet working hard and fruitfully on
> itself.[108]

Proust's definition of reading is what Barthes defines as bliss: being
in the presence of a lover and thinking about something else. In the
reading of good books, Proust writes, the reader's wisdom begins
where the author's concludes. It is Proust's deep reader who comes
closer to describing Nadezhda than Ruskin's 'dry' ideal, who

resembles more Osip Mandelstam. Nadezhda Mandelstam read her way into profound isolation, inspiration, and wisdom. Her reading led her to ask the questions about selfhood her writing addresses. Her reading of Mandelstam resulted in Proust's 'ideal': friendship in its 'uncontaminated form'.[109]

The Mandelstams were reading in an age anterior not only to the twentieth century, but to the eighteenth century as well. It is only recently, in the last three hundred years, that reading has become a silent act, a gesture of the eye and not of the tongue. 'To read without uttering the words aloud or at least mumbling them is a "modern" experience,' Michel de Certeau argues in *The Practice of Everyday Life*. In the last three hundred years the text has become a 'visual poem'.

> In earlier times, the reader interiorized the text; he made his voice the body of the other; he was its actor. Today, the text no longer imposes its own rhythm on the subject, it no longer manifests itself through the reader's voice. This withdrawal of the body, which is the condition of its autonomy, is a distancing of the text.[110]

The only contact the body now has with the text is through the eye. St Augustine thought reading to oneself was a bizarre subversion of the point of reading; for him, 'the spoken word was an intricate part of the text itself . . . Written words, from the days of the first Sumerian tablets, were meant to be pronounced out loud, since the sounds carried implicit, as if it were their soul, a particular sound.' Silent words on a page are dead, without spirit. 'Faced with a written text, the reader had a duty to lend voice to the silent letters.'[111]

Even the depth with which the Mandelstams read belongs to an earlier age of reading, a time when reading was 'intensive' rather than 'extensive', a vertical plunge as opposed to a horizontal perusal. It is best to read just one book all one's life, Mandelstam said,[112] in which case his was Dante's *The Divine Comedy*, the book he took to prison with him both the first and second times. He even carried a copy of it in his pocket in case he was arrested in the street. 'The coming of a new book into his life was like a first encounter with someone destined to be a friend,'[113] Nadezhda observed. Rolf Engelsing argues that

> From the Middle Ages until some time after 1750 . . . men read "intensively." They had only a few books – the Bible, an almanac, a devotional work or two – and they read them over and over again, usually aloud and in groups, so that a narrow range of traditional literature became deeply impressed on their consciousness. By 1800 men were reading "extensively." They read all kinds of material, especially periodicals and newspapers, and read it only once, and then raced on to the next item.[114]

Nadezhda Mandelstam, who personifies intensive reading, had returned to a time in which the text was seen as sacred.

IX

For Joseph Brodsky, Mandelstam was 'a modern Orpheus'.[115] The Orpheus of their story, however, the mourner who followed her beloved to the underworld only to lose him in a backward gaze, is Nadezhda Mandelstam. It is she who attended her husband into exile and who lived in the shadows after his death, singing his songs. And in gazing so hard at her loved one in the books she then wrote about him, she lost not only Mandelstam but also herself.

But there is another mythical figure represented by Nadezhda, apart from Echo and Orpheus, who comes closer to the Mandelstam's tale because she dominates Osip's second collection of poems, *Tristia*.

We shall die in transparent Petropolis,
before Persephone our queen.
When we sigh we swallow the air of death.
Every hour will commemorate our last moments.

Sea-goddess, stern Athena,
Lift off your great stone helmet.
We shall die in transparent Petropolis
where Persephone, not you, is the queen.[116]

Mandelstam's *Tristia* is a hymn to the goddess Persephone and her realm: death and the underworld. Petersburg, or Petropolis, has become her funereal kingdom. Mandelstam believed that ideally a man should abduct his bride from her family home, and so, like Persephone, who was stolen from her mother by Hades, Nadezhda was carried away from Kiev by Death and crowned queen of the afterlife. Living in Hell, Osip was unable to bear his fate without the presence of his wife.

There is a third person in this myth whose role is just as important as those of Hades and Persephone, and this is the woman who was left behind. The part of Demeter, Persephone's grieving mother and the goddess of the fruitful earth, was taken by Anna Akhmatova. And if Akhmatova's story is inseparable from the Mandelstams' it is not so much because of her friendship with Osip as because of her relationship with Nadezhda, which was precisely – as in all mother and daughter relationships – to do with inseparability.

Scathingly called by Andrei Zhdanov, Stalin's cultural henchman, 'half-nun, half-harlot', Anna Akhmatova was the eternal maiden, wife and mother. Akhmatova's life-cycle, like Demeter's, was seasonal: the maiden became the wife, who became the mother, who bore the maiden and buried the dead, who died herself and was renewed as the maiden, who became the wife and mother and so forth. Anna Akhmatova married three times (although the third time was not strictly a marriage because Nikolai Punin never divorced his wife, but then no one was sure any longer what the process of marriage or divorce actually involved and so formalities didn't much matter). She buried all her husbands, two in unmarked graves: Punin died in a prison camp in Siberia in 1953, the same year as Stalin. Also losing her son to concentration camps, she was adopted as both Russia's virgin queen and its spiritual mother. Her motherhood was epitomized in her representation of loss and grief rather than in maternal instinct, but the reality of her relationship with her son was irrelevant to her readers. 'She was, essentially, a poet of human ties: cherished, strained, severed,' Joseph Brodsky said. 'In that sense, the whole nation took up the pen name of Akhmatova.'[117]

Like Mandelstam, Akhmatova carried on writing well after it had begun to threaten her life and the lives of those around her. Poetry sustained her, she said, it gave her the strength to go on. Writing was an act of political defiance but it was also something over which she had no control. It 'happened' to her; try as she might she could not shake off the resounding noise of a poem in her ears, insisting on being heard. When her epic *Poem Without a Hero* was forming itself in her mind she wrote poems to it begging it to let her be. And like Osip Mandelstam, the only time she sat down to write a Soviet poem was in 1950 when she was trying to save the life of her child. 'I can say that I never abandoned poetry, although the frequent hard knocks of the oars against my numbed hands clinging to the side of the boat beckoned me to sink to the bottom.'[118]

Akhmatova was allowed to survive just as long as she knew who controlled the boat's rudder, and in case she forgot this her stammering, shy child, a Middle-Eastern scholar (who later became a professor of History), was arrested in 1933 while he was consulting a colleague about the translation of an Arabic poem. Lev spent nine days in prison, his colleague was still there sixteen years later when he died. Lev Gumilev was arrested again in 1935 along with Nikolai Punin, Akhmatova's third husband, and Akhmatova burned all her papers, in case they incriminated her family, then wrote a letter to Stalin. Lev and Punin were released so quickly that it left Punin in a state of shock, but Lev was arrested again in 1938 and this time he was tortured. 'It will be difficult to protect him,' Mandelstam had once said to Akhmatova of her son. 'There is death inside him.' Lev Gumilev would have been shot, only the officials who ordered his death were shot themselves. Instead he was sent to a Siberian work camp for five years. In 1949 he was arrested once more and sentenced to ten further years in work camps. Akhmatova again burned her writing and during the years her son was away she petitioned for his release, worked to send him money and queued for hour upon hour outside the prison walls so that she could leave parcels for him through the faceless window. This experience was the source of her cycle, *Requiem*:

> In the terrible years of the Yezhov terror, I spent seventeen months in the prison lines of Leningrad. Once, someone 'recognised' me. Then a woman with bluish lips standing behind me, who, of course, had never heard me called by name before, woke up from the stupor to which everyone had succumbed and whispered in my ear (everyone spoke in whispers there):
> "Can you describe this?"
> And I answered: "Yes, I can."
> Then something that looked like a smile passed over what had once been her face.[119]

Lev Gumilev believed that his mother was indifferent to his fate; after all, when he was a child she had been more interested in fame and lovers than in him. He was led to believe that because of her celebrity she only had to say the word and he would be released. He never forgave Akhmatova for his sufferings and he never believed in her own.

Anna Andreevna produced her first striking line of poetry when, aged seventeen, she changed her name from Gorenko, which means 'grief' and 'burn', to the alliterative Akhmatova.[120] Her father, she said, didn't want his name associated with her poetry, so she was saving him from embarrassment. She also said that the name Akhmatova came from her Tartar grandmother, but Nadezhda Mandelstam doubted that this Tartar grandmother ever existed and believed that she was dreamed up by Akhmatova's poetic imagination. Before she had written a word of poetry everyone was convinced that Anna Andreevna would be a poet – 'my father even teased me by calling me a decadent poetess . . .'[121] – just as during her years of silence in the 1930s and 1940s she continued to be treated with the reverence due to Russia's poetic voice. Her emergence as the greatest poet of feminine love since Sappho was achieved with the same suddenness as Nadezhda Mandelstam's appearance as Russia's memory. There was never a fledgling Nadezhda Mandelstam, or an immature Akhmatova. She arrived on the literary scene fully formed, like Pallas Athene from the head of Zeus.

'I was born the same year as Charlie Chaplin, Tolstoy's 'The Kreutzer Sonata', the Eiffel Tower, and, it seems, Eliot. That summer – 1889 – Paris celebrated the centennial of the fall of the Bastille. Midsummer night was and still is celebrated on the night I was born – 23 June.'[122] She was born in Odessa in what she called 'Dostoevsky's Russia' and brought up in Tsarskoye Selo, outside St Petersburg, Pushkin's home and the seat of the Tsar's summer residence. It was from this exclusive and cultured town that she imbibed her elegance, dignity, and aristocratic hauteur: Anna Akhmatova was pure Tsarskoye Selo. Her family, however, were not. There was no interest in aesthetics in the Gorenko household; Anna Andreevna was brought up on the socialist poetry of Nikolai Nekrasov, the only book they owned and which she was allowed to read on feast days and holidays. It had been a present to

Akhmatova's mother from her first husband, who had shot himself. In 1905 her parents divorced and Anna returned to 'the pagan unbaptised land' of the Black Sea. When she was thirteen, Anna knew Baudelaire and Voltaire – which she 'managed to get hold of somehow' – in French. Before then, she had instinctively known what poetry was, and from the age of eleven could be heard lying awake at night whispering her poems to herself, listening to their music in the dark.

She did not learn the formal art of poetry until her first marriage, when her husband showed her the proofs of his old schoolmaster Innokenty Annensky's 'The Cypress Chest'. This was the read that changed Akhmatova's life: 'Immediately I stopped seeing or hearing, I couldn't tear myself away, I repeated those poems day and night . . . They opened up a new harmony for me.'[123] Nothing her husband wrote made her feel this way.

In 1903 Anna Akhmatova met Nikolai Gumilev while she was Christmas shopping with a friend. She was barely an adolescent and he was five years her senior, but he was to pursue her for the next seven years, attempting suicide several times until she finally married him, in 1910. 'I believe it's my fate to be his wife. Whether or not I love him I really do not know, but I think I do,' Akhmatova wrote in 1907. As with Akhmatova's other marriages, her relationship with Gumilev was over as soon as it began. By the time she accepted him it was too late: Gumilev only fell in love with girls, he would never be able to relate to an adult woman.

For Gumilev, Anna was a mermaid, the barefoot child on the beach who leapt from the cliffs into the sea. He painted mermaids around the walls of his bedroom and she became the dominant theme of his poetry. 'It was as if [her marriage] had absolutely no significance for her,' a childhood friend said of the bride. 'She read poetry, and I found no images whatsoever in them of Gumilyov [sic] . . . in contrast to his poems, which were full of her until the end of his life. First as a water sprite, then as a witch, then simply as a woman hiding "evil solemnity".[124] 'From a serpent's nest,' Gumilev wrote,

> From the city of Kiev,
> I took not a wife but a witch.
> I thought her amusing
> Guessed she might be capricious,
> A gay and happy song bird.
>
> You call out and she frowns
> You hug her and she bristles
> When the moon comes out she starts pining.
> She stares and groans
> As if she were burying
> Someone and wanted to drown herself.

Gumilev had written poetry since he was six years old, but poetry 'took possession' of him when he was fourteen, after reading Pushkin and Lermontov's poetry about the Caucasus mountains and then seeing those mountains with his own eyes.[125] This comment sums up Gumilev: the poet as conquering explorer and swashbuckling adventurer, rather than the poet as aesthete or intellectual. He liked poetry to tell it as it is. Gumilev was a man of action, an innovator; it was he who inspired the move away from the Symbolists, the poets who dominated Russian poetry, and began the Acmeist movement, of which Akhmatova and Mandelstam were a part. Acmeism rejected Symbolism's allusiveness, religion, and mysticism, preferring a 'virile' return to clarity and precision. For the Acmeists, one of the group said, 'a rose has become beautiful in itself, for its petals, fragrance, and colour, not for its purported likeness to mystical love or anything'. Another member thought that the term 'Acmeism' contained an unconscious echo of Akhmatova, whose work had conformed to Acmeist principles before they had been formally defined.

Anna Akhmatova and Nikolai Gumilev were too alike. Neither were home-makers, both were restless, neither knew what to do with their son, who was brought up by his paternal grandmother, and both were more interested in poetry than in people. 'When I was young,' Anna Akhmatova recalled, 'I was very sociable, loved guests, loved to go visiting. Kolya [Gumilev] explained my sociability: when left alone, I constantly wrote poems. I needed people to rest from poetry, otherwise I would keep writing, never tearing myself away, never resting.'[126] Akhmatova either wrote poetry or rested from poetry; her relationships supplemented her poems and she appropriately wrote her first collection when Gumilev was away. Anna Akhmatova made a habit of marrying men who were jealous of her poetry. Considering the seductive effect Akhmatova had on her country, it is curious that her writing repulsed her husbands. Her case is a reminder that the flipside of desire is distaste, and that there is a violence to seduction, literary or otherwise, that quite easily leads to a kind of horror on the part of the seduced partner. Witness the extraordinary remarks made by her collaborators about Laura Riding as a castrating Medusa.

Akhmatova wrote nothing in her next two marriages. Her second husband discouraged it and burned her work, and her third husband was unsympathetic to her poems, but as soon as her marriage with Punin was over she began writing again. Her poetry inspired rivalry, as Gumilev wrote to her:

> I know a woman: silence,
> Bitter fatigue from words,
> Lives in the secret flicker
> Of her dilated pupils.
>
> Her soul is open greedily
> Only to poetry's bronze song,
> Before the pleasures life allots
> She remains haughty and deaf.

Nikolai Gumilev was a ladies' man, compulsively unfaithful to Akhmatova during both their courtship and marriage. Bored with married life, he took off to Africa six months after their honeymoon in Paris. It was then that Anna Akhmatova began to write, and by the time Gumilev returned she had completed her first collection of poems, *Evening*. When she went to meet him at the station, Gumilev asked Akhmatova whether she had been writing and whether he could to see her work immediately, then and there on the train platform. She showed him her poems and he nodded his approval. 'Good,' he said. But he thought 'for a woman to be a poet was – absurd', Akhmatova wrote[127] and for two poets to be married to one another was ridiculous . He would have preferred his wife to have been a ballet dancer.

Evening was more than good; it was perfect. 'It would seem that a small book of love lyrics by a beginning author should have drowned in world events,' Akhmatova said of its publication in 1912.'But time deemed otherwise.'[128] *Evening* was typical Akhmatova: clear, eloquent, disciplined verse, capturing in a few words the complexity of an erotic situation and focusing a dialogue through the lens of a chance detail or metonym. Love, for Akhmatova, was always something that never reached its destination; it was always diverted or too late:

> Under her dark veil she wrung her hands . . .
> "Why are you so pale today?"
> "Because I made him drink of stinging grief
> Until he got drunk on it.
>
> How can I forget? He staggered out,
> His mouth twisted in agony . . .
> I ran down not touching the bannister
> And caught up with him at the gate.

Panting, I cried: 'A joke!
That's all it was. If you leave, I'll die.'
He smiled calmly and grimly
And told me: 'Don't stand here in the wind.' "[129]

The cool impersonality of Akhmatova's art is not immediately apparent, and before her reader realizes how little the poet has given away, he feels seduced by Akhmatova's thus confiding in him. In this sense, and in no other, is her seductive appeal analogous to that of Anaïs Nin. Akhmatova presents her readers, in miniature, with scenes that could be taken from the last moments of a psychological novel. 'The genesis of Anna Akhmatova lies in Russian prose and not in poetry,' Mandelstam saw.[130]

Evening was followed in 1914 by *Rosary*, in 1917 by *White Flock*, in 1921 by *Plantain*, and in 1922 by *Anno Domini MCXMXXI*. Anna Akhmatova's second collection guaranteed her a secure position in Russian poetry, but after Lenin died in 1924 she found it increasingly difficult to find a place in the Soviet system. A 1929 entry in the *Literary Encyclopaedia* recorded her as a 'poetess of the aristocracy who had not found a new function in communist society, but had already lost her old function in feudal society'. In 1946 she was singled out for attack as 'a typical representative of empty poetry lacking in ideas and alien to our people'.[131] But her death knell sounded as early as 1922. In an influential lecture on the state of Russian poetry, 'Two Russias', given at the House of Arts in Petrograd by Korney Chukovsky, he compared the 'centuries of cultural tradition' of the sedate pre-Revolutionary Akhmatova with the 'thundering and rumbling . . . roaring and screaming' of the Futurist revolutionary bard, Mayokovsky. 'I love, but I am not loved; I am loved, but I do not love – this is her main speciality . . . Next to her,' Chukovsky said of Akhmatova, 'other poets seem like bombastic rhetoricians,' and with that remark he inadvertently buried Akhmatova under the rubble of the Revolution. She was seen thereafter as the representative of a dead past, cut off from the mood of the crowd who were being led along by Mayakovsky's pipe. By 1925 her poetry was unofficially banned by the Communist Party. 'It is only today that I realised the nature of my guilt before humanity, the crime for which they ceaselessly take their revenge,' she said in her old age. 'I wrote poems that people liked and continue to like. Apparently this is something not to be forgiven.'[132] Anna Akhmatova did not publish again until 1940. Mayakovsky had killed himself ten years earlier, in despair that his poetry would not last.

Nikolai Gumilev's concrete verse was respected in Petersburg circles and after he returned from Africa he introduced his young bride to the city's literati. She began to go with her husband to the poetry meetings that took place at the home, known as the Tower, of the Symbolist poet Vyacheslav Ivanov. Here, at her first meeting, she stood in front of the room of male poets and read:

> My heart grew chill so helplessly,
> Although my footsteps seemed so light.
> In all my anguish I was drawing
> My left hand glove upon my right.

She was immediately accepted by the fraternity as an equal, but it wasn't long before she broke away from the Tower to join the Poet's Guild, established by her husband, and concentrate on drawing up the modernist aesthetics of Acmeism. [133]

Nikolai Gumilev was killed by a firing squad on his thirty-fifth birthday, in August 1921. Akhmatova heard about his death while she was attending the funeral of the great poet Alexander Blok. Gumilev had been arrested a few weeks earlier, accused of conspiring in a counter-revolutionary plot, although Akhmatova never believed this and Gumilev used to joke that he made his pro-monarchy sympathies so obvious that no one could ever accuse him of undercover conspiracies. Akhmatova and Gumilev divorced three years before his death and both had remarried, but Nadezhda Mandelstam said that Akhmatova liked to believe Gumilev had been in love with her to the end, although she claimed that she had never been in love with him. Nine years later Anna Akhmatova found the site of the pit into which his body was thrown.

In a romantic elegy to the founder of Acmeism, the émigré writer Georgi Ivanov claimed that Gumilev had died not for the restoration of the monarchy or for the future of Russia but for the 'regeneration of poetry': 'Gumilev died in an attempt to hold by his own feeble hands, by his own personal example, that greatest manifestation of the human spirit – poetry – on the brink of a precipice into which it was ready to crash.'[134] When Akhmatova was asked why her son had been arrested she replied, 'Does there have to be a reason?' So too with the death of Lev's father: there was no reason for Gumilev's assassination, he died senselessly. He was a warrior-writer and he pushed himself to the front line, but he did not die for poetry. He was neither ready for death, as Mandelstam was after he recited his Stalin poem, nor suicidally possessed by words, like Laura Riding. Gumilev was a master of language; language had no mastery over him.

X

It was at the Tower, in the spring of 1911, that Akhmatova met Osip Mandelstam, who was a great friend of Gumilev's. 'At that time he was a thin boy, with a lily-of-the-valley in his button hole and long eyelashes,' she wrote in her memoir of him. To Mandelstam, she was a 'black angel' with the mark of God upon her. As with his relationship with Nadezhda, Mandelstam and Akhmatova's 'intensely personal and ardent friendship'[135] took off at once. They shared a sense of humour, knew what one another was thinking, rode around the bonfires of revolutionary Petersburg at night reciting poetry.

Mandelstam nervously introduced Akhmatova to his bride in 1924, remembering the disastrous meeting with Marina Tsvetaeva and knowing that Akhmatova did not tend to like poets' wives. But to Nadezhda's surprise Akhmatova accepted her and their friendship was consolidated the following year when they were both recovering from TB in the same sanatorium in Tsarskoye Selo. Nadezhda became Akhmatova's reader, memorizing Akhmatova's verse as well as Mandelstam's, and she observed the poet at work with as much reverence and curiosity as she did her husband. Akhmatova said that she had never seen anything in her life like the Mandelstams' relationship. Osip was terribly in love with his wife, she thought, and 'would not allow Nadya even a step away from him, would not let her work, was furiously jealous, and asked her advice about every word in his poems'.[136] When they were together, Nadezhda said of Osip and Anna, they reverted to the 'madcap' days of their youth before they knew her, and she watched them double up in laughter over a joke she didn't get.

The incongruous friendship between Russia's adored icon and her invisible widow, her symbol of grief and the embodiment of loss, continued long after Mandelstam's death and until Akhmatova's own, in March 1966. It seems to have been a difficult relationship for them both, maintained more through a need for proximity – to one another and to Mandelstam – than through mutual fondness. Brodsky tells a story in which Nadezhda said that she looked forward to dying because she would be with Osip again. ' "No," replied Akhmatova, upon hearing this. "You've got it all wrong. Up there it's now me who is going to be with Osip." '[137] And yet while sexual rivalry between the women certainly existed there was, as there so often is, an attraction and identification between the rivals, in recognition of their similar need.

Nadezhda Mandelstam's relationship with Akhmatova was, like that of Persephone and Demeter, one of a daughter with a mother. She struggled against her identification with the fruitful parent whilst also desiring the closeness, and was jealous of the secret relationship that the mother shared with the father, in which poetry replaced sex as the exclusive bond. Like a mother and daughter they grieved for the father, but like a mother and daughter they had an intimacy of their own. If, as Mandelstam observed, 'the genesis of Anna Akhmatova lies in Russian prose and not in poetry', then Nadezhda Mandelstam was born of Russian poetry and not prose. She was the literary child of Akhmatova's and Mandelstam's poems. When she had written *Hope Against Hope* and *Hope Abandoned* she said that she came to life, and she could only write her books because of what she had imbibed from the poets whose words she contained. 'Gradually the lines of those poets became her mentality, became her identity,' Brodsky argues; 'The clarity and remorselessness of her pages, while reflecting the character of her mind, are also inevitable stylistic consequences of the poetry that had shaped that mind.'[138]

One of the oddities of their relationship is that Nadezhda was always keen to distinguish herself from Akhmatova, to stress their difference, as if she felt in danger of collapsing into total identification with her. In the remarks she makes to differentiate herself from Akhmatova it becomes clear that Nadezhda saw in the poet what she had silenced in herself. Anna Akhmatova was the most jealous woman she had ever met, Nadezhda said, while her own most exasperating fault was her total lack of jealousy. Friends of Akhmatova's in her old age, on the other hand, comment on what they saw as precisely Nadezhda's 'jealousy' and coldness towards Anna Andreevna.[139] 'Nadia still felt no affection for Anna,' Lev's girlfriend Emma Gershtein says of the two women, '. . . even though she had helped to get Mandelstam released after his first arrest . . .'[140]

Anna Akhmatova was self-absorbed and selfish in her friendships, Nadezhda complained. 'Take her attitude to mirrors for example . . . She did not look into mirrors. She lived in them.'[141]

Akhmatova once called Nadezhda 'her second self' because, Nadezhda said, the poet saw herself in everyone: she used her flocks of admirers as mirrors in which she could be reflected. In *Hope Abandoned* Nadezhda sheds light on what she saw as the causes of Akhmatova's narcissism and Mandelstam's egomania: 'The loss of "self" leads either to self-effacement (as in my case) or to blatant individualism with its extremes of egocentrism and self-assertiveness. The outward signs may differ, but it is the same sickness: the atrophy of the true personality.'[142] Therefore Akhmatova and Mandelstam were just different versions of Nadezhda. For all three the self was an out-of-body experience. Akhmatova 'lived in' Nadezhda Mandelstam like a mirror because Nadezhda needed to contain in order to survive, and while Nadezhda had to contain someone, Akhmatova preferred to inhabit images of herself. Which is exactly what Nadezhda Mandelstam had become.

Nadezhda Mandelstam only lived on after Mandelstam's death because of her closeness to Akhmatova, she said, and proximity for Nadezhda meant a collapse of boundaries. For both women, as for Osip Mandelstam, *separation* was an issue and self-definition was difficult to achieve alone. They each expressed this difficulty through their relations with poetry. Either writing or reading it, they experienced poetry as a physical part of themselves: 'It's hard to judge one's own poetry,' Akhmatova told Georgy Adamovich. 'You have to remove yourself from it, get away from it, like a separation.'[143] Describing Mandelstam's poetry, Nadezhda said that an 'effort had to be made to understand him, and then an even greater effort was required so that, having understood him, one could extricate oneself from his power, from what he termed the "sense of the poet's always being right." In the struggle with the poet, no holds are barred.' Separating herself from the power of poets was an issue for Nadezhda, and her relationship with both Mandelstam and Akhmatova was caught between struggling against their poetic force and containing it.

Nadezhda had reason to be jealous of the friendship between Mandelstam and Akhmatova because it excluded her. It was a relationship between two poets, and Nikolai Punin was one of many who felt both inspired by and irrelevant in their company: 'It was a brilliant dialogue which made me both excited and envious – they would speak together for hours, perhaps without saying anything remarkable, but it was a *genuine poetic game* totally inaccessible to me.'[144] Punin was perceptive in seeing that Akhmatova and Mandelstam's conversations were a poetic game, and their game was organized around the seductive power of denying seduction. Seduction is terrifying and true seduction is sacrificial: neither Mandelstam nor Akhmatova were prepared to give themselves up to another's art any more than they were for another's ideology, and they fought against seduction as they fought against Stalin. 'We fight against that which seeks to seduce us,' Baudrillard writes, 'relentlessly seducing the other in order not to be seduced oneself . . . pretending to be seduced in order to cut all seduction short.'[145]

Nonetheless, Anna Akhmatova was disturbed that Mandelstam had not been seduced by her poetry or her person. She later claimed that early on in their friendship she had tried to keep him at arm's length because she sensed he was falling in love with her, but Nadezhda says this was not true. According to Nadezhda Mandelstam, Akhmatova liked to believe that she was a great seductress, and her assumption that anyone not yet in love with her was in grave danger of soon becoming so had deeply offended Mandelstam. 'The Akhmatova I knew,' Nadezhda said, 'was a fierce and passionate friend, who stood by Mandelstam with an unshake-able loyalty, his ally against the savage world in which we spent our lives, a stern, unwielding abbess ready to go to the stake for her faith.'[146] Mandelstam would never fall in love with a woman like this, Nadezhda said, however beautiful she was or however alluring her poetry. Akhmatova's independence and poetic power unsexed her for him. He saw her as his equal or even his superior and he could never love an equal; he could only love someone dependent on him. The Mandelstam's saw Anna Akhmatova much as Henry Miller and Anaïs Nin saw June: she was more man than him, more woman than her.

For all her male swains and followers, including the bevy of young poets like Anatoly Naiman and Joseph Brodsky who befriended her in her old age, Anna Akhmatova had a greater seductive effect on women than she did on men. Marina Tsvetaeva dedicated an entire cycle of poems to her; Nadezhda Mandelstam contained her; schoolgirls doted on her, and women in the prison lines relied on her to tell their story. 'Akhmatova never lacked admirers,' Nadezhda wrote, 'but one real reader, or rather listener, was more precious to her than all of them put together.'[147] Nadezhda had filled this role, but Akhmatova's strongest reader appeared in the year in which she at last abandoned her miserable relationship with Punin. (Because of the housing shortage she was not able to leave him in any satisfactory way; she simply swapped rooms with Punin's wife, who had spent the previous fourteen years with their child next door.) This was also the year in which Mandelstam died and her son was rearrested. Her 'one real reader' was the devoted and courageous daughter of Korney Chukovsky, the writer and critic who had given the talk 'Two Russias' that proved so disastrous for Akhmatova's reputation and to whom Mandelstam had turned in Voronezh when he was in despair. Lydia Chukovskaya, who would later shield Solzhenitsyn in her flat when he went into hiding, became Akhmatova's Boswell and she kept a daily record of the poet's life from 1938, which is now published in three volumes as *The Akhmatova Journals*. Available in Russia since 1989, like Akhmatova's and Mandelstam's poetry, these journals had been circulating in manuscript form for years.

Lydia Chukovskaya was thirty years old when she introduced herself to Anna Akhmatova, although she had known her poetry by heart since childhood. She had heard the rumour that Akhmatova had won her son's (temporary) freedom after writing to Stalin and had come to ask advice on getting her husband, the theoretical physicist Matvey Bronshteyn, out of prison. In their ensuing relationship, Chukovskaya took on the same role as Nadezhda Mandelstam in her partnership with Osip. A gifted writer herself – her novel about the Terror, *Sophia Petrovna*, is published in England as *The Deserted House* – she saw her duty as being the preservation of another woman's voice, and Lydia Chukovskaya became the narcissistic poet's Echo. 'Day by day,' she wrote,

> month by month, my fragmentary notes became less and less a re-creation of my own life, turning into episodes in the life of Anna Akhmatova . . . In the mental state in which I existed all those years – stunned, deadened – I seemed to myself less and less truly alive, and my own non-life unworthy of description . . . By 1940 I had virtually ceased making notes about myself, whereas I wrote about Anna Andreevna more and more often.[148]

We see nothing in these diaries of the diarist but we are given a vivid portrait of the imperious poet, 'stately, beautiful as ever', who would summon Lydia Chukovskaya to see her at midnight, first thing in the morning, and when it was minus 35C outside, in order to tell her the story of her life. Chukovskaya's husband, meanwhile, was executed later that year.

It did not take long for Lydia Chukovskaya to adapt to her role as Akhmatova's reader and memory. After her first visit to the poet's shabby, threadbare room in the grand Fontannay House, Chukovskaya walked home that night in a trance,

> trying to recall the poems. I had to remember them there and then, from start to finish, because already I could not let them go even for a second . . . I remembered everything word for

word. But later . . . I could not recall a single step down the
road . . . I had been sleepwalking: poems had guided me,
instead of the moon, and the world had been absent.[149]

Akhmatova was then working on her cycle about Stalin's Terror,
Requiem, and was convinced that her room was bugged. Very soon
the pattern between the poet and her reader was established. Afraid
of speaking her poetry, Akhmatova would break off in conversation, get out a pencil and paper and make loud small-talk about the
weather as she scribbled her verse down. She would then hand the
paper to Chukovskaya, who memorized the words, after which
Akhmatova would strike a match and burn the evidence. 'It was a
ritual,' Chukovskaya wrote, 'hands, match, ashtray – a beautiful
and mournful ritual.'[150]

The genuine poetic game Akhmatova had played with Mandelstam became a beautiful mournful ritual with Chukovskaya, which
is about as apt a description of seduction as one can get. This way
Lydia Chukovskaya preserved all of Akhmatova's late work. She
was sitting up editing the final volume of the *Akhmatova Journals*
when she died in 1996.

XI

The last time Anna Akhmatova and Osip Mandelstam met was in
the autumn of 1937. This was the year in which they were most
intimate, Akhmatova told Lydia Chukovskaya. The Mandelstams
were homeless and had illegally come to Leningrad for two days:
they were not allowed within a one-hundred-mile radius of main
cities. Someone told Osip that his father did not have any warm
clothing; Mandelstam, ailing and emaciated, then took off his
jumper so that it could be given to Emil Veniaminovich. That was
all that Akhmatova could remember of their meeting. 'It was all
like a terrible dream,' she said. The terrible dream continued: the

following spring, in 1938, the Mandelstams were offered a two-month holiday at a rest home not far from Moscow, after which Vladimir Stavsky, the secretary of the Writers Union, had promised to review Mandelstam's situation and to see what they could do about helping him to make a living. The Mandelstams expected that soon Osip would be 'restored' and able to return to full and open literary activity, and that in order for this to happen the Writers Union were concerned that he regain his full health. The couple could not believe their luck, and Mandelstam wondered for a moment if their present comfort was for real and not just a trap.

He must have known at some level that of course the holiday was a trap, that they were only being waited on hand and foot in a warm environment so that the secret police knew where they were: the Writers Union rang the rest home twice to check that the guests were still there. The truth was that Mandelstam's frequent appearances in Moscow and Petersburg had become a problem for the Writers Union. Before offering him the holiday Vladimir Stavsky had already written to Nikolay Yezhov in state security on 13 April 1938 about the wandering poet. Mandelstam's Moscow friends were financially supporting him, Stavsky observed, and were busy making of him 'a figure of suffering, a brilliant and totally unrecognised poet'.[151] Stavsky's letter implored Yezhov to help the Soviet literary world deal with Osip Mandelstam, and Yezhov was happy to oblige. The subsequent report put together on Mandelstam recommended arrest and isolation, not only because exile had done nothing to amend his 'anti-Soviet' views, but also because he was posing as a martyr and his 'psychological imbalance' had made him 'capable of aggressive acts'.[152]

The warrant for Mandelstam's arrest was signed on 28 April 1938, and police arrived at the rest home before dawn on 3 May. Nadezhda was only half awake, having just had a nightmare, when they heard the knock. So for both Anna Akhmatova and Nadezhda Mandelstam, their final image of Osip Mandelstam resembled the stuff of dreams. Nadezhda later recalled that the night before his arrest Osip had been trying to explain something to her that he was now beginning to understand. ' "You know, I think I've understood something – perhaps it's nonsense, but you and I . . ." ' She never knew what he next said because it was then that she fell asleep and when she awoke Mandelstam was being pushed out of the door by two men. Nadezhda was so 'horror-struck' that they did not even say goodbye properly.[153] Stalin's instructions were no longer 'isolate but preserve', because Mandelstam was clearly not going to survive. His file now had 'Terror' written across it, underlined twice.

The relationship between Nadezhda and Osip Mandelstam ended in the middle of a conversation. There is something appropriate about this for Mandelstam, for whom poetry was a conversation, conversation 'a poetic improvisation', and reading a dialogue. His life was a series of truncated or diverted conversations that he nonetheless continued. He once told Akhmatova that his conversation with the executed Gumilev 'never was and never will be broken off'; Pasternak said of Mandelstam's work that 'he got into a conversation which was started before him,' while his relationship with Anna Akhmatova was a conversation conducted indirectly through Nadezhda. Like Mandelstam himself, who died on his way to the middle of nowhere, his conversations never reached their destination, where ever that may have been.

The fate of destinations and addresses fascinated Mandelstam. In an early essay published in *Apollon*, he wrote about the unknown destination of each poem. The reader was an anonymous addressee – where was the poem going? Would it ever get there? Mandelstam's epigram to Stalin got there by default: like all of his poetry, it was carried in the person of another. Seduction, remember, means diversion, and Nadezhda Mandelstam's seduction was the indirect means by which Osip's conversations could continue.

From the day of his arrest until after his death nothing more was heard of Mandelstam, save one letter he sent to his brother, Shura, asking for clothes, food, and money, although he acknowledged that there was probably little point in mailing them. If they reached him at all it would be too late. He also asked after his wife, sending his love to her. Nadezhda Mandelstam wrote her final letter to Osip in October 1938. 'This letter was never read by the person it is addressed to,' she later said. Her letter was never even sent; she remained both its writer and its reader, just as she became the deliverer of Mandelstam's poems as well as their address.

I have no words, my darling, to write this letter that you may never read, perhaps. I am writing it into an empty space. Perhaps you will come back and find me not here. Then this will be all you have left to remember me by . . .
Life can last so long. How hard and long for each of us to die alone. Can this fate be for us who are inseparable? . . .
In my last dream I was buying food for you in a filthy hotel restaurant . . . When I woke up I said to Shura: 'Osia is dead.' I do not know whether you are still alive, but from the time of that dream, I have lost track of you. I do not know where you are. Will you hear me? Do you know how much I love you? I could never tell you how much I love you. I cannot tell you even now. I speak only to you, only to you. You are with me always, and I who was such a wild and angry one and never learned to weep simple tears – now I weep and weep and weep. It's me: Nadia. Where are you?

'That these lines may reach their destination,' Mandelstam once said of a poem, 'perhaps hundreds of years are necessary, as many as a planet needs to send its light to another planet.'[154] His poetry has finally got there, although it encountered many diversions on the way. Or perhaps, by never leaving Nadezhda Mandelstam's person, it had reached its destination all along.

Afterword:
W. B. and George Yeats

If, as Dr Johnson said, a man who is not married is only half a man, so a man who is very much married is only half a writer.

CYRIL CONNOLLY

On the afternoon of 21 October 1917, four days before the Bolsheviks stormed the Winter Palace in St Petersburg and thus began the October Revolution, William Butler Yeats and his bride, formerly Georgie Hyde-Lees, were honeymooning in the Ashdown Forest Hotel. Things were not going well: far from celebrating his marriage, the fifty-two-year-old poet was in a 'great gloom', so he told his friend Lady Gregory. Yeats, who would later send up the domestic unhappiness between the Holy Trinity of Robert Graves, Laura Riding, and Geoffrey Phibbs, was for the moment caught in an unresolved triangle of his own. His bride of four days, whom he believed knew nothing of his misery, was an artistic and unusual twenty-four-year-old. Georgie Hyde-Lees, passionately in love with her husband and of course completely alert to his gloom as well as to its cause, determined to assuage his doubts about the wisdom of his choice. In order to convince Yeats that by marrying her he had done the right thing, she did what all great seducers do: she took a risk.

The best writing and reading involve risk as well, and what Georgie did pushed both activities to their extreme. Telling Yeats that she suddenly felt as if 'something was to be written through her', she sat down with a pencil and paper. Then, as if in a trance, and talking 'all the while so that her thoughts would not affect what she wrote', she produced a message for him: 'What you have done is right for both the cat and the hare.' This was a brilliant idea, and Georgie's trump-card was waiting to be played: she told Yeats that this cryptic sentence had come to her automatically, that her hand had been controlled by an outside force and she had no idea what she had been writing or what it meant. The message, whose symbolism she knew her husband would understand, would reassure him that he needed to be with a home-loving cat and not a tearaway hare, and after he had been suitably calmed, she would tell him the truth about its composition.

Georgie was triumphant. Her task was accomplished. Yeats stood by ecstatic; their marriage was saved by what he called this 'miraculous intervention'. His great gloom had been healed, but not by the writer or by what she had written. What saved the Yeatses' marriage was what Yeats saw as the peculiar nature of the writing itself. Anaïs Nin cast a spell on her readers by her sheer absence from her work, and here it was in Georgie's disappearance behind her writing that the charm of the seduction lay. She was eclipsed by the power of that which poured out of her. 'The strange thing was that within half an hour after the writing of this message,' Yeats wrote to Lady Gregory a few days later, 'my rheumatic pains and my neuralgia and my fatigue had gone and I was happy. From being more miserable than I can ever remember since Maud Gonne's marriage I became extremely happy. That sense of happiness has lasted ever since.'

One of Yeats's editors, George Mills Harper, calls this first attempt by Georgie Yeats at seduction a 'fumbling effort', as though the experiments between wandering hands that were going on in the hotel room were sexual and not literary, which in a sense they were. According to Yeats's biographer, Richard Ellmann, who got it from Mrs Yeats herself, Georgie, like many young brides, began her intimate relations with her husband by faking it. For a truly compulsive writer like Anaïs Nin, who also spent the early days of her marriage in the bedroom with her spouse absorbed in writing, only sexual arousal could be faked and never literary pleasure. But Georgie knew better.

Automatic writing, she surmised, is the perfect vehicle for performing a seduction on a compulsive writer because it is pure activity. It is a writing undertaken without concern for literary value or narrative content, without consideration for the intricacies of inspiration or creativity. This is why Elizabeth Barrett and Henry Miller practised it as well. It is writing for its own sake. Automatic writing represents for the writer what books represent to the bibliomaniac: the thing itself, the sublime, unadulterated object of desire, and it was in this form that Georgie offered herself to her husband.

Faking the means by which she seduced Yeats, Georgie strengthened rather than weakened the power of the act. For there is nothing natural about seduction. Seduction *is* an artificial process, a choreographed set of moves, a game of cat-and-mouse, and seducers continually tease the fine line between artifice and authenticity. Consider for example Valmont in *Les Liaisons Dangereuses* or Lovelace in *Clarissa*, both of whom were driven to death by the game they pursued. Like card-players, they knew that nothing was so serious as winning. The desire they felt was real enough but its expression was ritualized, turned into a masterplan over which neither seducer managed to maintain complete control. Nor did Georgie Yeats; she too got caught in her own trap. For no sooner had she set her game in motion than it span out of her control and the stakes were raised considerably.

After she had written these artificial lines the tables turned on her; Georgie Yeats found that her body tensed up and released itself and that what she had faked before was now coming in full flow. Her hand, as though grasped by another hand, found itself pushed along the page against its volition, writing illegible sentences of which she had no understanding. The words she was forming seemed to come not only from another being but from another world. She was spoken through by different voices; spirits Yeats could call 'communicators', 'controls', and 'unknown writers' were making themselves known to him – the messages they brought were all for Yeats, not for his wife. They had 'come to give you metaphors for poetry', Georgie wrote. This *was* automatic writing and during the week following 5 November Georgie produced ninety-three pages of it. Over the next thirty months, 3600 more pages appeared – and these are only the scripts that survive.

Before long Yeats established an exchange in the form of a question-and-answer session between himself and the spirit world that was mediated through Georgie's person. While he set the direction of the scripts by posing the questions, Georgie, through her 'controls', produced the answers. Some of the questions he raised and the answers she recorded became the substance of Yeats's difficult, esoteric book, *A Vision*. It is possible to see this extra-ordinary work as the result of a literary collaboration, but neither Georgie nor Yeats would take responsibility for doing the writing. Georgie declined to have her name associated with its authorship at all, declaring herself only the medium through which the communicators spoke and Yeats was happy to concede to his wife's demand. His book, he announced, was written by neither one of them, and in this sense the story of Georgie and W.B. Yeats diverts from the others considered in these pages.[1] Neither saw what they were doing as being reading or writing. Yeats was 'communicat-ing' with what his wife wrote and Georgie's 'writing', she stressed, flowed not out of her but through her.

What took place in the Ashdown Forest Hotel was ghost-writing with Georgie Yeats, the most spectral of all, ghosting the ghosts. The ghostly writer in 'The Private Life', Henry James's story about Robert Browning, comes back to mind and Georgie can be seen to be divided like Clare Vawdrey between the shadowy self writing in the dark upstairs and the figure dining down below. The part of her that wrote was unknown to both her husband and herself and it remained that way, but this was the person with whom Yeats chose to engage when he began his relationship with Georgie's writing. Georgie threw herself into writing in desperation, and trading her body for words cost her dear, exhausting her in the first years of her marriage when she wrote every day, seeing practically no one and spending each evening in her husband's study helping him work. Why did she go to this extreme to woo her husband? To understand her motivation it is necessary to go back to Yeat's life before his marriage.

Yeats had spent the previous thirty years pursuing Maud Gonne, with whom he had fallen in love when she turned up, six foot tall, at his family home in Bedford Park, London on 30 January 1889. Maud Gonne was a passionate activist for Irish nationalism and had just read Yeats's *The Wanderings of Oisin*, which, whilst failing to seduce her, at least left her impressed with its treatment of Irish myth and legend. Yeats's poem would in fact set the tone for the Irish literary revival, but even this achievement for her adopted country was not enough to win the heart of Ireland's femme fatale.

In her mid-thirties Maud Gonne married an Irish soldier called John MacBride. When he heard the devastating news, Yeats had been in love with her for fourteen years. It was now February 1903; he was thirty-seven years old and facing middle age disappointed and alone. Maud Gonne's presence in his life, however fleeting, had made committed relationships with anyone else impossible, and for the first five years after their meeting Yeats had nothing to do with other women. He had renewed his proposals to her annually during the years immediately preceding her marriage, and even now that she had converted to Catholicism – thus ensuring that divorce was impossible – Yeats did not entirely lose hope of one day winning her hand. His chance came again when John MacBride, who had separated from his wife after two years of marriage, was shot following the Easter uprising in 1916. Yeats proposed to Maud once more and was once more refused, after which he turned his attentions to her striking daughter, Iseult, who, aged twenty-two, was the same age as Maud when Yeats had first set eyes on her.

Iseult Gonne (her father was a Frenchman and not John MacBride) had known Yeats all her life and was convinced that her mother was right to reject him: his passion alone was not enough on which to base a marriage. But, like a good Oedipal daughter, Iseult was determined not to be left out of this love affair and she proposed to the poet herself when she was fifteen years old. Yeats refused her then but thought better of it now: he had more in common with the daughter than the mother. Maud's only concern was with revolutionary politics, and Yeats had somewhat recklessly made it the condition of their marriage that she should give this up, while Iseult was interested in literature and the arts and liked to spend time reading with the poet. Lady Gregory, having briefly considered marriage to Yeats herself, approved of the match between the fifty-year-old bachelor and the child of the woman he had loved for nearly thirty years, but the two parties concerned thought better of it and after a meeting in a coffee house in London agreed that they would not wed.

Iseult remained in his mind, however, and it was when Yeats received a letter from her during his honeymoon that he was thrown into the disturbance and confusion that led Georgie to decide it was time to seduce her husband. It was Iseult Gonne who represented the restless 'hare' in Georgie's faked message. Against her husband's passion for his muse and its displacement in his obsession with her daughter, Georgie pitched a sentence of automatic writing. She gambled on her belief that the writing would erase in him the importance of the rest, displacing sexual desire with script.

Yeats's relationship with the Gonne women recalls Thomas Hardy's novel of the 1890s, *The Well-Beloved*, in which Jocelyn Pierston, a sculptor from the barren and stony isle of Portland, falls in love successively with three generations of island women and is prevented by fate from marrying any one of them. He loves first the mother, then her daughter, then her granddaughter, and seeks in each an image of the feminine perfection he felt he had found in the first and could find in sculpture. He eventually marries an elderly widow.

In Georgie Hyde-Lees, Yeats gave up on his feminine ideal and chose instead an intelligent companion who, whilst having none of the romanticism of Maud and Iseult Gonne, had about her a literary intelligence and strangeness lacked by her predecessors. George, as Yeats called her, was the daughter of friends of his and he had known her since she was eighteen: she followed his interests in all things, he was to realize, and she had known of his interest in the occult and automatic writing long before she married him. Maud Gonne scoffed at their marriage, calling it 'prosaic', which was an ironic term given that the partnership was to be organized entirely around the creation of prose, and prose that reanimated Yeats, inspiring his strongest poetry.[2] When the 'almost illegible writing' had first appeared, Yeats found it 'so exciting' that he 'offered', he said, 'to spend what remained of life explaining and piecing together those scattered sentences'. This is exactly what happened: his vision preoccupied him until the day that he died, in 1939. Yeats gave himself up to his wife's literary appeal.[3]

Like the other compulsive writers in *Literary Seductions*, Yeats benefited from the presence of a third party in his literary life, only in this case the third person was not always another woman and not always alive. Yeats and George lived for years in a triangle with a ghost and it was through the commands of 'Anne Hyde' (who had died in the seventeenth century) that the Yeats's first child was conceived. The couple had been told by her in the automatic script to have a baby and expect a boy. Anne Hyde wrote that she looked on Yeats as her husband and on George as herself and so their son would be a reincarnation of her own child. As it was, when George gave birth to a daughter they named her Anne.

I want to leave you with the image of George Yeats sitting at her desk on her honeymoon pouring out words to seduce her husband, because the questions this haunting scene raises are those that inspired this book. Who are we when we write? Where are we when we read? What, or who, is it we desire when we read and write? Had Yeats thought George the subjectivity behind her script, he would never have been seduced; had George thought Yeats might choose Iseult Gonne over ghost-writing, she would never have found him seductive. Was George Yeats a diverted reader or a compulsive writer? Sitting there at the Ashdown Forest Hotel with her hand scuttling across the page, she combines and confuses the diversions of the absorbed reader with the trance and drive of the compulsive writer, whilst occupying neither of these roles. In reading you put yourself in the hands of a writer and let go, abandoning all to the dictates of the word, but George did this when writing. It was when she lifted a pen, not a book, that she had no idea where the signs were going to lead her. And if reading, as Schopenhauer says, is thinking with other people's brains, George was *writing* with the mind of another. When she gave her body on her honeymoon, it was to produce these essays by diverse hands.

Was George Yeats possessed by writing, like Anaïs Nin? Did her writing consume Yeats, as Laura Riding and Robert Graves consumed one another? Was she the container of her husband's work, in the manner of Nadezhda Mandelstam, so that the rest of her fell away? There is a sense in which all three are the case, but the Yeatses' is a story of literary consummation: it was writing that completed their marriage vows. George's great achievement, her seductive force, lay in saving her marriage by diverting her husband's attention away from his muse and his femme fatale, and redirecting it towards compulsive writing. She therefore ensured that Yeats's desire for her was experienced by him as a drive to write while his drive to write was experienced by him as desire for her. And it is at the meeting point between writing, reading and desire that I have paused to consider these literary seductions.

Notes

INTRODUCTION Literary Diversions

1 *The Letters of Robert Browning and Elizabeth Barrett 1845–1846*, vol 1, edited by Elvan Kinter (Cambridge, Massachusetts: The Belknap Press of Harvard University Press, 1969), p. 3

2 Ibid., Sunday, 16 November 1845, p. 271

3 Henry Miller, *The Books in my Life* (London: Peter Owen, 1952), p. 37

4 Henry James, 'The Private Life', *The Figure in the Carpet and Other Stories*, edited by Frank Kermode (Harmondsworth: Penguin, 1986), p. 191

5 Ibid., p. 194

6 Introduction to Maurice Blanchot, *The Siren's Song*, edited by Gabriel Josipovici, translated by Sacha Rabinovich (Brighton: The Harvester Press, 1982), p. 6

7 'The Private Life', p. 212

8 *The Letters of Robert Browning and Elizabeth Barrett*, p. 270

9 Antonio Skarmeta, *Il Postino*, translated from the Spanish by Katherine Silver (London: Bloomsbury, 1996) pp. 38–9

10 Ibid., p. 40

11 Ibid., p. 74

12 *The Letters of Robert Browning and Elizabeth Barrett*, p. 63. My stress.

13 Ibid., p. 271. Browning's stress.

14 Harold Brodkey, 'Reading, the most dangerous game', *Reading in Bed, Personal Essays on the Glories of Reading*, edited by Steven Gilbar (Lincoln, Massachussetts: David R. Godine, 1995), p. 102

15 *The Diaries of Franz Kafka*, edited by Max Brod (Harmondsworth: Penguin, 1972), p. 51

16 Michel de Certeau, 'Reading as Poaching,' in *Readers and Reading*, edited by Andrew Bennett (London and New York: Longman, 1995), p. 159. Certeau's stress.

17 Elizabeth Bowen, 'Out of a book', *Reading in Bed,* p. 59

18 Peter Brooks, *Reading for the Plot: Design and Intention in Narrative* (Cambridge, Mass. and London: Harvard, 1992), p. 277

19 *The Diaries of Franz Kafka*, p. 300

20 *A Writer's Diary: Being Extracts from the Diary of Virginia Woolf*, edited by Leonard Woolf (London: Granada, 1978), p. 142

21 I am indebted to Zachary Leader here, whose highly original book, *Writer's Block*, has kept me stimulated for years. Leader's interests are mine as well, and we share a central concern which lies at the heart of *Literary Seductions*: I agree that Blake's literary 'fluency' is 'less a sign of health than of mania,' and that the 'ease with which [Blake] dealt with difficult or intractable problems of composition' (p. ix) is the issue to be addressed.

22 *The Collected Letters of Joseph Conrad*, ed. Frederick R. Karl, 3 vols (Cambridge: Cambridge University Press, 1988), vol 2, p. 49

23 Walter Allen, ed., *Writers on Writing* (London: Phoenix House, 1948), p. 230

24 Ibid., p. 231

25 Quoted in Ernest Jones, *The Life and Work of Sigmund Freud*, edited and abridged by Lionel Trilling and Stephen Marcus, introduction by Lionel Trilling (Harmondsworth: Penguin, 1964), p. 461

26 Woolf, *A Writer's Diary*, p. 129

27 Julian Green, quoted in Maurice Blanchot, 'Outwitting the Demon: A Vocation', in *The Sirens' Song*, p. 88

28 Sigmund Freud, *Moses and Monotheism*, translated by James Strachey (Harmondsworth: Pelican Freud Library, vol 13, 1985), p. 350

29 *Writers on Writing*, p. 238–9

30 Quoted in Blanchot, 'Outwitting the Demon', p. 88

31 Leon Edel and Lyall H. Powers, eds., *The Complete Notebooks of Henry James* (New York, Oxford: Oxford University Press, 1987), p. 511

32 *The Diaries of Franz Kafka*, p. 318

33 Ibid., p. 163

34 George Barker, *Essays* (London: MacGibbon and Kee, 1970), pp. 11–12

35 Woolf, *A Writer's Diary*, p. 133

36 Adam Phillips, *Monogamy* (London: Faber and Faber, 1996), p. 94

ONE Seduced Readers: *Between the Sheets*

1 Quoted in Samuel Chew, *Byron in England: His Fame and After-fame* (London: John Murray, 1924), p. 5

2 See James Soderholm's *Fantasy, Forgery, and the Byron Legend* (Kentucky: University Press of Kentucky, 1996) for a full account of the games of forgery in the Byron-Lamb relationship.

3 See *On the Side of the Angels: The Second Volume of the Journals of Elizabeth Smart*, edited by Alice Van Wart (London: HarperCollins, 1994)

4 Rosemary Sullivan, *By Heart: Elizabeth Smart, A life* (London: Limetree, 1991), p. 149

5 *Necessary Secrets: The Journals of Elizabeth Smart*, edited by Alice Van Wart (London: Grafton, 1991), pp. 222-3

6 *By Heart*, p. 140

7 Ibid., p. 155

8 Ibid., p. 162. Rosemary Sullivan is quoting Paul Potts.

9 Ibid., p. 3

10 *Lady Morgan's Memoirs: Autobiography, Diaries and Correspondence*, 2 vols, ed. W. Hepworth Dixon (London: W. H. Allen, 1863), vol 2, p. 202

11 Michael Sadleir, *Bulwer: A Panorama, Edward and Rosina, 1803-1836* (London: Constable and Co Ltd, 1931), p. 236. My stress.

12 Ibid., p. 235-7

13 William St Clair, *The Godwins and the Shelleys: The Biography of a Family* (London: Faber and Faber, 1989), p. 161

14 Claire Tomalin, *The Life and Death of Mary Wollstonecraft* (London: Weidenfeld and Nicholson, 1974), p. 216

15 *The Godwins and the Shelleys*, p. 316

16 Letter from Harriet Shelley to Catherine Nugent, 20 November 1814, in Robert Woof, ed., *Shelley: An Ineffectual Angel?* (Kendal: The Wordsworth Trust, 1992), p. 46

TWO Literary Possession: *Anaïs Nin and Henry Miller*

1 Anaïs Nin, *The Early Diary: 1927–1931* (London: Peter Owen, 1994), p. 13

2 Anaïs Nin, *Henry and June: From the Unexpurgated Diary of Anaïs Nin* (Harmondsworth: Penguin, 1987), p. 113

3 *The Early Diary*, p. 55

4 Anaïs Nin, Preface to Bettina Knapp, *Antonin Artard* (Chicago: Swallow Press, 1969), p. x

5 Otto Rank's preface was published posthumously as 'Reflections on the Diary of a Child'.

6 Anaïs Nin, *Incest: From A Journal of Love, The Unexpurgated Diary of Anaïs Nin, 1932–1934* (London: Peter Owen, 1993), p. 359

7 Anaïs Nin, *Fire: The Unexpurgated Diary of Anaïs Nin* (London: Peter Owen, 1996), p. 62

8 Mary Dearborn, *The Happiest Man Alive* (London: Harper Collins, 1991), p. 176

9 *Incest*, p. 241

10 *Early Diary*, p. 81

11 Anaïs Nin and Henry Miller, *A Literate Passion: Letters of Anaïs Nin and Henry Miller, 1932–1953*, ed. and introduced by Gunther Stuhlmann (London: Allison and Busby, 1988) p. v

12 Noel Riley Fitch, *Anaïs: The Erotic Life of Anaïs Nin* (London: Abacus, 1994), p. 4

13 *A Literate Passion,* p. vi

14 Deirdre Bair, *Anaïs Nin: A Biography* (London: Bloomsbury, 1995), p. 31

15 Fitch, p. 7

16 *Incest*, p. 240

17 Louise Kaplan, *Female Perversions* (London: Pandora Press, 1981), p. 10

18 Ibid.

19 Ibid., p. 11

20 Bair, p. 267

21 *Henry and June*, p. 131

22 Bair, p. 287. Nin's stress.

23 Joan Riviere, 'Womanliness as a Masquerade', in Victor Burgin,

James Donald and Cora Kaplan, eds, *Formations of Fantasy* (London and New York: Routledge, 1987), p. 36

24 Anaïs Nin, 'On Writing', With an Essay on her Art by William Burford (New York: 'Outcasts' Chapbooks, 1947), p. 18

25 Anaïs Nin, 'On Writing', p. 24

26 Jean Baudrillard, *Seduction* (Basingstoke: Macmillan, 1990), p. 199

27 Bair, p. 141

28 *Henry and June*, p. 14

29 *Early Diaries*, p. 68

30 *Seduction,* p. 96

31 Anaïs Nin, *Winter of Artifice: Three Novelettes* (London: Peter Owen, 1991), p. 7

32 *Incest*, p. 87 and p. 124

33 *Early Diary*, p. 197

34 *Incest*, p. 383

35 Bair, p. 163

36 Ibid., pp. 132–3

37 Ibid., p. 120 and p. 129

38 Roland Barthes, *The Pleasure of the Text*, translated by Richard Miller (Oxford: Blackwell, 1994), p. 22. His stress.

39 Fitch, p. 9

40 Elisabeth Barillé, *Naked Under the Mask*, translated by Elfreda Powell (Minerva: London, 1993), p. 99

41 Philip K. Jason, *Anaïs Nin and her Critics* (Columbia: Camden House, 1993), p. 78

42 Ibid., p. 85

43 William Burford, in Anaïs Nin, 'On Writing,' p. 7

44 Robert Snyder, *Anaïs Nin Observed: From a Film Portrait of a Woman as Artist* (Chicago: Swallow Press, 1976), p. 38

45 Ibid., p. 36

46 Henry Miller, *Tropic of Cancer* (London: Flamingo, 1993), p. 14

47 Henry Miller, *Black Spring* (London: Flamingo, 1993), p. 23

48 *Anaïs Nin Observed*, p. 98. My stress.

49 George Orwell, 'Inside the Whale', *Inside the Whale and Other Essays* (Harmondsworth: Penguin, 1962), p. 12

50 *Henry and June*, p. 53

51 Ibid., p. 50

52 Henry Miller, *Black Spring*, p. 48. Kate Millett is wrong in her suggestion (in *Sexual Politics*) that Henry Miller was disgusted by the lavatory and the body's waste and this is why he associated it with sex. He loved the lavatory, loving its smell when he first came to Paris, and he wrote many eulogies on the pleasures of urinating and defecating.

53 *Black Spring*, pp. 43–7

54 Anaïs Nin, *D.H. Lawrence: An Unprofessional Study* , with an introduction by Harry T. Moore (London: Black Spring Press, 1985), pp. 10–11

55 Henry Miller, *The Books in my Life* (London: Peter Owen, 1952), p. 12

56 *Pleasure of the Text*, p. 58. His stress.

57 *Black Spring*, pp. 37–8

58 *The Books in my Life*, p. 25

59 Ibid., p. 13

60 *Tropic of Cancer*, p. 105

61 *Henry and June*, p.154

62 *Anaïs Nin Observed*, p. 9

63 Robert Ferguson, *Henry Miller: A Life* (London: Hutchinson, 1993), pp. 375–6

64 Roland Barthes, 'Authors and Writers', in *Barthes: Selected Writings*, ed. and with an introduction by Susan Sontag (London: Fontana, 1982), p. 186

65 Terence Hawkes, *Structuralism and Semiotics* (London: Methuen, 1977), p. 114

66 Italo Calvino, *If on a winter's night a traveller* (London: Picador, 1983), pp. 10–11

67 *The Books in my Life*, p. 29. My stress.

68 Erica Jong, *The Devil at Large* (London: Chatto and Windus, 1993), p. 113

69 *Pleasure of the Text*, p. 11

70 Ibid., pp. 10–11. His stress.

71 Roland Barthes, 'Writing Reading', *The Rustle of Language*, translated by Richard Howard (Oxford: Basil Blackwell, 1986), p. 29. His stress.

72 *Pleasure of the Text,* p. 26

73 'Inside the Whale', p. 13

74 Ibid., pp. 14–15

75 *The Books in my Life,* p. 37

76 *Black Spring,* pp. 14–15

77 Ibid., p. 24

78 Mikhail Bahktin, *Rabelais and his World,* translated by Helene Iswolsky (Indiana University Press, 1984), p. 318

79 Simon Dentith, *Bakhtinian Thought: An Introduction* (London: Routledge, 1994), p. 66

80 *Black Spring,* p. 26

81 Ibid., p.15

82 Henry Miller, *Tropic of Cancer* (Paris: Obelisk Press, 1938). Preface by Anaïs Nin, pp. 7–10. My stress.

83 *Incest,* p. 63 and p. 77

84 *Winter of Artifice,* pp. 80–1

85 *A Literate Passion,* p. 3

86 *The Books in my Life,* p. 34

87 Ferguson, p. 35

88 Ibid., p. 59

89 *Tropic of Cancer,* p. 10

90 *The Books in my Life,* p. 30

91 *Henry and June,* p. 170

92 Jay Martin, *Always Merry and Bright: The Life of Henry Miller: An Unauthorised Biography* (London: Sheldon Press, 1979), p. 77

93 Ferguson, p. 161

94 Alfred Perles, *My Friend Henry Miller* (London: Neville Spearman, 1955), p. 4

95 *Henry and June,* p. 15

96 Ibid., p. 45

97 Ibid., p. 38

98 Ferguson, p. 203

99 Ferguson, p. 197

100 *Henry and June,* p. 212

101 Ferguson, p. 1

102 *Henry and June*, p. 75

103 Ferguson, p. 105

104 Ibid., p.161

105 *My Friend Henry Miller*, p. 3

106 *Henry and June*, p. 60

107 Ibid., p. 54

108 Ibid., p. 15

109 *Incest*, p. 46

110 *Early Diary*, p. 156

111 *Henry and June*, p. 56

112 *D.H. Lawrence: An Unprofessional Study*, p. 14

113 *Henry and June*, p. 56

114 *A Literate Passion*, p. 24

115 *Henry and June*, p. 64

116 *Incest*, p. 117

117 Benjamin Franklin V and Duane Schneider, *Anaïs Nin: An Introduction* (Ohio: Ohio University Press, 1979), p. 197

118 *Anaïs Nin and her Critics*, p. 84

119 Otto Rank, *Art and Artist: Creative Urge and Personality Development*, with a foreword by Anaïs Nin (London and New York: W. W. Norton, 1989), p. ix

120 Ferguson, p. 317

121 Quoted by Noel Riley Fitch in 'The Literate Passion of Anaïs Nin and Henry Miller', in *Significant Others: Creativity and Intimate Partnership*, eds Whitney Chadwick and Isabelle de Courtivron (London: Thames and Hudson, 1993), p. 169

122 *Early Diary*, p. 180

123 Ibid., p. 52

124 Ibid., p. 80

THREE Literary Consumption: *Laura Riding and Robert Graves*

1 *Early Diary*, p. 170

2 Ibid., p. 171

3 Laura Riding, *Selected Poems: In Five Acts* (New York: W. W. Norton, 1973), p. 15

4   Robert Graves, 'Juana de Asbaje', in Paul O'Prey, ed., *Robert Graves: Collected Writings On Poetry* (Manchester: Carcanet, 1995), p. 120

5   Ibid., p. 119

6   Paul O'Prey, ed. *'In Broken Images': Selected Letters of Robert Graves, 1914–1946* (London: Hutchinson, 1982), p. 189

7   Laura Riding, *Poems: A Joking Word* (London: Jonathan Cape, 1930), p. 18

8   Letter to John Graves, quoted in Richard Perceval Graves, *Robert Graves: The Years with Laura 1926–1940* (London: Weidenfeld and Nicholson, 1990), p. 88

9   Laura (Riding) Jackson, *The Word 'Woman' and Other Related Writings*, ed., Elizabeth Friedmann and Alan J. Clark (Manchester: Carcanet, 1994), p. 10

10   Deborah Baker, *In Extremis: The Life of Laura Riding* (London: Hamish Hamilton, 1993), p. 16

11   Martin Seymour-Smith, *Robert Graves: His Life and Works* (London: Bloomsbury, 1995), p. 175

12   Robert Graves, *The White Goddess* (London: Faber and Faber, 1948), p. 13

13   Graves, 'Juana de Asbaje', p. 119

14   The comment was made by Allan Tate, quoted in Baker, p. 12

15   The ancedote was told to Martin Seymour-Smith, p. 7

16   Seymour-Smith, p. xiv

17   Robert Graves, *Goodbye To All That* (Harmondsworth: Penguin, 1960), p. 11–13

18   Robert Graves, 'The Future of Poetry', in *Collected Writings on Poetry*, p. 25

19   See Seymour-Smith, p. 2 for his analysis of Graves as the 'discoverer of the *poetic*'.

20   Perceval Graves, p. 213

21   *Goodbye To All That*, p. 15

22   Miranda Seymour, *Robert Graves: Life on the Edge* (London: Doubleday, 1996), p. 104

23   Quoted in Miranda Seymour, p. 59

24   *The Word 'Woman'*, p. 10

25 *Collected Writings on Poetry*, p. xii

26 Harold Bloom, ed., *Robert Graves* (New York: Chelsea House, 1987), p. 2

27 Randall Jarrell, 'Graves and the White Goddess', p. 20, in Bloom, above

28 *Goodbye To All That* , pp. 10–11

29 Anne Oliver Bell, ed., *The Diary of Virginia Woolf, 1925–1930,* vol 3, 2nd edition (London: Hogarth Press, 1980), p. 13

30 *Goodbye To All That*, p. 236

31 *The Word 'Woman'*, p. 10

32 Seymour-Smith, p. 77

33 Miranda Seymour, p. 79

34 Laura Riding, *Anarchism is Not Enough* (London: Jonathan Cape, 1927), p. 11

35 Baker, p. 87

36 Seymour-Smith, p. 114

37 *Goodbye To All That*, p. 279

38 Camille Paglia, *Sexual Personae* (Harmondsworth: Penguin, 1990), p. 15

39 T.S. Matthews, *Under The Influence* (London: Cassell, 1977), p. 319

40 Graves, 'Juana de Asbaje', p. 119

41 Robert Graves, *But It Still Goes On: An Accumulation* (London and Toronto: Jonathan Cape, 1930), p. 13

42 Robert Graves, *Goodbye to All That* (London: Jonathan Cape, 1929), p. 444

43 Seymour-Smith, p. 158

44 *Anarchism*, p. 220

45 Baker, p. 41. Her stress.

46 *Anarchism*, p. 220–1

47 *In Praeterita*, Riding's unpublished memoirs, quoted in Baker, p. 44

48 Baker, p. 45

49 Quoted in Seymour-Smith, p. 119

50 Ibid., p. 126

51 Laura Riding's statement was made in *Contemporary Poets* (1975), and quoted in Seymour-Smith, p. 121

52 Louise Cowan, *The Fugitive Group: A Literary History* (Baton Rouge: Louisiana State UP, 1959), p. 217

53 T.S. Matthews, p. 13

54 Laura Riding, *Collected Poems* (London: Cassell, 1938), p. xxvii

55 T.S. Matthews, p. 147

56 Ibid., p. 144

57 *Poems: A Joking Word*, p. 18

58 Ibid., p. 10

59 Laura (Riding) Jackson, *The Poems of Laura Riding* (Manchester: Carcanet, 1986), p. 2

60 Julian Symons, 'An Evening in Maida Vale', pp. 34–41

61 Laura Riding, *Collected Poems* pp. xxvii–xxviii

62 Ibid., p. xxviii

63 *Anarchism*, p. 119

64 Ibid., p. 97

65 Riding, *Collected Poems*, p. xviii. My stress.

66 Stanley Kunitz, ed., *Authors Today and Yesterday* (New York: The H. J. Wilson Co., 1938), p. 565

67 Graves, 'Juana de Asbaje', p. 119

68 *Collected Writings on Poetry*, p. xi

69 T.S. Matthews, p. 141–2

70 *Seduction*, p. 133

71 T.S. Matthews, p.156. His stress.

72 Robert Nye, *A Selection of the Poems of Laura Riding* (Manchester: Carcanet, 1994), p. 5

73 *The Poems of Laura Riding*, p. 9

74 Graves, 'Juana de Asbaje', p. 120

75 Blanchot, 'Kafka and literature', *The Sirens' Song*, p. 32

76 *Poems: A Joking Word*, p. 9

77 Martin Seymour Smith, 'Laura Riding's Rejection of Poetry', *The Review: A Magazine of Poetry and Criticism*, no. 23. September-November, 1970, p. 11

78 Baker, p. 16

79 Allon White, ' "The Dismal Sacred Word": Academic Language and the Social Reproduction of Seriousness', in *Carnival, Hysteria, and*

Writing, Collected Essays and Autobiography (Clarendon Press: Oxford: 1993), p. 128

80 *The Poems of Laura Riding*, p. 9

81 T.S. Matthews, p. 205

82 Baker, p. 347

83 Letter from Kit Jackson to Tom Matthews, quoted in T.S. Matthews, p. 317

84 Seymour-Smith, p. 343

85 Ibid., p. 157

86 Frank O'Connor, *My Father's Son* (London: Macmillan, 1968), p. 21 and p. 23

87 *Poems: A Joking Word*, pp. 15–18

88 Baker, p. 100

89 O'Connor, p. 69

90 Perceval Graves, p. 78

91 Ibid., p. 81

92 Letter from Graves to Marsh, 16 June 1929, *In Broken Images*, ed. O'Prey, p. 188

93 Laura Riding and George Ellidge, *14a* (London: Arthur Barker, 1934), p. 258

94 Robert Graves, *Greek Myths* (London: Cassell, 1958), p. 46

95 T.S. Matthews, p. 141

96 Robert Graves, 'The Duende', *Poetic Craft and Principle* (London: Cassell, 1967), p. 109

FOUR   Literary Containment: *Osip and Nadezhda Mandelstam*

1 Translator's introduction, *The Voronezh Notebooks: Osip Mandelstam Poems, 1935–1937*, translated by Richard and Elizabeth McKane, introduction by Victor Krivulin (Newcastle: Bloodaxe, 1996), p. 11

2 Joseph Brodsky, 'The Child of Civilization', in *Less than One: Selected Essays* (Harmondsworth: Penguin, 1986), pp. 143–4

3 Nadezhda Mandelstam, *Mozart and Salieri*, translated by Robert A. McLean (Ann Arbor: Ardis, 1983), pp. 27–8

4 Osip Mandelstam, 'Fourth Prose', in *The Noise of Time*, translated with

introductions by Clarence Brown (London, New York: Quartet Encounters, 1988), p. 181

5 Sven Birkerts, *The Gutenberg Elegies: The Fate of Reading in an Electronic Age* (London: Faber and Faber, 1994), p. 82

6 Nadezhda Mandelstam, *Hope Against Hope*, translated by Max Hayward (Harmondsworth: Penguin, 1975), p. 12

7 Ibid., p. 192

8 Ibid., p. 190

9 Nadezhda Mandelstam, *Hope Abandoned: A Memoir*, translated by Max Hayward (London: Collins Harvill, 1989), p. 11

10 'The Child of Civilization', p. 136

11 Joseph Brodsky, 'Less than One', in *Less Than One*, p. 26

12 'The Child of Civilization', p. 136

13 *Hope against Hope*, p. 319

14 Ibid., p. 188

15 Ibid., p. 242

16 Ibid., p. 192

17 Isaiah Berlin, 'Meetings with Russian Writers in 1945 and 1956', *Personal Impressions* (London: Hogarth Press, 1980), p. 158

18 *Hope Against Hope*, p. 227

19 Yalena Tagar, 'Ariel Ways', 1965. Quoted in Clarence Brown, *Mandelstam* (Cambridge: Cambridge University Press, 1973), p. 130

20 Konstantin Polinov, *Anna Akhmatova and her Circle*, trans. Patricia Beriozkina (University of Kansas Press, Fayetteville, 1994), p. xiv

21 Anna Akhmatova, *Requiem: The Complete Poems of Anna Akhmatova*, translated by Judith Hemschemeyer, edited by Roberta Reeder (Boston: Zephyre Press, Edinburgh: Canongate Press, 1989), p. 384

22 Nadezhda Mandelstam, 'Akhmatova', in *Anna Akhmatova and her Circle*, p. 113

23 *Mozart and Salieri*, p. 34

24 *Hope Abandoned*, p. 232

25 Ibid., pp. 182–3

26 *Marina Tsvetaeva: A Captive Spirit: Selected Prose*, with a New Introduction by Susan Sontag, edited and translated by J. Marin King (London: Virago, 1983), p. 169

27 Amanda Haight, *Anna Akhmatova: A Poetic Pilgrimage* (New York and London: Oxford University Press, 1976), p. 110

28 Viktoria Schweitzer, *Tsvetaeva*, translated from the Russian by Robert Chandler and H. T. Willetts. Poetry translated by Peter Norman. Edited and annotated by Angela Livingstone (New York: The Noonday Press, 1992) p. 75

29 *Hope Abandoned*, p. 467

30 *A Captive Spirit*, p. 169

31 Tsvetaeva quoted in *Mandelstam*, pp. 61–2

32 *The Noise of Time*, p. 110

33 *Hope Against Hope*, p. 14

34 *The Noise of Time*, p. 78

35 Nancy Pollak, *Mandelstam the Reader* (Baltimore and London: Johns Hopkins University Press, 1995), p. 6

36 Robert Alter, 'Osip Mandelstam: The Poet as Witness', 1978, quoted in ibid., p. 9

37 *The Noise of Time*, pp. 78–9

38 *Mandelstam*, p. 7

39 *The Voronezh Notebooks*, p. 20. My italics.

40 Ibid., p. 15

41 *Hope Against Hope*, p. 68

42 The most accurate account of this conversation is given in Berlin, 'Meetings with Russian Writers', pp. 181–2

43 *Mandelstam: Critical Prose and Letters*, edited by Jane Gary Harris, translated by Jane Gary Harris and Constance Link (London: Collins Harvill, 1991) , pp. 561–2

44 'A Child of Civilization', p. 132

45 *Hope Against Hope*, p. 82

46 Ibid.

47 Ibid., p. 225

48 Ibid., p. 83

49 Ibid., p. 331

50 *Hope Abandoned*, p. 22

51 *Hope Against Hope*, p. 15

52 Ibid., p. 22

53 Ibid., p. 258

54 Osip Mandelstam, *The Moscow Notebooks*, translated by Richard and Elizabeth McKane (Newcastle: Bloodaxe, 1991), p. 75

55 *Anna Akhmatova and her Circle*, p. 116

56 *Hope Abandoned*, p. 182

57 *Hope Against Hope*, p. 229

58 Ibid., p. 321

59 Vitaly Shentalinsky, *The KGB's Literary Archive*, translated from the Russian, edited and annotated by John Crowfoot, with an introduction by Robert Conquest (London: The Harvill Press, 1995), p. 185

60 *Hope Against Hope*, p. 243

61 *Hope Abandoned*, p. 180

62 *Critical Prose and Letters*, pp. 559–60. His stress

63 *Hope Against Hope*, p. 221

64 'Conversation about Dante', *Critical Prose and Letters*, p. 400

65 *Hope Abandoned*, p. 171

66 Ibid., p. 11

67 Ibid.

68 *Pleasure of the Text*, p. 67

69 Ibid.

70 *Hope Abandoned*, pp. 4–5

71 Ibid., pp. 8–9

72 Ibid., p. 137

73 Ibid., p. 255

74 *Hope Against Hope*, p. 435

75 *Hope Abandoned* p. 15

76 Ilya Ehrenburg, *Men, Years, Life,* vol II, *First Years of the Revolution 1918–21* (trans. by Anna Bostock in collaboration with Yvonne Kapp, London: MacGbbon and Kee, 1962), p. 108

77 *Hope Abandoned*, p. 20

78 Roberta Reeder, *Anna Akhmatova: Poet and Prophet* (London: Allison and Busby, 1995), p. 41

79 Nadezhda Pavlovich on her and Blok's reaction to hearing Mandelstam read, quoted in *Mandelstam*, p. 88

80 Yelena Mikhaylovna Tager, quoted in ibid., p. 69

81 *Hope Abandoned*, p. 308

82 Ibid., p. 182

83 Ibid., p. 260

84 Ibid., p. 232

85 Ibid., p. 260

86 Ibid., p. 478

87 Ibid., p. 234

88 Ibid., pp. 195–6

89 Ibid., p. 21

90 *Critical Prose and Letters*, p. 484

91 *Hope Abanoned*, p. 142

92 Ibid., p. 22

93 'To seduce is to appear weak. To seduce is to render weak. We seduce with our weakness, never with strong signs or powers.' *Seduction*, p. 83

94 *Hope Abandoned*, p. 135

95 Joseph Brodsky, 'Nadezhda Mandelstam (1899–1980)', *Less than One*, p. 155

96 *Hope against Hope*, p. vii

97 *Hope Abandoned*, p. 502

98 George Steiner, 'Our Homeland the Text', 1985, quoted in Pollak, *Mandelstam the Reader*, p. 8

99 *A Captive Spirit*, introduction, p. 16

100 *Hope Abandoned*, p. 303

101 Ibid., p. 234

102 *The Gutenberg Elegies*, p. 82

103 *Tsvetaeva*, p. 65

104 *Mozart and Salieri*, p. 12

105 *Hope Abandoned*, p. 297

106 When Akhmatova met the philosopher Isaiah Berlin in 1945, even though he was her first visitor from the West ever and the time they had for conversation was restricted to one night alone, she recited to him some of the cantos of Byron's *Don Juan* before reading to him the long poem on which she was working.

107 Marcel Proust, *On Reading*, introduction and translation by John Sturrock (London: Syrens, 1994), p. 26

108 Ibid.

109 Ibid., introduction, p. vii

110 Michel de Certeau, 'Reading as Poaching', in *Readers and Reading*, pp. 160–1

111 Alberto Manguel, *A History of Reading* (London: Flamingo, 1997), p. 45

112 *Hope Against Hope*, p. 269

113 Ibid., p. 271

114 Engelsing's argument is summarised by Robert Darnton, in 'The First Steps Toward a History of Reading', quoted in *The Gutenberg Elegies*, p. 71

115 'The Child of Civilization', p. 144

116 *Osip Mandelstam, Selected Poems*, translated by Clarence Brown and M. S. Merwin (Harmondsworth: Penguin, 1987), p. 38

117 Joseph Brodsky, 'The Keening Muse', in *Less Than One*, p. 52

118 'Akhmatova on Akhmatova', p. 23

119 Anna Akhmatova, 'Instead of a Preface', *Requiem, The Complete Poems*, p.384

120 See 'The Keening Muse', p. 35

121 Lydia Chukovskaya, *The Akhmatova Journals Volume 1: 1938–1941* (London: Harvill, 1989), p. 120

122 'Akhmatova on Akhmatova', in *Anna Akhmatova and her Circle*, p. 6

123 *Akhmatova Journals*, p. 97

124 *Akhmatova: Poet and Prophet*, p. 33

125 Earl D. Sampson, *Nikolay Gumilev* (Boston: Twayne Publishers: A division of G.K. Hall & Co, 1979), p. 10

126 *Akhmatova: Poet and Prophet*, p. 39

127 Anna Akhmatova, 'We met for the last time', *The Complete Poems*, p. 142

128 'Akhmatova on Akhmatova', p. 4

129 *The Complete Poems*

130 *Akhmatova: Poet and Prophet*, p. 47 Another critic, writing in *Apollon*, compared Akhmatova's lyric poetry to Japanese art, noting 'the same refracted perspective, a disregard for space distinguishing the

foreground from the background, one detail serving for the whole atmosphere. What is important is not the event as such, but the state of soul revealed through it . . .' Valerian Chudovsky quoted in *Akhmatova: Poet and Prophet*, p. 55

131 Leonid I. Strakhovsky, *Craftsmen of the Word: Three Poets of Modern Russia* (Cambridge, Mass: Harvard University Press, 1949), p. 82

132 'Akhmatova on Akhmatova', p. 35

133 More significant to the poets of St Petersburg than the Tower or the Poet's Guild was The Stray Dog, a bohemian arts club opened on New Year's Eve 1911 by Boris Pronin. Here, at candle-lit tables in the brightly coloured room, the audience would listen to the poets perform their latest work on the small cabaret stage, and Akhmatova and Gumilev reigned as the tsar and tsarina. Benedict Livshits has left a description of the regal couple's arrival at the club: '. . . swathed in black silk, with a large opal cameo at her waist, Akhmatova would glide in, stopping at the entrance, where, at the request of Pronin, who rushed to meet her, she would write her latest poems in the 'pigskin book' . . . In a long frock coat . . . without failing to notice one beautiful woman in the process, Gumilev would back his way through the tables, whether by doing this he was observing court etiquette or whether it was because he feared a dagger-like glance at his back.' Quoted in Amanda Haight, p. 29

134 Georgi Ivanov, preface to *N. Gumilev, Chuzhoe Nebo*, pp 3–4 (2nd Edition, Berlin, 1936), quoted in *Craftsmen of the Word*, p. 52

135 Nadezhda Mandelstam, 'Akhmatova' in *Anna Akhmatova and her Circle*, p. 113

136 Quoted in *Akhmatova: Poet and Prophet*, p. 177

137 'Nadezhda Mandelstam (1899–1980)', p. 155

138 Ibid., pp. 150–1

139 Anatoly Nayman, *Remembering Anna Akhmatova* (London: Peter Halban, 1991), p. 64

140 Emma Gerstein in *Anna Akhmatova and her Circle*, p. 138

141 Nadezhda Mandelstam, 'Akhmatova' in *Anna Akhmatova and her Circle*, p. 114

142 *Hope Abandoned*, p. 6

143 Georgy Adamovich, 'Meetings with Anna Akhmatova', in *Anna Akhmatova and her Circle*, p. 75

144 *Akhmatova: Poet and Prophet*, p. 42. My stress.

145 *Seduction*, p. 119

146 *Hope Abandoned*, p. 195

147 Ibid., p. 228

148 *The Akhmatova Journals*, p. 6

149 Ibid., pp. 11–12

150 Ibid., p. 6

151 Letter from Stavsky to Yezhov, quoted in *The KGB's Literary Archive*, p. 186

152 Ibid., p. 188

153 *Hope Abandoned*, p. 259

154 Osip Mandelstam, 'On the Addressee', *Critical Prose and Letters*, p. 73

AFTERWORD W. B. and George Yeats

1 Something similar happens in George Eliot's *Middlemarch*. Fred Vincy and Mary Garth each write a book and the community credits Fred with the authorship of Mary's, because she hadn't been to university and so would know nothing about literature, and Mary with the authorship of Fred's, 'because they never expected Fred Vincy to write on turnips and manglewurzel', which is something Mary, as a country girl, would know all about. As such, no one was praised for the writing because, George Eliot noted, 'it was always done by someone else'.

2 As Anaïs Nin and Nadezhda Mandelstam would do after her, George made a point of befriending her rival. Iseult and George, Yeats innocently said, enjoyed discussing clothes (a more comfortable fantasy for him to have than considering the other topic the two women might find in common), and Iseult was invited to join the Yeatses for their first Christmas as a married couple.

3 There is something quintessentially modernist about the purity of the Yeatses literary seduction. It dramatized the progressive fading out of the writer and foregrounded the writing itself; it achieved a clean separation between operator and effect. Along with those other scenes in high

modernism, like Bella Cohen's electronic pianola in James Joyce's *Ulysses* or the piano playing by itself in the bar of Joseph Conrad's *The Secret Agent*, George's writing dispensed with human agency altogether.

Index

Frances Wilson lectures in English
Literature at Reading University.

She is editor of **Byromania:
Portraits of the Artist in Nineteenth-
and Twentieth-Century Culture.**